Laguna, I Love You

Also by John Weld

Gun Girl
Stunt Man
Don't You Cry for Me
The Pardners
Sabbath Has No End
The Missionary
Young Man in Paris
Fly Away Home

Laguna, I Love You

The Best of "Our Town"

by JOHN WELD

illustrated by PHIL INTERLANDI

Fithian Press, Santa Barbara 1996

Published by Fithian Press
Post Office Box 1525
Santa Barbara, CA 93102

Book design: Eric Larson
Set in Bembo and Fritz Quadrata

LIBRARY OF CONGRESS CATALOGING-IN-PUBLICATION DATA
Weld, John, date
Laguna, I love you : the best of "Our Town" / by John Weld.
p. cm.
ISBN 1-56474-157-5
1. Laguna Beach (Calif.)—Social life and customs. I. Title.
F869.L15W45 1996
979.4'96—dc20 95-37388
CIP

Contents

"Notice the ease with which she handles; the surging power; the smooth, easy comfort...."

FOREWORD

Writing is a difficult and arduous way to make a living. At age seven I wrote bucolic doggerel which my proud mother thought showed literary promise. I rhymed cow with sow and dog with God. She managed to get it printed in the *Birmingham Age-Herald*. Seeing my name in print was so intoxicating I decided then and there to become a professional writer. That was one of my early mistakes.

When I was born I was the first male to appear on my mother's side for three generations. As a consequence I became overloaded with family names. John Willoughby Blasengame Weld. John, because my mother thought it was a good, sensible name for a boy; Willoughby, because one of my ancestors of that name had distinguished himself, though in what field I do not know; and Blasengame for an ancestor who was killed while serving in the Confederate Army during the Civil War.

From the beginning I was not called John but Jack, a name I did not like. After my father died (I was six months old) my mother married a man named Robert Curtis Lewis, and throughout my childhood I was not called John Willoughby Blasengame Weld but Jack Lewis, this in spite of the fact Mr. Lewis never went through the formality of adopting me.

After graduating at age sixteen from Castle Heights Military Academy, Lebanon, Tennessee, and spending a year at Alabama Polytechnic Institute (now Auburn University), I set out to see the world and record my adventures. I became a bellboy on the S.S. *President Monroe* and made a voyage to Europe. I wrote a vaudeville act and tried it out at the famous Palace Theater in New York. I drove with three other boys from Atlanta, Georgia to Los Angeles in a Model T Ford and became a stunt man in the movies. I dove off a Santa Cruz Island cliff a hundred and thirty-seven feet high, drove a car from an opening drawbridge in Long Beach and, among other doubling acts, parachuted out of the first airplane I went up in.

It was while I was working as a stunt man in pictures that I met Louella Parsons, a columnist for Hearst newspapers. She had powerful clout in the movie business and offered to get me an acting contract at Metro–Goldwyn–Mayer Studios, the beginning salary, seventy-five dollars a week. Wanting to be a writer, I asked her to use her influence and get me a job on a newspaper. She said she would.

Soon after she left for New York, I took my meager savings and followed her. She arranged for me to go to work as a cub reporter on the *New York American,* twenty-five dollars a week. I was twenty-one. It was 1926.

After a year on the *American* I went to Paris and got a job on the European edition of the *New York Herald–Tribune.*

During the five years I spent in Paris—1927–1932—I wrote two books, both novels. *Gun Girl* was about a bobbed-haired bandit who, to afford a drug habit, held up tobacco stores in New York, and *Stunt Man,* based on my stunting experiences. Both were published by Robert M. McBride in 1932. Columbia Studios became interested in *Stunt Man* and called me back to Hollywood to write a stunting scenario.

While at Columbia I met actress Gigi Parrish. She was new in films and had been chosen a "Wampas Baby Star." WAMPAS was the acronym for Western Association of Motion Picture Advertisers. Every year its members chose from the plethora of upcoming actresses those most likely to attain stardom. Gigi was a nickname. She had been christened Gertrude Katherine McElroy and was married to Dillwyn Parrish, an artist/writer. She and Lucille Ball got their start in the film business at the same time, working for Samuel Goldwyn in a musical, *Roman Scandals*. Thereafter Gigi played parts in dramatic and comedy films, most notably as John Barrymore's secretary in *Twentieth Century,* which also starred Carole Lombard.

When I met Gigi she was well on her way to film success. She was the most beautiful woman I had ever seen. Unbelievably, in 1937 during the Great Depression, she turned her back on the silver screen, divorced her husband and married me. I was impoverished. I didn't have the nineteen dollars to buy a wedding ring, so she paid for it.

We went to live in Laguna Beach, California where I finished *Don't You Cry For Me,* a novel of the western migration based on the Donner Party tragedy in California history. Gigi clean-typed it and Charles Scribner's Sons published it. The reviewer in the *New York Times* compared it to the *Book of Exodus,* the *Odyssey,* the *Aeneid* and *The March of the Ten Thousand.*

I have been a writer ever since. I am one of the earliest members of the Authors Guild, since 1933. For twenty years I wrote a column, "Our Town," for the *Laguna Beach Post,* which Katy (Gigi) and I published 1949–1965 and this is a compilation of the better ones. In them is much of the social history of the town during those years. I always ended the little essays with "Laguna, I love you." Hence the title.

Appreciation

Thanks to Katy Weld, whose name should be on the cover as co-author and amanuensis. Thanks to Nancy Bushnell for her computer skills, and to Gretchen Worth, who lives on Fripp Island in South Carolina and clean-typed hundreds of the columns.

Thanks to everyone mentioned in this book for having helped make Laguna Beach the unique town it is.

Thanks to the Laguna Beach Historical Society and the Laguna Beach Library, which has twenty-year-tapes of the *Post*.

An overwhelming thank you to Phil Interlandi for donating his *Post* drawings, a few of which have appeared in the *Laguna Beach Coast Line News,* Laguna's new newspaper.

And I mustn't forget to thank my sister Elinor Webb, who, at age ninety-three, still has faith in me and believes I have talent.

Thanks to June Andrews and June Ireland (mother and daughter), who pressed me to compile the columns. And to all my friends who buy a copy, thereby saving me from bankruptcy.

JOHN WELD
LAGUNA BEACH, CALIFORNIA

Laguna, I Love You

"Unusual little house, isn't it? Typical of Laguna....
Care to see the garage?"

CHAPTER 1

Welcome to Laguna

Let me tell you how with a little of Katy's money we bought a house in South Laguna. It was advertised in chalk on a blackboard outside Jack Lasley's real estate shack on Pacific Coast Highway. It was early December 1940.

BEACHFRONT HOUSE FOR SALE $4000.

Katy and I were on our way to a house we were renting in Three Arch Bay. I said, "There's something we may be able to afford," and braked the Model A.

Lasley took Katy and me in his jalopy down an alleyway which would have been Eleventh Street but it had no sign. When we got to its dead end we could not see the roof of the house he wanted to sell. However there was a gate and a picket fence; both were in need of paint and a few of the pickets were broken. He led us down a weed path to the cliff's edge. Halfway down it was the house, its roof about seventy feet above some rocks. The house needed paint and caulking. Steep wooden steps led down to a door. There was no porch.

"Oh, my!" Katy exclaimed. "We don't want to live here!"

I, too, was disappointed, but said, "Well, we've got to have a look. The gentleman has been kind enough to bring us here." And down we went.

The screen door was awry, but the moment we got into the living room the views on three sides were spectacular. There was a beach on both sides, and dead ahead as far as the eyes could see was the Pacific. Katy clasped my hand. She was enthralled. "Magnificent!" she exclaimed.

Lasley told us the property was owned by a widow who had moved into an old folks' home. She could not afford to make payments for the twenty-five hundred dollar mortgage and the bank was about to foreclose.

"When?" I asked eagerly.

"February first."

That was about two months away. I said, "Before she loses it to foreclosure we will give her five hundred dollars, take over the mortgage and pay your commission. How much is it?"

"One hundred fifty."

We did not hear from him until late in January when he telephoned to say that the widow had accepted our offer. Katy and I were ecstatic. We moved in.

The property was forty-two feet wide and two hundred and sixty-two feet deep. Eventually, aside from refurbishing the house, we bought two adjacent lots for twenty-five hundred dollars.

We lived in the house for eighteen years and in it I wrote several books. We sold it in the late 1950s for eighty thousand dollars thinking we were making a killing. Since then two other houses have been built on the property and each of them is valued at more than a million dollars.

We were living in the house when the Japanese bombed Pearl Harbor. Katy and I had found a gallon of battleship gray paint on the beach and, including the by-then-repaired screen door, we painted the house as far as the contents would go. I was eager to do what I could to win the war. Meanwhile our friend Max Miller, author of the best-selling *I Cover the Waterfront,* who lived in La Jolla, came calling with Ernie Pyle the columnist. Max wanted Ernie to see our "hangover house." Ernie was much amused with our paint story and wrote a column about Katy, me and the house:

> On our way to Los Angeles, Max Miller and I told spinach jokes and got around to serious questions of what each of us was going to do personally about the war in lieu of continuing to write our respective brands of deathless literature.
>
> We both were in a quandary, didn't know what we

> should do, probably couldn't do it if we tried, and got exactly nowhere with our problem. "I thought maybe you'd have an answer," Max said. "But I guess it's the halt leading the blind...."
>
> It being a literary day, we stopped in South Laguna to see another author, John Weld. We stayed a couple of hours and we all praised one another to the skies. It was wonderful. John Weld writes semi-historical novels. I don't doubt that some day his name will carry great respect. He and his wife Katy live in one of the most spectacular houses you ever saw. It is high on a cliff that rises smack out of the Pacific....

I asked Max and Ernie for suggestions as to what I might do in the war effort and learned they were in the same predicament. Max said, "I've taken a job at Consolidated-Vultee in San Diego, but I was in the Navy toward the end of World War One and I'm thinking of going back in."

Ernie said, "I guess I'll become a war correspondent and go where the actions are."

I was in the midst of writing another novel, *Sabbath Has No End,* about slavery in the South, when the Japanese bombed Pearl Harbor. At age thirty-six, I was too old to be a foot soldier, so to help in the war effort I went to work for Consolidated-Vultee. Meanwhile, Henry Ford had contracted with the government to build B-24s at Willow Run, Michigan. He sent his emissaries to San Diego to conscript as many Consolidated–Vultee employees as were available to help those at Willow Run. I was one of them.

I worked for Ford throughout the war, but as soon as it was over Katy and I returned to Laguna. There, thanks to my friendship with Henry Ford II, I became a dealer of Ford cars, hoping it would be a source of income while I wrote books. I soon found out that writing and running a Ford business were not congruent. Both suffered. Soon I was spending eight hours a day at the dealership and two at the typewriter.

Sherman Paddock, publisher of a throw-away weekly newspaper, the *Laguna Beach Post,* asked me to become his partner in that enterprise. I saw a chance to write a weekly column. I borrowed five thousand dollars from the Bank of America and bought a half-interest in the paper. This was a gamble. It was not making money.

As a partner, Sherm had several weaknesses. He was addicted to alcohol and cheated me by collecting whiskey for advertising and not reporting it. He also had a fondness for betting on horse races. He spent only a couple of days editing, getting the paper printed and distributed. The rest of the week he'd spend at Santa Anita, Hollywood or Del Mar racetracks. About a year after I had bought a half-interest in the *Post* he said, "John, I've got the chance of a lifetime, but I need money. How about buying my interest in the paper?"

I was inclined to do so. Politically we weren't in concert; he was far-right Republican and I wanted the paper to be nonpartisan. Moreover the paper was getting better. It recently had been awarded Best Weekly in Orange County.

I asked, "What're you going to do with the dough?"

"I've got a chance to buy a half-interest in a horse at Santa Anita."

I knew that the Internal Revenue Service had been hounding him for income taxes. He boasted that he had never paid a penny. To avoid confiscation he did not own anything except the clothes on his back—no real estate, jewelry, stocks, bonds or furniture. His ten-year-old Chevrolet convertible, from which he distributed the paper, was registered in his son's name.

I said, "If I buy your share I'll have to report it to the Eye Are Ess."

"That doesn't bother me. By the time they get to me I'll have spent the money."

"They'll attach the horse."

"Won't be in my name."

"How much do you think your share's worth?"

We haggled and agreed on eight thousand. I went to the bank, gave him the money and he high-tailed it to Santa Anita.

I did not see him for two or three weeks. One morning he came into the dealership. We chatted about the *Post*. It was being printed in Santa Ana. Recently I had decided to print it in Laguna, which would make it eligible for the County's legal advertising and give it a second class U.S. Mail permit. I had already bought on credit a much-used flatbed press and a Linotype machine. I told him this and he said, "Maybe I sold out too soon."

"How did you come out with the horse?" I asked.

"Won the first race. Paid ten to one."

"Then you're in the money."

"In the next race he broke a leg and we had to shoot the son-of-a-bitch."

"Oh, brother!—Was he insured?"

"Insuring a race horse is expensive. We couldn't afford it."

"You mean to say you lost all the money I gave you?"

"I paid some bills."

"How about the revenue boys? Have they gotten to you?"

Sherm grinned grimly. "Yeah. I told 'em they could have my half of the horse. Say, John," he went on, getting to the cause of his visit, "a jockey friend has given me a sure-win tip. I was wondering, could you loan me a couple of hundred bucks? You might want to put a couple on the horse yourself. His name's BetYourBoots and he'll be in the sixth race this afternoon—a long shot, figures to pay fifteen to one."

"I'm sorry, Sherm. What with the flatbed press, the Linotype, a lot on Ocean Avenue and soon to build on it, I'm up to my ears in debt. Even if I had the money I wouldn't lend it to you. It would contribute to your delinquency." I laughed to take the sting out.

"I'll pay you back tomorrow."

"If the horse wins."

He left, mad as hell.

With Katy digging up local news, helping to sell advertising and me writing a front-page column the *Post* grew in popularity and soon we stopped delivering it gratis. A banner across Page One read: HENCEFORTH THIS STERLING JOURNAL WILL BE DELIVERED ONLY TO SUBSCRIBERS. THE ANNUAL FEE IS ONE DOLLAR. *When coming to pay, stop in for tea.*

Within two weeks we ran out of tea but had three hundred dollars from paid subscribers. By the end of the year we had almost four thousand and the fee went to three dollars.

The Ford agency was limping along fairly well, and while I managed it Katy managed the *Post,* taking charge of the books, the circulation and generally being co-publisher. We built the building, installed the press, hired pressmen, an editor, three advertising salespersons and began printing the paper in our town. It became a rousing success. My columns appeared on its front page every week for eighteen years, from 1950 through the 1960s, and this book is a compilation of the better ones.

CHAPTER 2

Laguna, I Love You

I love Laguna. Not only platonically, but devotedly. Loved it from the first time I saw it—in 1932. There's something about it—or rather a combination of things—which make it irresistible. It's the configuration, the topography, the hills running down to the sea; it's the coves and beaches, the cliffs and caves and rocks and rills. It's the fabulous weather and the house-dotted hills against the sky. It's the sunsets and the prevailing wind which keeps the town clean.

Take a day—any day.

Arise with the sun. Put on shorts and shirt, go out and take a long look at the sea. Watch the sun come over the hills. See the bright, true colors of morning. Breathe the fresh, clean, dry air. Listen to the squashing of waves as they spew upon the sand.

Now follow the fishing boats as they glide by. On the horizon a laden ship will be either coming into Los Angeles Harbor or heading out on a long voyage.

Contemplate the unreal, other-world story-book look of Catalina Island which seems to be floating at anchor.

Spring and fall you can follow the whales as they wander north to feed or south to breed. And all winter long it's a fascinating sight to watch lobster fishermen pull their traps. Those heads are either lads diving for abalone or seals at play.

Take a barefoot walk on the beach. Poke a finger into an anemone. Skim a stone on the water, skip rope with a string of kelp. Adventure into the caves and listen to the sounds of waves pounding into a "blow hole."

And if you come to a stretch of beach someone has tried

"...and there's a lovely view of the ocean from here."

to fence in, don't be intimidated. The beach is yours, the sea is yours, and there's no one can ever take them away from you. Snooze on the warm sand or read a book, absorb the vitamin-giving sunshine. Trouble and strife are over the horizon and beyond the sky.

It is one of the great joys to come in a car around the bend at Emerald Bay and see the village scattered over the foothills. If you're coming from somewhere far away, like New York, the scene has a tendency to chill the roots of the hair. And if you've never been here before—you'll be likely to drag a foot; you'll want to stay.

Pointing out the virtues of Laguna, I have almost forgotten the most wonderful and beautiful of all. At sundown mix yourself a drink, go back onto the porch, plant yourself in a comfortable chair and watch the sky change, watch it go from yellow to rose to red to purple as night takes over. Lift your glass and drink a toast to this artful town and thank God for letting you pass this way.

Among Laguna's characters are two whose occupation is sifting the beach sands for lost jewelry and coins. The boardwalk benches are generally occupied by old gentlemen who find it stimulating to gaze dreamily upon the succulent "San Quentin Quail." Laguna has a slough of artists, would-be artists and those who lack artistic talent but call themselves artists. And we have zany characters like Eiler Larsen, who waves to people passing through; Elba Dryer, who shouts "Hello!" to everyone walking, and Leo Phillipson, the barber whose son is an honor student at Harvard University. Among us are an automobile dealer, Ed Clancy, who just happened to be in Guam December 7, 1941, on his way home. As luck would have it, he spent the next four years in a Japanese internment camp. Another resident is a retired general who spends most of his time pruning his roses. Here you will find the professional Irishman, Bart McHugh, who owns a toy store and is the closest thing to Santa Claus this side of Dublin.

In truth and in fact, Laguna has just about every type, including its share of freaks, widows and viewers-with-alarm.

There isn't anything it doesn't have, except a plethora of bachelors and plenty of parking space. I think you could find almost anything at Dorothy and Roy Child's Pottery Shack.

Eccentric Millionaire

Attended the auction at the Pyne "Castle" last week and found the place reveals its builder's characteristics, a worthy who has been dead for several years. Every Lagunan knows the cement-gray three-storied mansion on the north side of town. It was the home for years of the late Walter Pyne, recluse, faddist. He built it to house his numerous, some say imaginary, relatives. If so, few ever came to stay; apparently they could not endure his Spartan regime.

Pyne's wealth came from oil—discovered in the early years of the century on his ten-acre orange ranch in Santa Ana Canyon. It is said his income was $600 a day. In any case, his hobby was building, and the oil permitted him to indulge himself in a fond farewell.

Pyne's outstanding characteristic, everyone I talked with who knew him agreed, was close-fistedness. He could grip a dollar tighter, they say, than any man they ever knew; yet his penury was offset by a foolhardy extravagance. He bought the finest mahogany doors and equipped them with the most expensive hardware, but never engaged the services of an architect or engineer. In his house are innumerable doors and hallways.

Joe Jahraus, who sold Pyne lumber and cement, tells me that a great concrete wall, on which Pyne expended several thousand dollars, went out with the first rains because it did not have a proper footing. He had used the cheapest labor he could find.

All the wood in the house was fireproofed. To fireproof it, Pyne bought a wood fireproofing plant and had all the lumber for the house shipped there to be treated. To further insure it against fire he had all the walls, ceilings and roofs sheathed with asbestos.

Some say this fire complex may have come from a feeling

of guilt, but he hardly was a sinning man. In all the years he lived in Laguna he never drank alcoholic beverages or smoked tobacco or ate meat. He was a staunch believer in the efficacy of goat's milk, vitamins and dried fruits. He reminded me in this respect of Henry Ford, who believed that most of man's illnesses came from eating sugar. Pyne's libraries, of which there were two, were filled with books on diet and internal medicine. One thick volume I came across was entitled *The Stomach.*

Pyne never married. He was not exactly anti-social, but was hypercritical of his fellows, I gather, and had few friends. His sole companion, it seems, was his housekeeper, to whom he left his estate in trust so long as she lived. When she dies all of the property will go to the Christian Science Church.

Pyne was not a Christian Scientist. He attended the Presbyterian Church, but his mother, whom he apparently revered, was a Christian Scientist. So he left that part of his estate to that church, stipulating that it or the moneys it brought be used for an old people's home somewhere in southern California. The church is asking $125,000 for the real estate, and if those awful buildings weren't on the eight acres they probably would be worth more than that.

The main house has four or five parlors, several dining rooms, two of them with complete service for twelve, and innumerable bedrooms and baths. There are two complete heating systems in the main house—the second just in case the first ever failed. Apparently it never has—not since it was installed in 1925.

The decor and furnishings reflect the most abysmal taste. Pyne was a patsy for birdseye maple furniture. Grand Rapids should erect a statue in his memory, because that city owes him a great debt. I never saw so much birdseye maple in my life.

And the paintings! The walls were crowded with canvases painted by an artist who should have stuck to sign painting: Romanticized scenes of Laguna in reds, and yellows and blues. There were three pianos in the house, reflecting Pyne's interest in music. Before oil was discovered on his small ranch, he operated a piano store in Santa Ana.

I also noticed several pieces of athletic equipment in the house. One contraption which fascinated me was a treadmill of rollers on which one can walk while staying in one place.

Must have worked out well. Pyne lived to a ripe old age—well past seventy—despite the dried fruits and goat's milk.

Job Offer

My friend Harry Willats, owner of the Laguna Riviera Hotel and Colonial Dames Cosmetics, has passed along to me a job opportunity. It came to him special delivery and marked confidential because of his exalted position in the business world.

"I enclose a letter I just received," he wrote. "It is an inquiry—a search for a very special kind of executive for a big job. As I read the letter I visualized you as exactly the man they seek...."

This is the inquiry:

"We frequently are called upon to assist our clients in locating outstanding executive personnel. One of our current recruiting assignments is for an exceptionally top-level man—one who may be a personal friend or business associate of yours. Because of the unusual nature of the job opening, I would greatly appreciate your personal help in finding someone who may be qualified for this position.

"The man we are seeking would be given the title of vice-president of marketing with one of the country's most aggressive and successful companies in the consumer goods field. Salary is open, but our client is prepared to pay a base salary of $100,000 per year or more, plus additional executive compensations.

"Although the candidate must have had experience in the packaged consumer goods on a national basis, personal qualifications are considerably more important. He must have a quick mind, great imagination, and capacity for hard and sustained work...."

"Thanks, Harry," I replied. "I appreciate the thought. But

there are two reasons why I do not wish to have this job. One is, it would doubtless mean that I'd have to leave beloved Laguna, and this I am not about to do for money, power or fame. Imagine walking down the streets of Grand Rapids or Pittsburgh and not seeing a friend.

"The other reason is that emphasis on 'hard and sustained work.'

"Not that I'm lazy. It's just that the kind of work I specialize in and like to do—combing beaches, watching pelicans dive for fish and whales spout—is not somehow associated with munificent salaries.

"With all that money, of course, Katy and I could live higher on the hog, we'd be able to pay our debts and she could have a Magnin mink.

"But in such an important job I would doubtless have to do a lot of traveling and entertain people for whom I have no personal affection or regard; I'd probably have to eat in restaurants all the time and drink three martinis before lunch. There would be top-level meetings and conferences with advertising, promotional and merchandising people and I would have to make a lot of what at the time seem like important decisions (Should we enlarge the package or cut down on the contents?).

"All of that sort of thing is quite interesting, Harry, but I'm afraid it isn't for me. I've been through it once, which is enough. It is a little like going over Niagara Falls in a barrel—exciting the first time, but terrifying to repeat.

"You know, Harry, I find it is pleasant to be middle class. There is so little responsibility connected with it. And I have yet to find a greater aid to relaxation than going to bed at night knowing that it doesn't make any difference what time you get up in the morning.

"Thank you, Harry, for the flattering thought. I appreciate it and your regard. If you happen to run across the fellow who takes the job I wish you'd give the benighted bohunk my best wishes."

"Atta baby! Rev it up good and loud.... I hate the people who can afford to live in this town!"

CHAPTER 3: 1949

The Belles Are Ringing

A unique organization called the Eleven Belles held a carillon in Laguna Beach a few days ago to decide what they should do for the war effort. While they were here I appointed myself recording secretary and press agent, on account of I was in love with the entire membership and wanted to keep up with their scampish activities.

The membership is made up of the best known, most beautiful, respected and intelligent ladies of that fairy-tale land of Beverly Hills–Brentwood–Pacific Palisades called Hollywood.

In alphabetical order they are Sibyl Brand, wife of 20th Century Fox's boy-publicist, Harry; actress Irene Dunn; Maggie Ettinger, who is even more renowned than some of the people and companies she publicizes; Maxine Keller, wife of Robert, former vice-president of Chrysler Corporation; Fieldsie Lang, wife of movie director Walter; Dorothy Manners, who, besides being Mrs. John Haskell, is a famous newspaperwoman; Lorena Mayer, widow of movie king-maker L.B.; Louella Parsons, who needs no introduction, Nancy Sinatra, ex-wife of Frankie; and Sue Taurog, wife of movie director Norman.

The Club functions this way: No one is president, there are no dues, fines or assessments. One has to be invited to get in and, save death, there is no way to get out.

Whenever one of the members gets an idea for an outing she calls the others and they convene. Their main aim is to stir up hilarity. They've rung melodiously in Las Vegas and Palm Springs, and there's some talk of holding meetings in Hong Kong, Cabo San Lucas and Skagway.

Last week they conclaved in Laguna, where Maggie

Ettinger has a house, to decide what they could do to win the war.

Louella Parsons and Dorothy Manners could not make it to Laguna last week, so they sent a substitute—Cesar Romero.

My report: They had a wonderful night at the Festival of Arts. You should have seen the bus load of old ladies when they spotted Cesar!... At Del Mar racetrack Maggie ran into a client, John Elsbach, who had personally talked with a horse named Roman Holiday. She won more than a hundred dollars on him—the horse, that is. I've known Fieldsie since 1926, when she and I were swimmers on the Ambassador Hotel swim team. It was then we both came to know a local girl named Jane Peters, who subsequently changed her name to Carole Lombard. Until she was killed in an airplane accident, Carole and Fieldsie were all but inseparable.

Portraits of Two Painters

I don't know much about art, but I like the work of Ross Shattuck, Maggie Ettinger's husband. One of Laguna's distinguished painters, Ross has lived here for many years, but is not well known in our town because he has long been working as art director at Metro-Goldwyn-Mayer Studios.

Everyone will have the privilege of seeing a collection of his work beginning next Wednesday and running through March 30th. The Art Gallery, bless its heart, is holding a one-man Shattuck show and a number of his canvases have been gleaned from uptown, they being the highly treasured properties of persons prominent in the movie industry.

Besides being a very good and individual painter, Ross has the distinction of being married to one of the country's most extraordinary and successful women, Margaret Ettinger, justly famed Hollywood publicist and outstanding woman in her field.

He was born in Enderlin, North Dakota, about sixty years ago. Enderlin was little more than a water-tank siding in those days (its present population is 1,500) and Ross was born there by happenstance. Seems his father worked for the Harvey System of railroad restaurants and he and Mrs. Shattuck just happened to be in Enderlin the day Ross insisted upon presenting himself.

Much of his childhood was spent traveling the west and that vast and wondrous land made a deep and lasting impression on him, as his pictures plainly show. There is a wistful, almost painful loneliness about them, the kind of feeling one gets when one hears the far-off wail of a train whistle or the deep and tortured bay of a moonstruck coyote. In all of his work there is that nostalgia, that radiating beauty which penetrates one's innermost core.

Ross' interest in art manifested itself in grammar school, and when he was old enough to leave home he went to Chicago and attended the Academy of Fine Arts. He subsequently became a commercial artist, a career which was interrupted by World War I. Enlisting, he was wounded in France in the battle for Amiens. He spent months in hospitals. When he finally recovered he became the art director for the Philadelphia advertising agency, N.W. Ayer.

He continued to paint seriously in his spare time and it was in Philadelphia he held his first one-man show. He left Ayer to become art director for the largest advertising agency in the world, the J. Walter Thompson Company.

He painted Laguna, the Mother Lode country and San Francisco. Virginia City, Nevada, fascinated him because in its ruins lurked the over-all theme of his work—nostalgia—and he painted a great many pictures there. Then, as his coffer gradually became empty, he hit upon an idea to replenish it. He sold to ten sponsors pictures as yet unpainted and with the money thus raised went to Mexico and painted for six months. He called this the Shattuxeco Expedition. It proved so successful he did the same thing the next year, this time going to New Orleans on what he called the Louisiana Buy.

In New Orleans he painted the old houses and the streets in the French Quarter and these pictures are among his finest work. He was at the height of his creative productivity. It is ironic that Fate chose this time to lay him low with a heart attack. He returned to Laguna where he died.

William Grant Sherry is another dedicated and extremely capable painter who cut a wide swath through Laguna. A tall, handsome man, he caught Bette Davis' fancy and became one of her several husbands, the only one by whom she had a child. The marriage lasted through that miracle and a year or so thereafter. Bette was hard on husbands. She was egocentric and spoiled by her stardom. She bought an expensive beach-front house at Wood's Cove and they lived there until after the baby was born. Meanwhile she was busy in Hollywood, so hired a girl to look after the baby. The girl, Marion, was very pretty, quite young—no older than twenty. During the time Bette was away Marion and Sherry were often together and as his marriage began to crumble they fell in love. When Bette was home there were scenes in which she might have been acting on the screen; in fact all of them put together would have made the third act of a Class A screenplay. She soon demanded a divorce and custody of the child. Once he was free Grant married Marion and they moved to Florida.

Meanwhile the Sherrys became Katy's and my close friends and have remained so throughout the years. Three of his highly treasured paintings hang on our walls. They have two children and I was flattered that they named the boy John, after me. I include a letter from him written in Paris dated April 4, 1952.

> It is surprising that the showers of Spring have little effect on Parisians. Unless the rains come unusually hard the children go right on playing in the parks and their mothers and nurses simply raise their umbrellas and go on reading or knitting. Yesterday I was roaming around, looking for something to sketch. A young couple strolled along, stopping for an occasional kiss. A kiss in an April shower on a street in Paris—there's something very lovely about it.
>
> As I reached Rond Point a fine drizzle descended. Rond Point is on the Champs Elysees, halfway between

the Etoile and Place de la Concorde. I got under a big tree and began sketching one of the horse-drawn carriages waiting for a fare. I didn't get far before the wind began to blow and the rain came. Big drops fell on my sketch book so I beat it over to Le Cafe Rond Point and sat under a huge awning which covers its sidewalk tables and chairs. I ordered coffee and unfolded my *New York Herald–Tribune,* Paris edition. I remembered you, John, used to work there. I thought of you and Katy and other nice people living in Laguna. I saw girls dodging puddles in their high heels, a bicyclist unrolled a raincoat which had been folded under his seat. A taxi expelled three laughing occupants who ran for shelter; the guy who stayed to pay the fare got soaked which caused much laughter. By now the carriage driver had covered his horse with a blanket and was curled up in the carriage for a nap.

Nearby in the adjoining park was a carousel. Carved wooden horses hung by chains under a green and blue awning of a merry-go-round. Their glass eyes seemed to have more sparkle when children were riding them. In the park along Avenue Matignon every Sunday morning stamp collectors gather to talk, buy and exchange stamps. Last Sunday I went there to sketch them. My sketch book was mistaken for a stamp book and I was asked several times if I had any stamps to exchange. The couple I noticed kissing earlier were at a nearby table tete-a-tete. Soon the shower stopped and the sun broke through. Now I could see the upper half of the Eiffel Tower. People got moving, their umbrellas furled, and birds began chirping again. The carriage driver took the blanket off the horse and spoke to him affectionately. Now all he needed was the young, kissing couple to go for a drive through the park. I hope they did. I went back to our hotel to finish the sketches.

Marion joins me in love to you and Katy.

Grant.

My Friend Fred, April 1, 1949

Fred Beck is well known for his columns in the *Los Angeles Times* for the Farmer's Market.

He was living in Cathedral City, California. I wrote him this letter:

Dear Fred:

I follow with great pleasure your essays in the *Times* on the advantages of buying land in California. Indeed, your pieces are so moving, poetic and persuasive that I am writing for "further information" about your Cat City.

Nothing I'd like better than to own land anywhere in Southern California.

The other day, I came across the following advertisement in your paper.

BE THE PROUD OWNER OF ONE SQUARE INCH OF THE ROCKY MOUNTAINS! *Valid warranty deed. Excellent showpiece or gift. Mail $1 (full price) to* MIDGET RANCHES INC., BOX 1566, ALBUQUERQUE, N.M.

I could not resist the urge to send a buck. It was the "full price" that got me.

In fact, I sent two bucks—to buy an inch for you and one for me. Furthermore, I insisted that the parcels be adjoining. I wanted in this small way to thank you for the pleasure your writings have given me. It is my plan to add an inch every year until we both have a square foot. There I hope we'll plant a bay tree. That is, we'll plant a tree if we don't strike oil or gold first. One of my stipulations in the escrow was that the mineral rights come with the property.

The bay tree, as you know, is the tree of peace. When the tree grows big and strong and flourishes like those mentioned in the Bible, I figure we can clip some of the leaves therefrom and mail them to Mr. Kruschev. These simple offerings might befriend him.

It will be our contribution to World Peace, which he seems to favor.

Who knows, with him we might even win the Nobel Peace Prize, which amounts to maybe forty or fifty thousand dollars, and with this money we could buy acreage in Cat City.

There are 144 square inches in a square foot. That means I'll have to add an inch a month for twelve years before we can plant our tree. As I figure it, the square foot is going to cost $144. There being 43,560 square feet in an acre, an acre is going to bring $6,272,640 to the guy who's promoting this come-on. I think we ought to join him.

Your Pal, John.

August 1949

For years I have been of the opinion that women who yowl about the drudgery of domesticity are short-sighted. Just let them go out into the cruel business world, let them face the fierce competition, the dog-eat-dog savagery there and they'll be happy with housework.

Recently I've had misgivings. Katy got the idea she wanted to get a job. "I think I'll go into the real estate business," she said.

I don't know how many people in this area are occupied selling houses—something like one out of five, I guess. It is the citizen's second occupation, ranking just below painting seascapes.

She promptly got her sales license and the result is I seldom see her any more. Until she went on this wild tear, our lives it seemed to me were serene. As it is now she has to be up and out by eight-thirty, which calls for me to hit the deck at six-thirty and, while she dresses for the marts of commerce, get breakfast started. By the time she leaves the house, I am up to my elbows in the kitchen sink on account I have to do the dishes and make the bed before I can get to my typewriter. Until now I never tried to make a king-size bed. Ours takes me about fifteen minutes. And when, come every Sunday, I have to change the sheets and do the laundry—Holy Cow!

After five weeks of "keeping house" and tending the garden, my respect for my wife has increased immeasurably. Dishpan hands? I got 'em. Housemaid's knee? Aching back? All day, every day. I'm sick of the vacuum cleaner, particularly when I have to dust under the bed. I'd almost rather wash the windows. Which reminds me: Who was that diabolical enemy of mankind who invented the jalousie window? He should be drawn, quartered and fed to the pigs, or, better yet, be made to spend his life cleaning the dam' things.

For years, trying to be a good husband, I've helped around the house—wiped the dishes and swept the porch, that sort of thing. But I've never done any chores consistently, and I never realized what an unending struggle it is to keep ahead of the laundering and ironing. I also have to do the shopping and errand-running, pay the bills and try to keep the checkbook balanced. But where I have the most trouble is with the mending. Every day I thank God we don't have any children.

Another thing I don't like is that when Katy comes home after a hard day showing houses she's too tired to cook, so we go out for dinner. It's not only expensive, but the food's not as good as when she cooks it.

When Katy starts bringing money home I'm going to hire a cleaning woman and a cook.

CHAPTER 4

I Am a Camera

Stopped the car to give an older man a lift to Dana Point. He was short, square, grizzled and blue eyed. His sunburned face was a map of wrinkles showing a devious way through a long life. I had never seen him before, but he greeted me as if we were friends and said, "Thanks. I can't drive any more."

"Why?" I asked.

"Went through a stop light. Cost me sixty bucks and they took my driver's license. Now I have to go shank's mare."

"Couldn't you see the sign?"

"Sure. Thought I could make it. I got good eyes."

"How old are you?"

"Seventy-nine."

"You don't look it," I said.

"Never smoked or drank," he said, as if that was a reasonable explanation for longevity. "Never been sick a day in my life."

"You look fine," I said. "You've got twenty years left in you."

"Oh, I'll live to be a hundred all right," he said confidently. "Only the prospect ain't so pleasin', what with my old woman gone and me not able to drive a car. First car I ever owned," he went on, "was a nineteen-and-twelve two-cylinder Buick. It's still sitting in my garage right now. I keep it to remind me of the good old days. I was born in Buffalo, used to work in the old Pierce Arrow factory. Got fifteen dollars a week for working ten hours a day and half a day Saturdays. I've forgot more about cars than that cop'll ever know. Wouldn't mind it so much," he went on, "if the old woman was alive. She was a

"We'll have to go back. I left my purse at the Jolly Roger."

good driver."

"How long has she been gone?"

"Eighteen months now. Greatest girl ever lived. Was seventy-five when she died. We got along just fine. There couldn't have been a happier marriage. I was her second husband. Her first was a boozer and a chippie chaser. She worked hard all her life. Saved fifty thousand dollars in her lifetime and left it all to me. Never would spend a nickel on herself, was the kind who always ate the necks and the wings and the gizzards and gave the good parts to the kids and me."

"How many children do you have?"

"She had one by her first husband and we had one, a boy. He weighed twelve pounds and three ounces when he was born. She had a hard time pushin' him loose. The doctor had to use the calipers three times. He grew up all right. They had him in the army. He never was what you might call a real smart boy, but he made a radio out of a pasteboard box when he was just a kid, so he isn't dumb. Works for the telephone company, is married and lives in Long Beach. His wife has a part-time job helping distribute newspapers. They got a new station wagon."

"Where do you live?" I asked.

"I got me a nice place here in San Clemente. Not long ago I sold some trust deeds and built me a triplex. My daughter-in-law did not like me selling the deeds. She gave me the devil. I get a good income from the rentals. Before she died I took my old lady on a trip to Australia. Was the first indulgence she ever permitted. We had a fine time, but she thought we spent too much money. She was a jewel. They don't make 'em like that no more." He looked at me, suddenly aware he had been talking.

"I'll get off at the bus depot," he said. "Thanks for the ride."

Green Stamps, Coupons and Rebates During WWII

I dutifully fill this column every fast-passing week trying to entertain, amuse or enlighten those who have nothing better to read. This week I am geared into entertainment.

As we pass through this lopsided world of odd balls, squares, cranks, freaks and other assorted characters, we hear tales, some factual, some fanciful, a few funny. A story currently going the rounds is about a smart lad in a factory, one of those modern well-tailored places where they use computers for everything but eating. Seems that the president of the company was about to be married and our hero was assigned the task of taking up a collection to buy him and his bride a wedding gift.

He extracted two dollars from each of the five hundred employees and bought five hundred packs of cigarettes—the kind with the coupon on the back—and four cases of whiskey, each bottle of which offered a one-dollar rebate. He traded in the coupons and the rebate dollars for a three-hundred-dollar silver coffee service, the wedding gift. The cigarettes he presented to his contributors, giving each of them a pack, and he used the whiskey for a company pre-wedding party. Thus everyone had value for their contributions.

The boys in the shop thought the purchaser should be rewarded for having handled the matter so beautifully, but when they proposed to buy him a gift, the young man demurred, saying he had been more than adequately rewarded for his effort. Seems that he had bought the cigarettes and liquor at a supermarket which dished out trading stamps and had gotten enough to buy several state lottery tickets, one of which had won five thousand dollars.

"Each employee got ten bucks," he told me.

Idwal Jones

Went to see old friend Idwal Jones on Glenneyre the other day. He has lived in Bluebird Canyon for years, is an intellect of the first rank, a scholar, a man-of-letters, a novelist, prolific contributor to magazines, bon vivant, wine connoisseur, newspaperman, columnist, editor, teacher and drama critic. He has also been rancher, prospector and motion picture publicist.

We talked of the wine tasting at Pomona, in which Idwal and I participated for several years, of current books and of M.F.K. Fisher, a mutual friend who is also a writer, and of a book Idwal has been working on for three years.

"Can't get the blasted thing as I want it to be," he said. "I've done it over a half dozen times, and still it isn't right."

I thought of the people who know little of the pain of composition; they often regard writing as a dilettantish pastime, a mere setting down of words in their proper order when the inspiration dictates.

The truth of the matter is: Writing is the most demanding of the endeavors. Idwal has had published fourteen books. All have been rewritten, some as many as a dozen times.

"No book I've ever done has come out as I conceived it," he said. "I'm always dissatisfied, even after it is published."

I first met Idwal while we were working on the same newspaper in New York, *The American,* thirty-some years ago. He had made a work-as-he-went trip around the world from San Francisco. I was a cub reporter and was fascinated by his use of words. I'll never forget one of them—transmogrification. It means a humorous transforming, a pun or a paraphrase.

Idwal is a Welsh name. He was born in Wales and still has a Welsh brogue. He probably knows California history as well as any man alive. He believes Norman Douglas, who died about two years ago, was the greatest writer of his time. Douglas wrote the classical *South Wind,* and if you haven't read it recently I suggest you give yourself the pleasure.

Ride with Irving Stone

We got on the horses and started up the mountain. There are few places where two persons can be more intimate than on horses. Horses are so indifferent about what people say. The trail was steep and deep in sumac, and we did not say anything for some time.

Irving Stone, my companion, was on a holiday—a well-earned one. He had just finished *The President's Lady,* about Rachael Jackson, and was obviously tired, though he tried not to show it. And he was taut, too, the way you get after a sustained effort. He had been working for a year—getting up every morning to face a frightening piece of blank paper. And he had been working for many years, learning and perfecting the exacting art of writing.

We did not speak for some time, but let the horses have their heads and lug us up the mountainside. Below lay the Sierra slope and the magnificent, inexpressibly beautiful Pacific. About us were the hills of home, of Southern California, and it was April, it was spring.

After a while Irving's horse stopped of her own accord to breathe deep-chested, the way climbing horses do, and this man that I know so well, this hard-working man, this loyal, gifted and fortunate friend crooked a knee over the saddle horn and, squinting against the strong sunlight, said, "I think if I had to do it over again I'd be a cowboy."

Having written a novel or two, I could see his point. "Well," I said, "now you've got old lady Jackson out of your system, I hope you're going to lay off for a while. I hope you're going to take a good long rest."

"The way I feel now," he said, "I may never write another line, much less book—as long as I live."

"You're getting some sense," said I.

"If Rachael Jackson sells," he said, "I'm going to save my money and become a reader. I'm tired of writing."

"Know how you feel," I said as we heeled our horses. He didn't respond. We rode on up the mountainside and as the world fell away did not talk much—a "Say!—look at that!" and a "Hey! isn't that something!"—until we got to the top. Now there were no more slopes to climb, only the mesa to traverse. We let ourselves through a barbed-wire gate and rode along the ridge, and I, riding behind, had a chance to observe my friend.

Suddenly Irving seemed less tired, as if he had caught his second wind, and our horses were breathing easily, too. We had come to the crown of the hill and were suddenly relaxed and free.

After a brisk lope he reined and waited for me to come up. "What do you know of Mary Lincoln?" he asked.

"Only that she was a shrew," I said.

"That's what everybody says. I wonder if she was."

"The history books say Lincoln was a saint and she was a termagant."

"Lincoln must have had his faults, too," Irving said. And suddenly I realized what he was up to.

"You reprobate!" I exclaimed. "You said you were going to quit, take it easy."

"I was just wondering," he said, and we rode on.

"He's been in Laguna too long—he thinks they're all illegals."

CHAPTER 5: THE 1950S

The World Beyond

Milton Stapp and Trudy Beckworth, who used to live in Laguna and now reside in Seattle, from time to time send me copies of messages they get from what they call the other world. These messages purport to be the utterances of M. Root, who died some years ago. They come through Trudy by means of an Ouija board and she is remarkable for the rapidity with which she short-hands them. The last one, just received, has to do with fortune-telling. "A man of strength does not need the advice of a fortune-teller or that of a spirit-world friend to guide him in making decisions."

Milton and Trudy are as convinced that they are communicating with Mr. Root as they are that they're alive. While I certainly believe that death is not the end of life, I cannot bring myself to believe spirits of the "world beyond" can communicate via an Ouija board.

I got to know Mrs. Houdini—the vivacious and tiny wife of the great magician who died in the '20s. She tried repeatedly over a period of years to communicate with the spirit of her remarkable husband, who before he died told her the times and places he would speak to her. Though she was faithfully there she never heard his voice.

Conan Doyle, creator of Sherlock Holmes, was intensely interested in the subject and vowed, as Houdini did, that once he died, he would pierce the barrier separating life and death. He's been dead for years but I don't believe he has ever been heard from.

The first I learned about the Ouija board was from my mother, who was a strong believer in clairvoyance. It was from her, I learned, that fortunes could be told by reading palms, tea leaves and bumps on people's heads.

Mother was extremely psychic, but I always felt that these were games she played for amusement. When the Ouija board had its great vogue in America, shortly after World War I, she explained its function to me.

Once we had gotten our fingers set lightly on the little three-legged Ouija table, I asked, "What is it like out there?" and to my surprise the table started moving quickly from letter to letter. Mother jotted down the reply: "Very spiritual." There were other questions and other answers, but to me none made sense. Finally the table slithered off the board and fell to the floor.

This was an indication, Mother told me, that "he" was displeased. "He" was my long-deceased father. When Mother was talking with her Aunt Natalie, who had been dead for several years, Aunt Natalie predicted I would grow up to be rich and famous. Mother took this for gospel. To me it was nonsense. Her close friend, Nancy Fullwood, became known as a "spirit writer." That is to say, she would hold pen in hand over a blank sheet of paper and a spirit named Sanatora would come along and write words of prediction. She published a number of books with Sanatora's poetic sooth-sayings, but the only people who bought them, I think, were her friends.

I wish there was some way for us to communicate with those who have died. I'd like to hear Walter Huston tell jokes, which he did so well, and sing "September Song."

As a French Scholar Sees Us

Acording to an attractive twenty-five-year-old French woman, Michelle Vuillermont, American men emasculate themselves by playing a subservient role to the American woman. Michelle has been attending Claremont Graduate School in Pomona on a Fulbright Scholarship. After a year here she left last week to return home. Before she went she made these penetrating observations.

"American men cater to women too much," she said. "It isn't gallantry exactly; it's more the subjective approach. They seem to be afraid of the female. This is different from the French man's attitude. The French woman is subjective. She regards the man as supreme; she nurtures, fosters and sustains him and adheres to his pronouncements. She makes a man feel like the king he thinks he is. The American woman, by contrast, seems to make the man feel more like her servant.

"From the economic point of view it is equally unreal. The American male takes a girl to dine. He may spend more money than he can afford and turn himself inside out to be entertaining. All the girl has to do is sit there and smile. In France men and women share expenses and the women contribute their share of entertainment."

I asked her if she liked Americans on the whole, and she said, *"Beaucoup."*

"I think one of your outstanding characteristics is your puritanism," she went on. "You seem to have a strange two-sided kind of morality. Sinning is all right if you're not found out. By and large I find you fairly indifferent to indiscretion. You're also generous and self-sufficient. You don't seem to have any deep-seated fears, such as one finds in Europe. You have not been ravaged by war in this century, as we have—twice; you've known war only second-hand, remotely. Yet you do not appear to be a particularly gay people—not like the Danes, for example, or the Greeks."

Miss Vuillermont likes almost everything about California, including its women's fashions. "They are so colorful and casual. Women adorn themselves well, for the most part, but I must say, when I first came to Pomona I was shocked by the way girls came to breakfast—in muumuus and wearing bandanas to cover their curlers."

She thinks American women put too much emphasis on their appearance. "The American woman seems to have no inner resources. In my opinion she would be more attractive if she sharpened her knowledge and her wit. I have found few American women who, outside the home, can talk intellectually."

She likes our climate and the way we live—out of doors. She even likes our food, which is praise from Sir Hubert, and even thinks California wines are as good as French.

"You have such a variety of food," she observed. "Mexican, Chinese, Swedish, French and German. But of them all I think I like your barbecued beef the best. There is the spirit of pioneers in this kind of cooking."

Never Thought I'd Work for Henry Ford

The greatest single contribution to modern times was made by Henry Ford, who, in 1914, established the eight-hour day and more than doubled wages at one stroke (from the then-prevailing $2.40 a day to $5.00). In doing so he started an American revolution, freeing his workers from proletarian servitude and making them customers, thereby contributing much to everyone's way of life.

Though lacking formal education Ford had many revolutionary ideas which proved to be sound, yet he had a host of zany ones, too. One was that many of man's bodily ills come from eating refined sugar. He was convinced its little crystals never dissolved in the system and damaged the fine membranes. In his personal relations Mr. Ford left much to be desired. He could be as cold as a process server.

The first time I met him, in 1931, he made me so angry I didn't cool off for a week. The meeting occurred in Cherbourg, France. I was a reporter for the Paris edition of the *New York Herald-Tribune*. He had just arrived in Europe for the first time since his famed "Peace Ship" visit in 1915.

Assigned to interview him upon his arrival, I went to Cherbourg on the train, arriving about midnight. *Europa,* the German ship on which the world-renowned automobile manufacturer was traveling, was scheduled to arrive from New York some time between five and seven A.M. Rather than retire to a hotel room (I might oversleep) I decided I would lie down on a bench in the dock's waiting room, a precaution which proved idle because I overslept anyway. When I awoke the tender had left the dock to go out and pick up the ship's passengers.

As I stood frustrated on the dock watching the tender pull away, a white launch detached itself from the *Europa* and headed toward me. It came directly to the dock where I was standing and off stepped Ford, his wife and cohorts. When I introduced myself I was not aware that to him for the nonce all newspapermen were anathema. It seems that reporters in New York had provoked him.

He brushed me off, saying, "How do I know you're a newspaperman?" I showed him my press card. Meanwhile he was striding straight ahead and his secretary-guardian was trying to fend me off. Mr. Ford said, "I'm tired of being misquoted by you fellows."

"I promise you I'll not misquote you, sir."

"Well, I'm not going to give you the chance." He climbed into one of the two Lincolns which had been sent to drive him and his party to Paris.

"But Mr. Ford," I pleaded. "I've been waiting here all night! Won't you at least tell me your plans?"

The manufacturer slammed the door and the car got under way, leaving me boiling in the dust.

On the way back to Paris I wrote what had happened, thinking to tell the public what a mean son-of-a-bitch the famous man was, but Eric Hawkins, *Herald's* managing editor, wouldn't print it.

Mr. Ford finally consented to an interview. All of the American correspondents in Paris as well as members of the French press were present. Throughout the questioning the manufacturer sat arms akimbo on a divan. His current conviction was: Men should work for six months in factories and six months on farms. It was evident that he did not have much patience with people who did not believe as he did.

I remember Hank Wales, correspondent for the *Chicago Tribune,* tried to compliment him on the sturdiness of his cars. "I drove Model T ambulances during the war," Hank said, referring to World War I, "and they were absolutely marvelous. They would go up to the front lines through the muck and mire and always bring us and the wounded back. You would have been proud...."

Far from receiving this compliment graciously, Ford said, "I don't want my cars used in that way. I don't believe in war."

All of us reporters were offended by the man's rudeness. That one day I would work in public relations for him seemed ridiculous. However I did.

In character and temperament Henry Ford was like the Model T, that is to say stubborn, ornery, lean and simple.

During World War II I was working for Consolidated-Vultee in San Diego, where PBYs and B-24s were being built. Ford got a contract to build B-24s at Willow Run, Michigan, and sent emissaries to San Diego to hire all the Consolidated help they could get. Although I did not like Mr. Ford because of our encounter in Cherbourg, the job and salary I was offered were too good to turn down.

I went to work in his public relations department as editor of the *Ford Times,* a monthly magazine distributed free to the public by Ford dealers. For years Mr. Ford did not believe paid-for advertising was profitable and refused to advertise in newspapers, magazines or on billboards. But he was shrewd enough to get plenty of free advertising by getting his name on the front pages of newspapers across the country. Whatever he said was good copy and newsmen would dog him to get a quote. He had opinions about everything and most of them were startling. He liked to shock. When I was introduced to him at Ford headquarters in Dearborn I did not remind him of our encounter in France. Several times I was with him to monitor interviews, but though I disagreed with some of the things he said I did not dare suggest that any of them should be altered.

Another way he got free advertising was through jokes about the Model T. For years jokesters made up hundreds of these and they were widely circulated. One of his favorites was about a farmer named Purdy and his wife who lived in a Louisiana swamp. Neither of them had ever seen an automobile until one day a Model T came bouncing along the mud-caked, wagon-rutted road. Pappy Purdy was in the cornfield hoeing weeds when he saw the strange contraption. He let out a holler and ran to the house. Ordering his wife to get under the bed, he snatched up his shotgun and from a window watched until the auto was abreast of the house. He then let go both barrels.

The frightened driver jumped out and took off lickity-split through the potato patch, but the Model T kept on going, guided by the wagon ruts.

His wife asked from beneath the bed, "Did you git him, Pa?"

"Gol' durn it, naw," came the reply. "But I sure as hell made it turn that feller loose."

One of my favorite Model T jokes was a letter printed in the *Toronto Globe* in 1921. It was written by George Napier:

> I had just arrived from Scotland and went west to Saskatchewan where I worked on a farm. The farmer bought a Model T Ford and I drove him to town in a wagon to get it. The dealer drove with him in the car as far as the bridge crossing the river, then left him to drive home on his own.
>
> When I got back to the farm with the wagon, the farmer, not knowing how to stop the car, was driving around and around the house. Meanwhile the kids had jumped in and were having their first automobile ride. Their mother came out with cookies and every time the car came around she would toss some to them. Finally, about suppertime the contraption ran out of gas.
>
> One day the car wouldn't start. When a horse got balky the farmer used to tell me to kick it in the belly, so I said to him, "Kick it in the belly!" Instead he hit it with a hammer and the car ran over him. I asked what happened, and he said, "The son-of-a-bitch threw me."

Mr. Ford loved jokes like that, but he had little sense of humor.

Political Opinions are Dangerous to Friendships

There has been considerable talk recently anent women's suffrage and their use of the franchise. I can remember, as a child, seeing ladies in ankle-length skirts, shirtwaists, high-button shoes and big hats atop piled-up hair parading down the streets of Birmingham, Alabama, demonstrating for their rights.

They were adamant, and their determination made strong men quail. They believed that once women got the vote they would vote as a block and thus negate them. There was even much talk of a woman president.

With the presidential campaign in full swing, I am reminded of an apropos anecdote.

Our friend Walter Huston and his wife, Nan, were divided in their choice of candidates for the presidency. He preferred the Democrat and she the Republican. Their discussions of the issues and criticisms of the candidates often became intense and even heated. Each tried to persuade the other to support their candidate but neither would change his or her mind. As voting day drew near Nan said to Walter: "Inasmuch as our votes will nullify each other, why should we bother to go to the polls?"

He agreed to refrain from voting if she would. "There'll be just two fewer votes," he said. "Neither will have any effect on the outcome."

When voting day came Nan decided that to go back on one's word was a small thing compared to the importance of electing the right man to run the country. She hied herself to the polling place and cast her vote.

When she and Walter met that evening, she waited until the polls had closed to ask if he had kept his word. "You did not vote?"

"I did not vote."

"I knew I could trust you, darling," Nan said. "But I must tell you that I voted. In doing so my man got two votes—mine and the one you did not cast against him."

Good man that Walter is, he forgave her. "She told me she took advantage of my integrity for what she was convinced was the good of the country," he said.

Despite her two votes, his candidate won.

Cat Nip

TLW and I were sitting in an Italian restaurant on Pacific Coast Highway. It was late. Our table was against the front wall beside a window through which we could see the traffic hurrying through the night.

Shortly after we had ordered, a yellow tomcat appeared on the windowsill outside and began pawing the glass. He opened his mouth a few times, as if speaking to Katy, but we couldn't hear his meow because of the glass.

Katy said, "It's a tom." I couldn't verify her observation. His attitude toward me was one of utter indifference.

"Poor thing," she said.

I dislike it when people get sentimental about animals. I don't know why. "Looks pretty fat to me," I said. About that time another cat must have approached the window outside, because the Tom started spitting that hate which only cats can express. He disappeared, only to reappear presently and began licking a paw.

"He's hungry," Katy said.

"How do you know?"

"I can tell," she said. And it suddenly occurred to me that there was some rapport between her and that yellow cat. He was concentrating, using his animal mesmerism.

As we went on eating he watched her every move. Presently, she tore apart one of the rolls we had been served and buttered it.

"You're not going to feed him?" I protested.

"Just a little bite," she got up, the half roll in her hand, but had hardly risen before the cat jumped down and disappeared. She could have been leaving the table for a number of reasons, but that cat knew with unerring instinct that she was coming to feed him. He had read her like a psychiatrist and was right there at the front door when she opened it.

"How do you suppose he knew you were coming to feed him?" I asked when she returned.

She shrugged. "Cats have marvelous perception."

"There is some strange communication between the two of you," I said.

"Cats aren't fond of bread," she said, "but he ate it." She loaded another piece of bread with meat sauce and, when we left, served it to the cat, which was right at the front door when I opened it. For a few moments we watched him. He licked the meat up, then, aware we were watching him, began tearing at the bread with his teeth. He chewed a piece of it but, as soon as we turned away, spit it out.

Somehow, that annoyed me.

Christmas Cards

Received a Christmas card December 15th from Señor Fred Beck, the pixilated poet of Cat City and Malibu Beach. It bore his likeness as Santa Claus.

The tender message: "I hope you don't believe in Santa but Merry Christmas."

Dear Frederico:

I not only don't believe in Santa Claus I don't have much faith in myself. I took stock the other day and found little credit. I can tell a joke well, can swim ten strokes under water, am a faithful husband and a martini-maker of the first rank.

That's about all I could come up with. I like to think of myself as being handsome, personable, kind, considerate, cheerful, smart and generous to a fault, but get the impression others see me as mean, narrow-minded, acerbic, calculating, sarcastic and cynical.

However, I tell you one thing, Fred—I believe in

you. You are the brightest, wittiest, kindest, most generous friend I know, and I know a whole slew.

We are all acquainted with people of superior talents who do not receive the acclaim they deserve. If you got your just desserts, my friend, it wouldn't be jello or a pie in the face, you would be as famous as Addison Sims of Seattle and as beloved as a French poodle.

June Andrews is another genius who hasn't had her share of acclaim. She has a beautiful, true, melodious voice and can sing rings around everybody in the warbling business. Not only that—she has an encyclopedic mind into which she can dip for lyrics old-timers have long forgotten.

June should be gracing the great music halls of the day. She should be twenty-four sheeted across the country. Her income should be in the hundreds of thousands. Instead, as wife of orange-grower and humanitarian Victor, she lives inconspicuously in Emerald Bay.

If I had an organization and wanted it run properly I'd call on a managerial genius who lives in our town—Muriel Reynolds, who should be on the President's cabinet, but instead keeps house, and very happily for husband Larry, no managerial slouch himself.

These talented people are all about us. Roy Childs is the merchandising genius. Jack Taylor has a marvelous sense of design. Betsy Rose is the best newsperson in Orange County. Richard Campbell is an inventor of the first rank. Harry Willats is superior to Hilton in running hotels.

These people live comparatively unsung in Laguna. They live quietly and the world hardly notes them. I'm sure they wouldn't trade places with those in the limelight.

To postmen, those bearers of tidings, bills and junk, to bus and taxicab drivers who have to work and stay sober during the holidays, to hospital workers who administer to the maimed and to the maimed themselves, we wish the best at this Yuletide.

> To rich and poor, loaner and debtor, to the crazy and nutty, the daffy and dotty, to relatives, friends and foes, our best wishes for a Merry Christmas and a Happy New Year.

We string Christmas cards we receive from the parlor ceiling to show how many friends we have. Gives us a feeling of amity. We got more than a hundred this year, a couple of them the four-dollar kind.

Quite apart from family, friends and business associates, they came from our plumber, the man from whom we buy fresh fish and several other business people. Camelback Inn in Phoenix always sends us one, though we haven't been there for at least ten years. Once in a while we get cards from people we can't remember.

The most meaningless card we received was one from which, when I opened it, Santa popped up like a jack-in-the-box and stuck his tongue out. This brought gift-giving into sharp focus—a Bronx cheer being what the man-of-the-house usually gets.

Some of the cards' designs show imagination, but for the most part they are traditional—pictures of Santa, trees, sleighs and reindeer. A certain number are photographs of the senders. One couple sent us a picture of their house. It's in Taos. They had to use a ladder to get in and out of it.

Then there are those Christmas letters which purport to tell all that has happened to the senders and their progeny during the previous year.

The travels of the Budge Weltys, of Bartlesville, Oklahoma, were told by their two cats, Dirty and Gertie.

Merry Christmas to the faithful readers of this column and yuletide greetings to Herbert Hoover and Harry Truman, neither of whom read the *Post*. To Papa Kroch, an elder statesman, who does; to Douglas MacArthur, a great egoist, and to all the losers on this planet.

Joyeux Noel to Henry Ford II and our President, Dwight

D. Eisenhower, to Mr. Kruschev and to Fidel Castro, who is out there sawing away on the limb he's sitting on.

"I live in the Art and Culture Center of the World, and I ain't artistic and I ain't cultured..."

CHAPTER 6: JUNE 1953

Hospital

Myford Irvine and I were sitting in the escrow department of the Laguna Federal Savings and Loan Association completing last details pursuant to the purchase of the twenty-two-acre hospital site in South Laguna. Mike had with him a check from the James Irvine Foundation, of which he is president, for $58,500—final payment for the property. For several days thereto we had been through a series of resolutions, conveyances, deeds, affidavits, whereases and wherefores. And as James McBeth, the escrow officer, was getting the big batch of papers in final order Mike said with a sigh, "Never had so much trouble giving money away in my life."

The Irvine Foundation has bought the property and deeded it to the Laguna Beach Community Hospital Association with the proviso that, if the community is unable to erect a hospital within five years, the property will revert to the Santa Ana Community Hospital.

We have to raise a million dollars from people not only in Laguna but in all of the towns in southern Orange County, and it ain't going to be easy.

Hospital Board Meeting

We are all sitting in the Fireside Room of Hotel Laguna waiting for the opening bids to build a hospital and Adolph "Papa" Kroch tells me he and his wife Trudy, who have just come back from Chicago where he has book stores, are to take off in March on a flight to Hong Kong to see daughter Gretchen. They'll be in the air 40 hours.

"Do they have bunks for sleeping?" I asked.

"Oh, yes," says he, "but I won't use one. I want to have my clothes on if we go down."

Victor Andrews, a member of the hospital board and a big-time farmer, confided that the well he has been digging on his Bakersfield ranch was giving him trouble. They struck water at sixteen hundred feet, but in trying to improve the flow went deeper—to two thousand.

Three guesses what the trouble was they ran into?—They struck oil.

I never saw a more disappointed farmer. "Well, what's eating you?" I ask, appalled. "Isn't the oil any good?"

"Fine," says he. "Thirty gravity. But at this point it's the last thing we want. We've got a hundred and fifty thousand dollar crop of potatoes and cotton in the ground. We can't irrigate with oil."

What's he going to do?

"I'm not sure," he replied. "We filled up the last hundred feet with concrete, but it stopped the water altogether. Now we haven't got oil or water. I guess we're going to have to blast the concrete—try to find our way back to the water. We may go back for the oil later," said he. "But right now we've got to have water or lose our crops."

Vic's attention is drawn elsewhere and I get into conversation with Joe Rosan, whose Rosan's Inc., in Newport, is one of the area's important factories. He tells me the *Explorer*, the army's satellite now circling the earth, may be held together by his product, a patented screw that he invented.

"Don't you know?" I ask,

He shakes his head. "Everything about that spudnick is top secret," he says, "even the screws."

Bill Lambourne, one of our town's councilmen and a leading real estate broker, tells me the real estate business here is booming, and I reply that Laguna real estate turns over here more frequently, it seems to me, than anywhere else. "This sort of thing can't go on forever, can it?" I ask Bill.

"It has for the fifteen years I've been here," says he.

"Don't you think it has reached the zenith?"

"Not by a long sight."

I said I could remember when a good 75x100 foot lot could be bought for $1,000—since the war, too. When they reach $4,000 a lot, I allowed as how I thought the millennium had come.

"Today the average is $7,500," Bill tells me, "and it will go to $10,000 within the next decade. There's only so much of it, and people keep coming here wanting to live. Question of supply and demand."

I don't know which is worse—inflation or depression. One seems to be about as bad as another. Main thing in a depression is to eat, and in an inflation is not to overeat. Also talked with Charlie Haskins, one of the most astute men I know, who started his first bank 40 years ago at a crossroad—I think in Montana. And with Paul Dodd, also a Security First National Bank vice-president, who had to get back to Los Angeles to attend a General Motors cocktail party. Client relations, you know. And Roy Childs who has a money-making machine (Pottery Shack) at the corner of Brooks and Coast Highway; he is planning to build a new house on Diamond Street. And Josephine Tice, the board's secretary, whose ancestors came to this country in the seventeenth century,

The room is loaded with people—bidders as well as board members and other interested persons, and finally the bids are ready to open. What do you know?—the low bid is just under a million dollars. We are all delighted because it is within our estimate. Now we'll see if we can get the federal government to give us an equal amount.

As a rule this space is devoted to pointing out the foibles of mankind and criticizing the modes and manners of our time, but today we have an anecdote.

It is about two tenacious gentlemen, Adolph Kroch, president of the South Coast Community Hospital board, and J.E. Riley, a contractor who is there to bid for clearing and leveling the twenty-three acres where hopefully the hospital will stand.

The board had allocated $55,000 for the job, this being the amount donated for that specific purpose by the James Irvine Foundation. Most of those on the hospital board were hopeful the job might be done for less than $50,000.

Turned out they were idle dreamers. As the bids were opened the faces of board members fell lower and lower. One was for $83,000, one for $78,000, one for $69,000, one for $73,000 and one for $92,000.

By the time the penultimate bid was opened no bidder was anywhere near the allocated figure. Then Mr. Riley's bid was opened. It was for $57,000. While this was above the sum allotted, it was within our means and was therefore a great relief to the distraught board.

The most disappointed person present at the bid-opening was "Papa" Kroch. He had been riding herd on everybody to garner money for the job.

Papa thought that even Riley's bid was excessive. To discuss the matter he invited him to his home on Pearl Street, fed him a sumptuous lunch, including a cocktail and excellent wine, and during the repast, talked to him in three tones, paternal, pleading and persuasive, in an effort to get him to lower his bid.

But Riley said that, far from making a profit on the job, he stood to lose several thousand dollars, "Even if everything goes all right, which in such a job it rarely does." He had bid his low figure because he had a lot of heavy equipment which, if left standing idle, would cost him money.

Papa took another tack.

Would Mr. Riley then, consider making a donation to the hospital?

What could Mr. Riley say? Mellow with wine and some of Trudy Kroch's delicious food, he accepted the proffered pen and wrote a pledge for $1,000.

Thus, the hospital is getting its site cleared for just a little more than the amount allocated. Papa said, "Mr. Riley deserves a vote of thanks." And added, "Greater love hath no man than to lose his shirt and then give away his pants."

Strong Man

One of the acts in the recent fund raising "Extravaganza," produced at Irvine Bowl by the women's auxiliary of the South Coast Community Hospital then a-building, was Paul Anderson, without question the strongest man in the world. A huge fellow (twenty-five-inch biceps) he weighs well over 300 pounds, has a hard time in this life finding a bed or a chair which won't collapse under him.

Marge Swanson, in charge of securing hotel accommodations for the performers, reserved a room at the Riviera for Anderson and his company, but by curtain time Anderson confided to Muriel Reynolds, the show's chairman, that he wasn't going to spend the night. "I'm going home where I'm sure of the furniture," he said.

Rooms were at a premium that Saturday night, so Muriel asked Marge to call quickly and cancel his reservation. "Maybe they can rent the room and save us the expense," she said.

Marge called right away.

"We're glad you called," the clerk said, "but Mr. Anderson has already used the room, and we don't think the place will ever be the same. If he were coming back we were going to charge you double. As it is, you're getting away cheap."

I Meet William Randolph Hearst

Bill Holt, who lives in Emerald Bay, reminds me of the only time I met Mr. Hearst. It happened in 1925. At the time I was earning a precarious living as a stunt man in the movies, doubling for such actors as Richard Barthlemess, John Barrymore and Tom Mix, and Bill was putting himself through school by chauffeuring the actor James Kirkwood. Thus we were both rubbing shoulders every day with fame and wealth, though little of either was rubbing off on us. One day I met a girl I liked very much named Pepi Lederer and she invited me to a fandango at her house, an address in Beverly Hills.

Nobody told me that Pepi was Marion Davies' niece and that the address she had given me was a baronial mansion. But I got dressed up in black tie and, having no car, prevailed upon a friend to drive me from my boarding house near Western and Sunset. When we arrived we were so impressed by the neighborhood that, to save embarrassment, I asked him to drive his ancient jalopy past the house and let me out half a block away.

I was certain I had made a mistake in the address but rang the doorbell anyway. Picture my surprise when an imposing butler in tails and starched collar greeted me. He allowed as how, yes, Miss Lederer lived there, took my hat and rain coat and announced me to a group of seven persons in a sunken living room.

The seven were Miss Davies, Mr. Hearst, James Kirkwood, his actress wife, Lila Lee, Charles Paddock, the then world's fastest runner, his girl friend Bebe Daniels, and Lita Grey Chaplin, wife of Charlie.

All of these people were world famous and to say I was nonplused is to demonstrate the paucity of the English language. Miss Davies was very kind. She came to the bottom of the stairs and gave me her hand, said Pepi would be down presently, and introduced me to each of those present. Kirkwood, acting as bartender, asked what I would like to drink.

It was prohibition time, and I was fresh out of Georgia. Indeed I was so innocent that the only liquor I had tasted was corn whiskey. We called it White Mule. It was known as "sitting down" whiskey, meaning one shouldn't drink it standing up.

Mr. Kirkwood mixed me a scotch and soda and I took it and went over and sat down on the nearest vacant seat, a divan three-quarters of which was occupied by Mr. Hearst, a huge man. People who know me would not believe I was speechless, but I was, and the Great Man offered me no help. Indeed, he did not even look at me. He had a big, long, sad face with a pelican-like dew lap under his chin and seemed to be anywhere but with us. I wished acutely I could speak to him of the big issues of the day, of world problems and politics, but I never felt so ignorant in my life. He was a man who, almost single-handed, had started the Spanish-American War, who had been seriously spoken of as "presidential timber," a publisher of many newspapers—how could a 20-year-old naive ignoramus, such as I, talk to him?

"I've heard so much about you," I said.

He turned his slant-eyed face on me and said, "Is that so?"

"It's my ambition to be a newspaperman," I said.

"What do you do now?"

"I'm a stunt man."

"Very interesting."

For the moment I couldn't believe he was talking. These were the only words we exchanged because at this juncture Pepi came in and rescued me. Meanwhile Bill Holt, now my friend in Laguna, was sitting out in the cold, waiting for Mr. Kirkwood. We did not meet that night and I did not learn until almost thirty years later that we went to the same party, he as a chauffeur and I as a guest.

My First Automobile

I read that our national economy rests heavily on the automobile, that one out of seven persons in the United Sates depends directly or indirectly for their livelihood on it and its roads.

I remember with strong affection the first car I owned. It was a 1920 Stutz. Usually a Stutz is referred to as "Bearcat," but this one was a touring car. It had belonged, the salesman told me, to Jack Pickford, Mary's brother. It was a four-door, lemon-yellow beauty, long and snazzy with a canvas top, leather seats, brass-framed windshield, spare wheels set in front-fender wells and a leather-bound trunk in the rear. The gear-shift and hand brake levers were outside the driver's seat. The four-cylinder engine had a basso roar that was hard to ignore. I always drove it with the top down because I wanted it to distinguish me. Those days in Hollywood it was important to develop a personality and an identity. The car cost one hundred and eighty-two dollars and I paid twenty-five dollars down. I bought it in 1924 from a used-car lot on Sunset Boulevard. It must have been six or seven years old and when it was new had probably cost two thousand or more dollars. It was a wonderful contraption. All it needed to operate perfectly, and all I gave it, were gasoline, oil and water. It was rugged. In shifting one had to "double clutch," that is quickly kick the clutch pedal twice. It got about eight miles per gallon, but gasoline was cheap in those days—about fifteen cents a gallon.

I was earning a precarious living as a stunt man in the movies. Whenever a scenario called for a particular hazardous endeavor by an actor or actress I might be called upon to perform it. When I was not working, which was most of the time, I was looking for a job. I would go from studio to studio—Fox on Western Avenue, Warner Brothers on Sunset, Paramount on Vine, FOB and Columbia on Gower, United Artists or Harold Lloyd's on Santa Monica, MGM in Culver City and Universal and Republic in San Fernando Valley.

In those days there was no Central Casting and we actors had to go from one casting office to another. Clark Gable and I had become friends and lived near each other. He had an old Dodge touring car, but we usually went on job-hunting jaunts in the Stutz, figuring that way we got more pizzazz. He was what is called a dress-extra, which means he owned both a tuxedo and full-dress suit and when he had to wear either of them he was paid ten to fifteen dollars a day instead of the extra's seven-fifty.

Clark was the last actor I ever expected to become a leading man. He had a large face, prominent ears, overhanging eyebrows and a heavy body. During our peregrinations we exchanged backgrounds and talked about what we should do with our lives. He was serious about acting, while to me it seemed a dilettantish way for a man to make a living. I said as much and he retorted, "Well, it's a hell of a lot better'n risking my neck as you do."

"I don't want to stay in stunt work," I said. "I want to be

a writer."

"Well, I sure as hell don't want to go back to the oil fields," he said.

"I think the place for you is in the theater. There's no way for you to become a movie star. Your ears stick out. And if you get leading roles you'll have to change your name. Clark's too namby-pamby. You'll have to make it Ace or Duke or King, something gutsy."

"How about Bozo?" he suggested and we both laughed.

A friend borrowed the Stutz one day to go to the beach. On the way he was speeding and smashed into a truck. The cost of repairs was more than the car was worth so I abandoned it—not without shedding several tears. Today, properly restored, it could be worth a fortune.

"Most successful year I've ever had."

CHAPTER 7: AUGUST 1953

Don't Call Him Doc

His father had been a manufacturing chemist and he himself had been and still is a registered pharmacist. He was in the medical corps of the Navy during World War I, and subsequently spent many years traveling the country selling surgical supplies. So it is quite logical Carl Waterbury, who has retired to live in our town, should be called Doc. Indeed, he is known as Doc from one end of the country to the other, but of late he is discouraging use of the appellation.

The reason he does not want to be called Doc goes back to that time in Buckhorn Mineral Wells, Arizona, when he was mistaken for a real doctor and, in an emergency, was called upon to save the life of a bona fide doctor's wife.

Buckhorn Mineral Wells is a health resort between Superstition Mountain and Mesa and is owned by Carl's friend, Ted Sliger. Sliger started out to build a motel, but in sinking a well he struck hot water so turned the place into a spa. It has become one of the best-known health resorts in the southwest. The San Francisco Giants baseball team does its preseason conditioning there.

Carl always stops at Buckhorn on his frequent trips across the country and he and Sliger have lots of fun teasing each other in that way men do when there is affection between them.

This time when Carl arrived Sliger greeted him as Doc and, for a gag and because he considers it good business to lend a medical atmosphere to his establishment, introduced him as Dr. Waterbury to a medical doctor with whom he was in conversation. The M.D. was interested in meeting a fellow practitioner and inquired what field Carl specialized in.

Not wanting to embarrass his friend by making him out a liar, Carl went along with the deception and tried to duck the question by saying he had been a surgeon but that he was retired. It seemed a harmless lie at the time and he thought nothing more about it until the next morning when, about five A.M., the M.D. knocked on his door in a state of considerable agitation.

"Doctor Waterbury!" he whispered hoarsely. When Carl opened the door the M.D. told him his wife was ill and asked him to come help him make a diagnosis. "When it comes to my family," he said, "I don't trust my own judgment."

Carl did not deem it prudent to reveal the truth about himself. He felt it would do no harm if he went and did what he could without committing himself.

The doctor's wife was indeed ill. She had vomited herself empty and was exhausted from heaving, besides which she was in great pain. "This is worse than having a baby," she told Carl between heaves.

The two men examined the lady's abdomen, Carl assuming what he considered a professional manner. Finally the M.D. asked the inevitable question: "What do you think it is, Doctor?"

Carl knew enough about the human body to venture a opinion. He said it looked to him as if her condition was ectopic, meaning an abnormal tubular pregnancy—a very serious ailment.

"But so far as I know my wife isn't pregnant," the M.D. said.

"Well, whatever is the matter with her," Carl said, "she is very, very sick, and in my opinion we should get her to a hospital at once." Thus playing his hand close to the belly, so to speak.

Together they carried the doctor's wife to Carl's car and drove hard for the nearest hospital, in Mesa, six miles away.

As chance would have it, one of the first persons they encountered at the hospital was a surgeon friend of Carl's and Carl says he never was happier to see anybody in his life. With an adroitness that would have done credit to the late Houdini, Carl turned the patient over to the surgeon and that worthy wasted no time in getting her onto an operating table.

It is a good thing he did, because Carl's conjectured diagnosis proved to be correct. Had the lady not been operated on quickly she probably would have died. As it worked out, she recovered and is alive and well today. Her husband, the M.D., still believes Carl is a doctor.

Specialization

The medical profession has become highly specialized in the last decade or so, but it occurs to me that it hasn't gone far enough. There's the skin specialist and the heart specialist and the foot specialist and the bone specialist and the gastrointestinal man and the U-G man and the ear doctor and the eye doctor; there's the proctologist and the otolaryngologist, the navel doctor and the nasal doctor, and a specialist for practically any part of the body or any disease it is heir to.

And then there is the general practitioner.

Now I claim it is asking a great deal of one man to become proficient and keep abreast of the advancements in treatment and technique of all the ills of man. And I am of the opinion it might be wise to split the classification of general practitioner into at least four categories.

The first would be the diagnostic doctor. He would be the one to decide whether or not you are ailing and what, if anything, is the matter with you.

The second would be the curing doctor. He would treat you and prescribe for you.

The third would be a specialist for hypochondriacs: that is, he would treat those who imagine they are ill.

And the fourth would be a doctor for hopeless cases.

The general practitioner is called upon to do all these things, but it is the rare one who does them all well. I think the departmentalization above referred to would lend efficiency and thoroughness to the profession.

The diagnostic doctor would not be called upon to diagnose such simple ailments as the common cold, unless there were complications. But he would be free to study symptoms exclusively, and he would save many of us a great deal of time, anguish and money by establishing what ails us at the outset.

The curing doctor would not have to take histories or waste your time or his by trying to find out what's wrong. The hypochondriac doctor would be chosen, of course, for his bedside manner.

And of course the man who treats the hopelessly ill should be a poet and a philosopher. He also should be a man who understands death's vast benefits. He should not try to keep alive those who are at the end of their tethers.

There comes a time in all our lives when it is a privilege to die. When that time comes we don't want some over-anxious doctor pumping us full of drugs and glucose to keep us alive for a few extra gulps of this life. The dying doctor would be a liaison between life and death, would be a man who would ease you on your way instead of trying to hold you back. If there's a specialist to bring babies into the world perhaps there should be one to shove us gently off this mortal coil. Most of us, I think, both the living and the dying, would consider it a blessing.

Real Estate Notes

Now that Mrs. William Wrigley, who had lain paralyzed in Pasadena for many years, has passed on to the nether shore, Catalina Island is for sale, I understand, by her heirs. The price is in the neighborhood of $25,000,000. The Wrigleys paid $4,000,000 for it in the 1920s. The day will come and many of us will see it when the Island's hills and dales will be covered with homes. It should be a fantastically lucrative real estate development.

Two factors are going to populate it: (1) a cheap production of fresh water from sea water; and (2) the development of the helicopter.

It will be a residential paradise. Because it is an island, its every aspect can be controlled as rigidly as a private club. Its twenty-odd miles in length should afford every kind of playground imaginable, from lawn bowling to golf, horseshoes to archery.

This immensely valuable piece of real estate has been lying dormant for years awaiting its time. The Spanish explorer Viscaino named the island Catalina in 1602, after Cabrillo had called it Victoria. Both found many Indians living there. They dressed in seal skins and lived in conical huts made of palm fronds. They made admirable canoes of tules to carry as many as twenty persons to and from the mainland.

When the island belonged to Mexico it was used as a penal colony. The authorities would send its worst criminals to Catalina and drop them off to get along as best they could. Most of them managed to make their way back to the mainland in the basket-like canoes.

Today it is one of the most beautiful tourist attractions in California.

Omnibus Outing

Always wanted to take the local bus tour, got around to it few days ago. Bus was driven by lady Regina Reiner, who is co-owner of line with husband, a Continental bus driver. She is probably the only lady bus driver in Orange County who works the afternoon shift and has a good time.

I got on at the depot on Ocean Avenue, took a comfortable seat alongside an old lady who reminded me of my Aunt Toady and we took off, Regina double-clutching, headed south. That is, we went east as far as City Hall, turned down Forest Avenue to humpy-bumpy Glenneyre street, *then* south.

"Be glad when they repave this cow path," Regina said over her shoulder. "It's awful hard on our equipment."

We stopped at the library corner to let on a lady with a load of groceries and two children, took the post office hill in high.

"Only time I get bored," Regina said, replying to a question, "is when the bus is empty. Most of my customers are regulars—older people who don't or can't drive cars, and children—and I probably know them and the details of their daily lives better than I know those of my relatives. Children like to ride in the backseat," she said parenthetically. "Don't ask me why."

When we passed the corner of Brooks street where the Pottery Shack is, Roy Childs, its owner, caught sight of me, gave me a double-take. *What is a Ford dealer doing riding a bus?* He finally decided he must be mistaken, went on with his pursuit, i.e., running the most lucrative business in town.

At Diamond we turned down to Coast Highway, rolled past the Old Brussels restaurant where Lucien Brack, a Belgian chef, prepared superb French cuisine; and as we climbed the hill at Victoria Drive, Regina said, "Take a look at that view! Where else in the world will you find anything to compare?"

Manhattan, Spring 1954

We came into this overpopulated island from Los Angeles in one of those modern miracles of science, a DC8 jet, which magic-carpets one through the ozone at nearly six hundred miles an hour. The flight was supposed to take four hours and forty-five minutes, but the Atlantic seaboard was fogged and the behemoth's pilot couldn't find the ground. We were thirteen hours en route. We could have made almost as good time in a Piper Cub.

First thing I did was buy a copy of the *New York Times.* If for no other reason, it is a pleasure to come here to read this great newspaper. I read it while eating breakfast in an Automat, which offers the best corned beef hash anywhere, and learned that the sea otter, which used to be plentiful along the California coast, is making a comeback.

This is good news, and if I had stayed in California I might never have known about it. Sea otters are about the cutest and friendliest of nature's whims. They sleep floating on their backs, chin on chest and a paw over each eye, the article informed me, and to keep from floating away they pull a little kelp over them. The reason they were almost extinct is because during the eighteen hundreds, to make fur coats and caps, their skins brought from two hundred to three hundred dollars apiece.

Another good reason for coming to New York is the availability of oysters on the half shell. I like them with tomato sauce, lemon juice, horseradish and a drip of Tabasco. Superb.

Then there is the subway—a never-closing theatre chock full of wonderful characters playing life's little dramas. While riding in the subway I watched a man put his hand in another man's pocket. I notified the man that he had been robbed but he did nothing about it. When I got off I mentioned the incident to a policeman and he told me that what I had seen probably was a dope delivery. "Happens all the time," he said.

I like New York for its astonishing vitality and rhythm. It's a city in which one walks for several reasons: the shop windows, the cost of a taxi, the passing parade and to exercise.

It is a thrilling and absorbing experience to saunter the canyon called Fifth Avenue. The shop windows artfully present the best merchandise the world offers. Because it is the city's show place, the avenue from 125th Street to Washington Square is kept spic and span. There were even public ashtrays planted at intervals in the sidewalks. Cross my heart.

Antique hansom cabs and bored horses still stand on Central Park South near the Plaza Hotel, as others did during the gay '90s, and, clopping rhythmically, the horses still take lovers through the park.

The pigeon population seems to have doubled since we were here in 1957 and poses a problem. Most of them have forgotten how to fly. They strut up and down the sidewalks as if they owned the real estate. Oftentimes it is difficult to keep from stepping on them. They're as insouciant as the San Marcos pigeons in Venice.

Not even in London are hotel doormen so dressed up—in admiral coats with gold braid and caps with chicken guts. Even in winter they are prone to wear only one glove, leaving a bare hand for accepting tips. In almost any direction you look you'll see window washers working the hell-and-gone up yonder. I have a great affection for the genial, ever-helpful, long-suffering New York policemen, eighty percent of whom, according to the *Times,* are Irish.

It is a generally held belief, I think, that New Yorkers are the best groomed, but I don't think it's true. I think San Franciscans beat them a mile. Though the weather is cold we've seen few fur coats. The style here is caracul. Men wear Homburgs or Astrakhan caps. The walking stick is coming back, but so far we haven't seen anyone wearing spats.

When one tires of walking, there are the expensive, ever-present and wonderfully peripatetic taxicabs. New York cab drivers are entertaining egomaniacs. They know everything about world affairs, politics, art, love, and how to bring up children.

One who drove Katy and me today has been "hacking," he told us, for thirty years. Of the four sons he has reared, two are doctors and two are lawyers, while papa keeps on driving. He works ten hours a day, six days a week, earns about two hundred dollars, mostly in tips. "I wouldn't work in an office if you paid me double," he told us.

Thinking of California, I asked if he didn't yearn to live somewhere else. His reply: "There ain't no other place." Then he told me he had once driven a cab in Beverly Hills. "Everybody goes to bed at nine o'clock," he said. "I almost starved to death. Nobody in New York City goes to bed at nine o'clock—at night, that is."

Art Notes

All my life I have been fascinated by the art of painting, but the longer I live and the more I study it the less I seem to know. My most recent confusion comes from a situation which has arisen at the Detroit Institute of Art. Seems that twenty-eight patrons of the museum forked up $200,000 to purchase a painting. It's an unfinished picture of a madonna and child and two angels attributed at least in part to Leonardo da Vinci. There is some doubt as to its authenticity.

Now this is the situation. If Leonardo did paint so much as the background or a foot of one of the angels the picture is worth at least one million dollars. But if he did not and the picture was painted, as some experts aver, by unknowns, it is worth very little, maybe a couple of hundred bucks.

This does not make good sense. What is the first purpose of painting? Is it not to please the optic sense?

The painting in question is very old and very beautiful. Despite the fact the madonna is unfinished—that is she was merely sketched in, and perhaps the artist left her thus for effect—the religious theme is superbly done and the coloring, detail and composition are masterly.

The question arises: Why the vast disparity in value? The picture is a picture is a picture, Leonardo or no Leonardo. If it is of the great master's period and is well painted enough to be attributed to him by experts, it should have a high value. When one buys a picture is one buying art or history?

While in New York recently, I saw the Picasso show at The Museum of Modern Art. Picasso has been painting for many years and has performed through many stages of art. In the early years of this century—1905, '06 and '07—he went through his so-called blue period. Examples of this period were among the works shown.

In my estimation the pictures Picasso painted in those years are his best. They have a softness about them, an idealistic, romantic quality which is pleasing. There is also a religious feeling in them which is not found in his work of recent years. Much of his recent work is almost purely technical. From it one gets the feeling that the artist is cynical, indifferent to his audience and utterly arrogant.

I am not protesting his right to deviate from the norm. The point is that, though his weird, feelingless pictures sell today for fabulous prices, I do not think they will always be so valuable. It would be my ignorant guess that they will become mere curiosities.

But not so the works of his "blue" period. The pictures he painted then have a powerful individuality. They will always have the power to evoke a viewer's inspiration, which is the aim of art.

Long after we have learned all about outer space, Mars and the Moon, we probably won't know why some artists sell well, some poorly. Public fancy is a poor critic, and money seems to have little relationship to merit.

Please do not get the idea I am an opponent of "modern art." On the contrary, one of my favorite painters is John McLaughlin, who lives and paints in Dana Point. If you want to experience the feeling an artist can put into geometrical designs, have a look at his work. His pictures of practically nothing have a strong power which commands attention.

Good Samaritan

You know how it is: do what you consider a good turn and get a slap in the face for your pains.

Happened to me just now. Two weeks ago this space carried a paragraph, to wit:

> Lady called me, didn't give her name, said Ella Bucholz, whose waiter husband was killed recently on Coast Highway, is destitute and suffering from cancer. She's at the Iverson Apartments in Dana Point, needs help.

Harmless little piece. I thought it might do the lady some good, that some of her friends might call and do what they could.

Well, I'll tell you, it didn't work out that way. From all reports the power of the press is alarming.

First, James Torrens, the printing salesman, came in and said Mrs. Bucholz was not sick or destitute, that he had seen her that very day, hale and hearty, up and about, and that she was employed as a waitress, was doing fine.

I said I was glad to hear it.

Then he came in later to say he had made a mistake. Had the wrong woman. The woman he had talked to was a Mrs. Wehrt who had telephoned me in the first place and wouldn't give her name. He said Mrs. Wehrt was very upset because of what I had written.

I said I was sorry.

Then John Knowles, the attorney, called me to say he represented Mrs. Bucholz in the negotiations with an insurance company involving the death of Mr. Bucholz. "No sooner did your column appear," John said, "than the insurance company called and made a ridiculous offer, inferring if Mrs. Bucholz is dying she would not be in need of much money."

"You've certainly thrown a monkey wrench into the works," John told me.

I said I was sorry.

Then I got a note from Mike Jackson, feature editor of this sterling journal. To wit:

"John Knowles called and asked if you could run a retraction item in your column on Ella Bucholz, the woman somebody told you had cancer and was destitute. Turns out she has no cancer, and while far from affluent is not destitute. Knowles says he realized your motives were of the best, but that you got the facts wrong."

Then another lady called, wouldn't give me her name, said Mrs. Bucholz was very unhappy about what I had written because at least three persons had come into her house and started to pray over her.

Then John Knowles called again and asked me to please run the following. To wit:

"Ella Bucholz, whose waiter husband was killed recently on Coast Highway, is *not* suffering from cancer as was recently reported in the *Post*."

Then Mrs. Wehrt called to ask what on earth I had been thinking of to write such nonsense as I had about Mrs.

Bucholz. "I didn't tell you she had cancer," Mrs. Wehrt said. "I told you she had tuberculosis. And I didn't want you to write it up. I wanted you to do something about that insurance agent who won't give Mrs. Bucholz her just dues. It's an outrage, that's what it is."

At this point I am inclined to agree with Mrs. Wehrt.

And I'm sorry.

I'm glad Mrs. Bucholz hasn't got cancer but apparently she can use plenty of help.

CHAPTER 8: THE 1960S

My Mother Is an Astrologer

This year, 1962, dear reader, we go to the polls to elect a president of our great nation for the next four years, and I am beginning to wonder whether the person we elect will last that long. History tells us that about every twenty years, as if controlled by audacious fate, a president dies in office.

The pattern goes back a long way. Let's start with William Henry Harrison, who died in office in 1841. Abraham Lincoln died in 1865, James Garfield in 1881, William McKinley in 1901, Warren Harding in 1923, Franklin Roosevelt in 1943. Whoever is elected to serve this time—either Richard Nixon or John Kennedy may be assassinated. If so the vice-president will become the chief executive, so it is important, which it usually isn't, that he be of top quality.

I got this history from my mother. Before she died she was one of the country's well-known astrologers. Her professional name was Deborah Lewis and she wrote monthly articles on international affairs for *American Astrology.* She became a celebrity by predicting, three months before it happened, the Japanese attack on Hawaii, December 7, 1941.

Her interest in astrology came out of her interest in the occult. She studied Hinduism, Buddhism and other religions. She was an Episcopalian but learned to read Hebrew so that she could delve into the Mishnah and Gemara. She had a firm conviction that she had lived on this earth before.

She did not like to do personal horoscopes and in doing them read the clients rather than their charts. She particularly disliked doing women's horoscopes. Invariably they wanted her to tell them about romances in the offing. What she gave them

"Looks like everybody in town has some sort of talent."

were pearls of common sense. She avoided telling them their faults.

"People, by and large," she told me, "see themselves as too flawless to accept censure." She would tell clients that there are no bad configurations. "Any position of the stars can be beneficial," she would say. "If fortune turns against you, learn from the experience and turn the adversity to account. Indeed, through misfortune we often find opportunity." To those who came wanting to know when their "ship was coming in," she would say "If you just sit and wait, the chances are it never will. Your best route to riches and happiness is through diligence and hard work."

A man who had read some of her magazine articles wrote her from northern Canada saying it would be valuable to him to know precisely what day the ice would break sufficiently to permit navigation on the upper Mackenzie River. If she could tell him, he wrote, he would reward her handsomely. She replied, giving him a date and adding, "Don't bet on it." Lo and behold, that spring she received a check for one hundred dollars from the Canadian. "You hit it right on the nose," he wrote. "That astrology is quite a science."

"I want you to know," she wrote back, thanking him, "the date I gave you was based on weather forecasting. It did not have anything to do with astrology."

I asked her what she did with the check.

She said, "I kep' it."

It will be interesting to see if her prognostication about Presidents dying in office comes true.

Kennedy won the election and was assassinated in 1963. Ronald Reagan, during his presidency, was shot in 1983 but survived.

Did you know that at one time a woman was actually nominated for the Presidency of the United States? Her name was Victoria Claflin Woodhull and she was the nominee of the Equal Rights Party in 1872. She ran against Ulysses Grant.

Vicky was a character worth a book. She arose from what the cliche artists call abject poverty to run a brokerage house on

Wall Street and made lots of money. She published a weekly magazine, precipitated a scandal about the celebrated Henry Ward Beecher, engaged in an almost unending litigation with him, was arrested more than once, and lectured widely, chiefly on the subject of free love—a daring topic of the day. Sometimes she was for it and sometimes she was against it. Being a woman, she figured she had the right to change her mind.

She died in England, whither she had fled, in 1927 at the age of eighty-nine and left a large, landed estate.

Victoria Woodhull's character was so contradictory as to defy description. She had an almost hypnotic effect on audiences and individuals. Some people adored her, thought she was a saint; others thought she was a charlatan.

Whatever the truth about her, if she had become President she would certainly have enlivened history. By comparison, look at that drab character who beat her, "the people's choice," Ulysses Grant. Like Eisenhower, he was a good general, a poor businessman and a lazy President.

An historian wrote the following about Victoria:

"She was beautiful and bright, but had none of what's called cant. Though quite an enigma, her picture on bills would have looked better than Grant's."

CHAPTER 9

Reincarnation *or* Next Time Around

I'm in a quandary. Don't know what I want to be when I come back in the next life. Sometimes I want be a pelican and sometimes I want to be a seal. Can't make up my mind.

I'm rather partial to the pelican idea. Pelicans are philosophical and independent. I would like to be philosophical and independent. Seems to me the pelican would have made a much better national bird than the eagle. The eagle is handsome and a good fisher, but he's dumb as a dodo.

If I come back a pelican I could spend my life coasting on the updrafts from waves and diving for my supper. It must be fun to site your prey, lock your wings and take a header! *Bop!* As a pelican one could head on down to Panama when Southern California weather gets cold and go over to Catalina for weekends. Must be absolutely wonderful to pick up a wind and have it take you.

On the other hand, the life of a seal offers much. Now that seal skin coats are no longer fashionable, a seal's life is one long holiday of play and basking. Even when he is foraging he's playing and he can float on water or bask on land. Furthermore, there's a good family set-up when you're a seal. You have your calves and they love you and play with you. There's no community property and the only thing you have to worry about is whether the federal government will change the law which makes it a crime to kill a seal.

Or, come to think of it, I could come back a cormorant. The hell-diver combines the best features of the pelican and the seal. He can fly and he can swim; he can dive and he can soar. Of course, he doesn't do any of these these as well as a special-

"Surfing is just not what it used to be."

ist. But he does all well. He gets around, in or out of water.

There is, of course, another possibility: If I had a choice I could elect to come back a Homo sapien. I've found life on this cinder a very pleasant affair. And a human being can do something neither the seal nor the pelican can, he can hate the Russians. I wouldn't give up that right for anything—not unless they're serious about this peace business. If they are serious about ending the cold war and outlawing the atomic bomb and are not just trying to lull us to sleep, I'll quit hating them. But that's a big if.

This is a cliché, I know, but can you imagine what mankind would be able to accomplish if he didn't waste his energies on the stuffs of war? Why, we could have all the schools and hospitals we want: we'd all be healthy and smart. And we could have three-day work-weeks and we could build a beautiful resort at Bahia de Los Angeles and a six-lane highway to it, and we could all go fishing. We could fly and we could swim and we could loll. We wouldn't have to wait for the next life: we could have it all in this one.

Female Foolishness

TLW had a cold sore, couldn't wear lipstick for a week. She looked so beautiful without I asked her henceforth to eschew it.

Being a dutiful wife, she went without it as long as she could. She was back on the stuff as soon as her lip healed, said she looked too conspicuous without it.

At what age should girls start wearing lipstick? Saw ten- and eleven-year-olds wearing it the other day. Is this good?

Was a time when men rouged their lips, the clowns. I predict someday someone will come up with a lipstick dye which won't come off. He'll become one of the richest men in the world, runner-up to the fellow who invented Maybelline.

The Telephone as an Instrument of Torture

The telephone is a wonderful gadget, the workings of which I have never understood. It has become a very important part of our lives, and, unquestionably to a marked degree, been responsible for our country's high standard of living.

But there are times when this little device is an instrument of his Satanic Majesty, old Beelzebub. Ours turned out to be that the other day.

I came home to our land yacht (mobile home) to be greeted by Katy: "Operator Number So-and-so in Palo Alto has been trying to get you," she said. "Somebody's calling you collect."

"Who in the world do we know who'd do that?" I asked.

"His name's Noel Kane."

"Noel Kane!" I exclaimed. "Why, what could he want? I haven't seen him for ten years, not since the war."

"It must be urgent."

Just then the phone rang. It was the Palo Alto operator. Would I accept the charge? I told the lady I was puzzled why Mr. Kane would be calling me collect. "If he wants to talk to me," I said, "let him pay for it." And from the other end of the wire I heard Noel's plaintive voice. "I haven't got any money, John, that's why I'm calling."

When I had accepted the call, Noel told me he and his family had come back to Palo Alto after several years in Mexico to find that the government had put a clamp on their bank account for back taxes. "I'm desperate," he said. "We haven't any money to eat or to pay our hotel bill. Will you please help us out?"

The request seemed incongruous to me because Noel and I had never been close friends; indeed I had good reason to believe he never liked me. We had worked in the same office at Consolidated-Vultee during the early days of the war.

"I heard you had a Ford agency in Laguna," he said, "so I figured you were loaded."

"Thanks for the compliment," I said, thinking to myself—

this man is truly poor if I am the only one he can call for help.

"I'll get the whole thing straightened out Monday," he said, "and send the money back to you. I'll even pay for this call."

The question arose as to how I would get the money to him, and he said it was imperative that he get the money that night. "Telegraph it," he said.

When we had concluded our conversation, I called Western Union and asked if they would send Mr. Kane a hundred bucks. Sure, they said, but they would have to have the cash in hand. "And you'll have to bring it quick," the manager said. "I've been here since five o'clock this morning, and I'm about to close the place."

"Will you accept my check?"

"Sorry. Against the rules. It'll have to be cash."

Not having enough money on hand, I went by the liquor store where Jules Marine cashed my check, and raced to the Western Union office, the while thinking that I wouldn't do all this for my grandmother—running around like crazy for a guy I hardly knew.

"The money will be in your friend's hands within half an hour," the Western Union manager said.

Well, that's been a month ago, and I've never heard a word from Kane since—not even a note saying he received the money.

The next time anybody calls collect I'm not going to be home.

Charpentier's Food and Drink

Most unique restaurant in California—Henri Charpentier's in Redondo Beach. Henri is the famed French chef who is credited with inventing the crepe suzette, for which he should be canonized. His restaurant seats twelve. He serves one meal a day—dinner—to one party, no less than nine, no more than twelve. To partake at his table is a superb experience, the epitome of dining.

Henri runs his place strictly on a reservation basis. He is taking reservations today (March 8, 1956) for 1958, and if you think I'm exaggerating, call up and ask. He's booked solid till then. Our niece, Connie Farrer, made arrangements for us and when she and her husband, William, were guests there last year, she thought it would be nice to give a party on her mother's birthday and kill two obligations with one meal. Turned out she almost did. We ate too much.

The restaurant is in a tiny shack of a house on Pacific Coast Highway—a most unobtrusive place. There is no sign. Vines almost obscure the front door. The only way you can tell it's Henri's is by a small ceramic figure of a chef over the doorbell.

Inside there's nothing fancy either—old fashioned furniture from Grand Rapids, age-yellowed photographs of famous personages. Henri himself answers the doorbell in white chef's costume, including, of course, a towering chef's hat. He is a well upholstered, jowly gentleman who has lived seventy-eight vastly interesting years. At the turn of the century he served such notorious characters as Diamond Jim Brady, Bet-a-Million Gates, Charles Canfield and Lillian Russell. He has cooked for Presidents, Kings, Queens, and millionaires galore. As a matter of fact, he himself lost $1,000,000 in the stock market crash of 1929.

"How?" I asked.

He shrugged. "Was spread too thin," he said. And he added: "It is just as well. I would not want to be rich. Money is too much of a responsibility."

He has worked in some of the outstanding restaurants and hotels of the world. "But I have never been so happy as I am here," he says. "I own the place."

Possibly the great Charpentier's favorite customer was Diamond Jim Brady, an horrendous glutton and party-giver, who used to spend as much as $75,000 annually at Delmonico's when Henri was there.

I don't know that I'm quoting Henri exactly but I think he said that Jim Brady would eat two dozen oysters on the half shell as a starter, following them with a quart of soup, a whole fillet, two or three lobsters and a quart of ice cream. Anyway, the figures were appalling. To top even this, Henri says Brady would drink three of four bottles of champagne at one sitting.

For dinner we had delicious cold California lobster over which was a vichyssoise sauce, served in a bed of parsley and variegated carnations; a clam bisque soup flavored with chives and crushed, crisp bacon, a chilled green salad with delicate French dressing, two whole charcoal-broiled chateaubriands (there were nine of us), new potatoes in a fine sauce, and finally crêpes suzettes as only the master can make them—thin and ablaze with a wonderful brandy-and-cointreau syrup. There were three kinds of wine.

It was a dinner such as you dream of and one which none of us will forget.

Throughout the meal, while Mary, the chef's right-arm labored in the kitchen, Henri sat in a rocking chair and told us of his life and experiences. He was born in France and at an early age became a ward of the famous chef, Escoffier. Escoffier taught him to cook.

I've made a reservation for February 24th, 1958, and can hardly wait. That's my birthday.

"You are not going before the city council with that idea for the village entrance! With our luck, they'll go for it!'

CHAPTER 10

The American Dream

The theme for a great American story is rags to riches. Such success stories are profuse, but last week I heard one that is really a dilly. It is that of Francis Cabang, owner and operator of the widely known and much patronized Royal Hawaiian Charcoal Broiler. This is his story as he told it to his fellow Rotarians.

He was in extremely humble circumstances on a farm in the Philippines, one of ten children. For a time he attended a school where English was taught, but after a year and a half he had to leave school to help support his family. He worked on the farm for a while, then at the age of sixteen made his way to the United States, the land of opportunity.

In time he got a job on a ship which took him as far as Hawaii, where he worked as a laborer on a pineapple plantation. He practiced English, saved his meager earnings and bided his time.

The day he arrived in California he considers the most fortunate of his life, though his ambition was a long way from realization. He wanted to get into some kind of business. I don't think you could imagine a more unlikely candidate for a successful restaurateur than this penniless Filipino.

Through an employment agency he got a job on a ranch in the San Joaquin Valley, laboring in the fields, chopping lettuce and topping carrots. A hard, conscientious worker, he always found work, but the time came when he tired of such menial labor. He had come to America to make his fortune, and working in the fields hardly seemed the way to get ahead.

He made his way to Los Angeles and another employment

agency. Though he did not know it the guardians of fate were about to put him on the road to success.

That road was Highway 101 and it led to, of all unlikely places, Laguna Beach where he found a friend. There he got a job as dishwasher in the Hotel Laguna.

No more would he work in the fields. Henceforth a kitchen would be his domain, and he took to it like the proverbial duck to water.

As time went on he worked his way up to busboy, then waiter, and eventually fry cook, baker and finally cook. Whatever he did he did well. He was quick to learn and always willing to work and was in a fair way to becoming a second chef when the Japanese bombed Pearl Harbor. Almost at once Uncle Sam tapped him on a shoulder.

"My naturalized son," Uncle Sam said, "I need you."

Francis Cabang served four years in the Army—twenty-five months of it overseas. Guess where. The Philippines? No. Europe. But he did spend it cooking, and he learned a lot, not only about cooking but about Democracy and morality and the ways of man. And he won several decorations including the Bronze Star.

After the war he returned to the Hotel Laguna and its kitchen. Though he had come a long way, the world was a long way from being his oyster. One day Hal Hanna, his friend, suggested he open a restaurant of his own and offered to put up some capital.

They rented an old house on North Coast Boulevard—the restaurant is still there—and hung out a sign: ROYAL HAWAIIAN CHARCOAL BROILER. Francis, who knows every job from growing food to waiting on the customers, did everything. But his principal genius proved to be organization. His restaurant not only served delicious food, supervised by him, but served it smoothly, efficiently and courteously. It was not long before the Royal Hawaiian became popular. People stood in line. Since its founding in 1948 it has become one of the most popular restaurants in Orange County.

Eventually Francis bought out his partner's interest in the

business and later bought the property upon which the restaurant stands. A year or so ago he went home to the Philippines and married one of the country's most beautiful daughters. Today he is a proud father.

Francis Cabang stands at the top of his field. He is a fine American and a fine example of what honesty, industry and perspicacity can accomplish—even when one has to start at the lowest rung of the ladder.

License Plates

It was inevitable, I guess, that some poor, harassed columnist would make fodder of the 1956 automobile license plates. A new three-letter language appears to have come into our ken.

There is a theory that the genius who figured out the three-letter combinations is a subversive and that he is using the Russian alphabet, but I think he is a cross-word puzzle fan. He has included the AUK, the YAK and the GNU, while avoiding any arresting combination, such as BVD, COD, PDQ, and GOD. He is sometimes ungrammatical, such as in the instance of GIT. I have yet to see any three-letter words of the profane variety.

The new language has some amusing sidelights. John Schaffer says he saw an old broken-down dog of a car with the imposing letters HRH, and that there's a car owned by a restaurant operator in San Clemente with the letters HSH. They tell of a dyed-in-the-wool Republican in Santa Ana whose fellow Rotarians fined him for having the letters HST on his license plates. When I applied for The Little Woman's plates I requested the letters TLW, but they weren't available. I saw a Ford Thunderbird skeedaddling down the road with GMC on its tail. And I saw another car driven by a gentleman of my acquaintance with a pretty girl, not his wife, curled next to him, bearing the license letters HMM.

Out of this new language has come a game; trying to make sentences of the passing car plates. The day you see TEE HEE following each other you've won the turkey.

Sometimes when I have nothing else to read I peruse the

telephone book. You may be interested to know that Joy Little is listed as Little Joy, and that there's a Low J.G. on Jasmine Street.

Social Notes

Mary K. Brown, erstwhile national woman tennis champion AND national woman golf champion, recently moved from Emerald Bay to Irvine Terrace in Corona del Mar. In her mid-sixties, she still plays superb golf, is a five handicapper and shellacked us the last time TLW and I played with her.

Aileen Riggan Soule, Olympic diving champion in 1920 is visiting the Wendell Finleys in South Laguna. When I tried out unsuccessfully for the Olympic swimming team in 1924 Aileen's name was a household word. She won the gold medal in 1920 at the age of fourteen, the silver medal in 1924 and the bronze in 1928. Though she has a daughter in Wellesley, she has changed physically hardly at all—weighs about the same today as she did in 1928 and is even prettier than she was then.

I asked Aileen what she thought of the recent performances of the Russians in the winter Olympics, and she replied, "They gave notice in 1952 that they were going to be tough. The answer to their perfection obviously is training. For example, skiers are not permitted to use lifts in Russia; they have to walk up the mountains they ski down. Americans are not used to such rigorousness. Perhaps we are becoming flaccid."

Is Honesty the Best Policy?

Since the Sixty-Four-Dollar TV quiz show exposé, honesty is breaking out all over. Yesterday I heard a radio announcer say, "Portions of the foregoing program were recorded." I almost fell out of bed.

Hereto, when such facts had to be revealed, as prescribed by the Federal Communications Commission, it was done during the musical bridge and the word "transcribed" was used for recorded, on the supposition that most people did not know what it meant and so would be under the delusion that the entire show had been "live."

If this honesty kick continues we can expect politicians and bankers and automobile salesmen and columnists and comedians and lawyers and lovers and all kinds of truth-shaders to come clean.

"Madam," the salesman will say, "this car is no better than its competition. They are all made of the same stuff and in many instances by the same parts makers; they work on the same principle, burn equal amounts of fuel, and one will last as long as another. But please buy this one for my sake. I need the money."

And the lawyer: "I am sorry to tell you, sir, but you haven't a chance in this cruel world to win a judgment in this case. The other fellow is right as religion, and unless we bribe a juror or the judge we're sure to lose."

And the banker, in making a 7.2 percent loan: "Your collateral is more then sufficient, and we could let you have the loan at a lower interest rate and make a good profit, but all the other banks are getting rich so why shouldn't we?"

And the insurance agent: "You are paying too much for this dying insurance, my friend. As a matter of fact, along with millions of other simple-minded males in this country, you are helping build up the most fantastic profits and surpluses for the insurance companies—and getting nothing in return. All you will get is a funeral."

And the lover: "Darling, you and your perfume and your magnetism attract me and I yearn to possess you, but marriage is out of the question. Do I need to remind you that I am a male and, as such, a polygamist? So let us enjoy the moment and then kiss each other goodbye."

And the lady: "If you think I'm going to jeopardize my future for a passing fancy, you're as nutty as an almond orchard. If you want my favors, buster, let's make it legal—which means I'll own half of you."

And the minister: "As a congregation you are a niggardly

and carping group. I find little charity among you. For the most part you are self-centered hypocrites. But you're all I've got, so settle back while I preach you this hackneyed sermon."

You can see what chaos truth will create. I think we'd all better write our congressmen and tell them to desist before it is too late.

Opulent Odyssey

Journeyed to Belvedere, just above San Francisco, to attend the christening of Cordelia Pollard and to help her parents, Margaret and Richard Pollard, get packed for a move to London, where he will assume the post of chief of the *Life Magazine* office and she will continue to work for the Asia Foundation (actually the CIA).

Our visit included half a dozen "Farewell to the Pollards" parties, most unique of which was a visit at the last moment from their family physician. He came bearing a black satchel containing going-away presents. The presents: needle pokes in the posterior to guard Peg and Dick against influenza.

Another of the parties was a colossal wing-ding which required three houses and to which, it seemed, all San Franciscans came. Did meet there one of our favorite columnists, Herbert Caen.

Caen is a shy guy who has developed a fine defense of humor to off-balance people who invade his privacy. His innate kindness emerges through his very excellent *Chronicle* column which is always clever but rarely at the expense of others. He loves San Francisco the way I love Laguna Beach. Peg told him I was the Herb Caen of Laguna Beach. Made him proud, I hope.

Day or so later the Pollards, a German nurse named Anna, Katy and I together with the two adopted babies—aged two months and eight months—got into the Pollards' station wagon, started south dragging a U-Haul trailer full of luggage and golf clubs. The Pollards were to take the jet to New York from Los Angeles.

It was almost noon before we got away and the morning, to understate, had been hectic. Movers were aswarm in the house, myriad last minute errands had to be run—for more nipples (one-holers), an electric bottle warmer which could plug into the car's cigarette lighter, for ice to keep the formula fresh, to the post office to leave change of address, to the Goodwill with clothing and magazines and to the library with books—ad infinitum.

But now at last we were on our way, the car loaded with us and the innumerable things babies need—diapers by the dozen, cribs, sterilizers, blankets, toys, etc., sandwiches in a bag (we did not plan to stop, save for gas, until we reached Solvang).

Reilly, the eight-month-old, rode in the front seat and Cordelia in Katy's lap. En route I kept up a teensy-weentzy patter to keep the babies amused, was a little hoarse by the time we reached Alisal Ranch about sundown.

Alisal, at Solvang, was one of the first Spanish land grants, it having been deeded to one Jose Carrillo, a soldier who came to Alta California in 1769 with Father Serra. It comprises 10,500 acres. A guest ranch as well as working ranch, it is nestled in the beautiful Santa Ynez Valley.

Did stay there for two days, while the Pollards got rested for another round of parties in Los Angeles.

Rode south through beautiful Santa Barbara County, now aglow with the flowers of spring, tra la.

Of Graves and Scholars

Interring the bodies of the dead has always been a real estate problem. By and large, man doesn't like to be reminded of the precariousness of life and the inevitability of death, so he doesn't hanker to live next to a graveyard.

This psychological truth comes to mind because it looks as if we might, on account of a cemetery, lose the chance to have a branch of the University of California in our backyard.

The university has been seeking a site in Orange County

on which to erect a major branch of that great institution of learning and had about decided, I understand, on a portion of the Irvine Ranch just back of Corona del Mar.

The site under consideration is magnificent—rolling hills overlooking the azure and tranquil Pacific and the offshore islands. Here is an ideal location for a university. It abounds in inspiration. A campus here could make the one at Westwood picayune.

If the university is so placed the entire south coast will be vastly benefited. Skip the economic advantages and think of the cultural dividends: music, drama, art, lectures by distinguished scholars, major athletic events. There's no question: it would be the greatest thing that could happen both to the university and the area.

Negotiations were going well. Everybody was enthusiastic; then, almost as an afterthought, there arose an obstacle. Seems that a firm known as Pacific View Memorial Park has a lease on forty acres adjoining the property under consideration. When the university officials learned of the proposed necropolis they threw up their uncallused hands in horror. Locate their institution of culture and learning next to a yard for the dead?—Don't be silly.

Nevertheless, that's what the powers-that-be decided.

Members of the Irvine family, who are always trying to do the best for Orange County, said they'd see if they couldn't persuade the cemetery boys to move their operation elsewhere—perhaps over yonder beyond the foot of Saddleback Mountain.

But as soon as the undertakers were asked to change the location of their Valhalla, they swung into action. As yet no body has been interred there; indeed, they were not ready to open for business. Forthwith they dispatched a truck to Los Angeles, picked up six bodies of corpses from the morgue of the General Hospital and hurried them back to the south forty where, at night, they were planted in a neat row. Now the area was a graveyard in fact.

I asked my friend John Vibert, president of the cemetery,

why those particular acres for the "park" had been chosen and was told: because of the magnificent view.

If this boneyard prevents the university from locating in these parts I'm for boycotting it. On the other hand, I don't think the university officials should let a graveyard deter them from placing the branch of learning in a place well suited for both learning and dispersing souls.

My Friend Myford

It is ironical that Myford Irvine, president of the Irvine Company, was one of the cemetery's early occupants. One of the richest men in the state, he took his own life and shocked everyone who knew him. He was in his early fifties, presumably in the best of physical health.

"He had everything," people said. "Why did he do it?"

I don't think anyone can answer that question, and I doubt if "Mike" could have put it into words. But anyone who has descended into melancholia knows that reason does not reside there—only hopelessness. I do know, though, that Laguna and all of Orange County became immeasurably poorer when Myford elected to slide off this sometimes frustrating sphere.

His outstanding characteristics were kindliness, generosity and responsibility. Perhaps he was too responsible. I had the feeling at times that he would not have chosen the exalted job of president of the great Irvine Company, but having inherited it he did his best to fulfill it with honor and distinction. Had he been master of his own destiny I think he would have preferred a more humble station in life.

For he was a humble man. He was also shy, and he did not seem to have a high regard for himself. He was a member of the board of directors of the South Coast Community Hospital and rarely missed a meeting. He would sit through these meetings without offering an opinion unless one were requested of him. Victor Andrews, then hospital president, called one day to ask him about a matter and was surprised when Myford said, "I'm flattered that you value my opinion."

He had few friends and was a lonely man. He could not show affection because people usually wanted something from him. And this must have frustrated him, because he liked to help others.

After Irvine Coast Country Club opened I often played golf with Myford, usually with Tom Henderson and Hadd Ring or Les Steffensen. None of us, I venture, can say we ever really got to know him. He tried hard, but he could never be one of us "boys." His laughter was always a little louder than the joke called for.

The Irvine Company in those days was taking in more than one million dollars a day, but with all his wealth, Myford had a curious streak of penury. One day he drove a golf ball out of bounds and because of a high fence could not retrieve it. The next day he drove over the ground with his wife, and found the ball, but she would not let him pick it up. "Somebody might see you," she is reported to have said.

I tell that incident not as criticism of Myford, but to show this facet of his character. It seems to me that incongruous forces were struggling within him. He was highly elated at times, deeply depressed at others. If he could have waited for a while, the day he died the melancholia probably would have passed.

He did not leave all of us in Orange County bereft. No one was more concerned with this community's welfare.

CHAPTER 11

Long Distance Swimmer

Horace Hough is a health faddist currently training in our waters to swim to Hawaii. I had the good fortune to catch him ashore at Wood's Cove this week for an interview. To be more precise, Horace was there, dripping wet in his G-string shorts, but Pascal Dinwoody, his press agent, did most of the talking.

Horace is a big fellow with a beautifully proportioned physique and a small head which is out of proportion on a thick neck. "How," I asked him, "do you propose to make this crossing?—by way of the Great Circle or as the gull flies?"

"We shall take off from Laguna Beach," Pascal said, "because the water is warmer here than it is in San Francisco or Seattle, both of which are considerably nearer our goal."

"Will you go by yourselves," I asked, "or will someone accompany you?"

"He will be accompanied by a supply boat, of course," Pascal said. "A flotilla of yachts will escort us as far as Catalina. And we're endeavoring to get the Marine Corps to send a squadron of planes."

"How will he sleep?"

"Horace has developed the faculty of sleeping in the water," Pascal said. "That is one of the phases we've been working on here. We have developed a plastic hood which permits him to breathe even though waves break over his head. But for this we could not make the attempt."

"What about storms?"

"In the event of storms we will pick him up, mark our position and, when the storm has abated, drop him back in at the point we took him out."

"All I know is he does a lot of fishing."

"How long do you figure it will take?"

"To Hawaii—about six months. Horace can do fifteen miles a day without taxing himself. If we do not lose too much mileage by drifting while he sleeps we may make it in less time."

"Why are you doing this?" I asked Horace.

"Tell him, Horace," Pascal said.

"Because it has never been done," Horace said. "And we're doing it to call attention to Eisenhower's and Nixon's physical fitness program."

Pascal said, "This is only the first leg of what we hope will be a swim around the world."

"It'll take us several years," Horace said.

"Who's going to finance the expedition?"

"The chambers of commerce of the cities we will touch. We figure," Pascal went on, "that we'll give Hawaii so much publicity it can't help but become the fiftieth state by the time we get there."

"By the time we get to Guam," Horace said, "it may become the fifty-first."

"Could be," Pascal said.

"How can you cash in on a thing like this?" I asked.

"I'll write a book," Horace said.

"What will the book be about?"

"The swim," he said.

I envisioned an entry: *Swam fifteen miles today, slept well, saw a school of tuna.*

Pascal said, "Horace will also lecture."

"On the swim?"

"On the denizens of the deep, the flora and fauna of the sea. He's already got a three thousand dollar advance."

"I'll also lecture on the human body," Horace said, "How to train it and what foods to eat. Lecturing pays well."

"What foods will you eat?"

"Sea bread is my favorite—builds up the muscles; yogurt, black strap molasses, apples, buttermilk and bouillon."

"What about meat?"

"No meat. Meat is poisonous, but lots of seafood. Seafood

contains iodine."

"We'll even put a little iodine in his brandy.' Pascal confided. "He loves it."

"He's gonna drink brandy?"

"Just now and then. To keep warm."

"And wear grease?"

"We'll need lots of grease."

"What about sex?—Isn't that going to be a problem?"

"I'm not married," Horace said.

H. Allen Smith, a world-traveler, read the above interview on his way to Hawaii and added it to his diary entitled:

> WAIKIKI BICHNIK
>
> John Weld suggested on my way to Hawaii that I keep an eye peeled for Horace Hough who is trying to swim non-stop from Laguna Beach to Honolulu. I'm going to keep a sharp lookout for Horace. I might even drop him some black strap molasses, just to help out.

Press Agentry

See by the papers they had a cow on Wall Street. It was a press agent's idea to "symbolize the fact that the stock exchange serves the farmer as well as industry—that Wall Street is linked to Main Street. Bulls are common on Wall Street, but this is the first time in over a hundred years there's been a cow." Yak. Yak.

An aspiring young actress jumping into a Central Park lake clutching a photograph of a famous man used to be a regular occurrence Saturday afternoons in time for the morning papers. Her pretty picture, with the wet dress plastered to her torso, oftentimes made front pages.

When I was doing publicity for the film version of "Green Pastures," I thought up what I considered a good stunt. The Negro playing God in the picture was a big man with a resonant voice and a pontifical manner, and I conceived the idea of having him preach a sermon in a church. I could see the headline: GOD PREACHES IN AIMEE SEMPLE MCPHERSON'S ANGELUS TEMPLE. I telephoned Sister Aimee and asked her if she would go along. Aimee is a press agent in her own right. I told her that I thought we could make front pages all across the country. She said she would take the matter up with her board of deacons, meaning her mother.

She called me later to say that, while she favored the idea, she had been voted down.

I'm kind of glad the stunt never came off, because the actor who was playing God in the picture shortly thereafter got arrested for sexual harassment and the whole thing might have backfired.

Art Note

One of the Southland's best portrait painters, B. Breakspear Farrar, recently completed a portrait of the late Henry Goodcell, an early Laguna resident. It will hang in the San Bernardino Bar Association building. Mr. Goodcell, one of whose sons, Roscoe A. Goodcell, lived on Graceland Drive, was secretary of the Bar Association for a number of years. He first brought his family to Laguna in 1883. "The only building hereabouts," Robert says, "was a ranch house where the City Hall now stands. Joe Thurston was fourteen at the time and used to sell melons to the summer picnickers on the beach. We would camp on the sand where the boardwalk is now. By 1889 there were a number of board-and-bat cottages along the main beach."

Robert's grandfather was an English sea captain who was converted to Mormonism. He left his ship in New Orleans and went to Salt Lake City. Once there pressure was exerted to make him take another wife in addition to the one he had. This he refused to do. He moved his family on to Nephi, Utah Territory, where he farmed for three years. The first two years grasshoppers ate his crops, but the third he managed to bring in a good harvest and, with the money derived therefrom, brought his family by covered wagon to San Bernardino.

"I always know you've had enough when you stare at Catalina and start yelling 'Land ho!'"

CHAPTER 12

Thank-You Letter

Personally I dislike thank-you letters, but along with the McKee Thompsons of San Marino, TLW and I were guests recently of Governor and Senora Alvarado Obregon in Hermosillo, Mexico. At Katy's urging I wrote this letter:

Dear Señor and Señora Obregon:

The Thompsons, my wife and I thoroughly enjoyed the ceremony of your inauguration and the grand ball which followed and want to thank you for your hospitality. It is heartening to know that a man of your background (son of a former president of Mexico and successful businessman) would accept the responsibilities of such a high public office when already your life was full of activities and excitements. You are a wealthy man; your interests are varied and you have shown no ambition for political honors. You saw your father assassinated by a fanatic at the height of his political career. Ever since that day, in 1924, politics must have stirred sour juice in your stomach, but, being a good man, you have placed service to country and compatriots above personal desires.

At your inauguration I was struck by your declaration of intentions. It is heartening to know that you consider Mexico's first need is education and that you are going to build more schools. Before Mexico can move forward politically, economically and culturally her people must be educated. You cannot legislate away disease and inequalities. People must rid themselves of these scourges, and it is only through education that they can be taught to do so.

There is a great surge of prosperity in your country. Building activity is in evidence everywhere, and thousands upon thousands of acres are being cleared annually and planted to cotton, alfalfa and other crops. But there can be no real prosperity when people are illiterate, when hordes live in ignorance and when they can earn but a few pesos a day with their hands.

As you said so well: Mexico needs capital, it needs roads and it needs dams and power, but primarily its people need education. With education the other things will come.

Thank you for inviting us, and best wishes from all of us in your new job.

Burmese Boy

Interesting visitor to Laguna last week: Roland Thoon, a Burmese lad, son of the attorney-general of that celestial land. Sent to this country for his schooling (to become an engineer), he is the ward of former Lagunans, Peg and Dick Pollard. Dick is former *Life-Time-Fortune-Sports Illustrated* editor in San Francisco (they are now in London, he as bureau chief for *Life Magazine*) and Peg works for the Asia Foundation.

In the two years he has been here Roland has become superficially as American as corn-on-the-cob, though in his philosophy, gentle demeanor and religion he is still distinctly a Buddhist. He has been going to school at Thacher in Ojai, is presently enrolled in Menlo Park College pending entrance next year to Stanford. The only reason he is not going to Stanford this year is at sixteen he is considered too young. A tall, handsome, lean youth, he's a prince of the realm, his father being the Thomas Jefferson of Burma and that country's richest man. At one time he owned five hundred elephants.

Two years ago, when Roland first arrived at Thacher, he was considered stuck-up and generally disliked by his classmates. When he graduated this year he was voted the most popular member of his class. While he was four years old his country was invaded by the Japanese and his father was the only member of the government who was not slaughtered. He went into hiding, taking his family with him. Their money was worthless, and the only way they could get Japanese scrip (which the Japanese soldiers printed for themselves) was to raise and sell chickens. Because his father dared not show himself, Roland was sent forth to do the selling.

On one occasion an explosion wrecked part of their camp and the Japanese, suspecting Roland was a spy, seized him and shipped him to confinement in Japan. He lived on little more than rice and water for the duration.

Despite this horrendous experience he has a wonderful spirit and fine sense of humor. Some interesting bits of information about his native land:

While women are considered useful and even essential, in the social scale they are equal to the pet dog.

A male Burmese would not deign to so much as enter a kitchen, much less wash or wipe a dish.

Burmese girls cannot marry until they are nineteen, boys until they are twenty-one.

Most Burmese are vegetarians.

It is against their religion to drink spirituous liquors.

The Burmese Government is democratic and strongly opposed to Communism.

Reminiscence

I read in the paper where a doctor states that a daily bath is not healthful. I learned this thirty-five years ago when I lived on a ranch in the backwoods of Colorado. There we used to bathe once a week whether or not we needed to. Even once a week was not healthy—not the way we did it.

The ceremony would be performed in an iron washtub and I can tell you with authority that even on warm days it was a trial and on cold days an ordeal.

The water would be heated in a great copper kettle on the wood-burning range and poured into a galvanized iron tub set in the middle of the kitchen floor. Cold water had to be brought in from the well to take the sting out of the hot, and, after hanging clothes on the milk separator, you would squat down in the tub, knees to chin, and get as wet as possible. Then, standing up, you would proceed to soap yourself.

For privacy a calico curtain was drawn between the kitchen and dining room, and I remember Aunt Anna, who was a big woman and about sixty, used to hang a "Don't Come In—Bathing" sign on the kitchen door. I've always been curious as to how she got into that little tub.

It was next to impossible to rinse the soap off. We always had soap in our ears and under our arms, no matter what we did, and there it would stay from week to week, until summer came when we could go swimming and wash it off in the river.

One winter Hiram McNeil and I built a raft which we intended sailing down the creek from Colona to Delta and thence down the Gunnison to the Colorado and on to God-knows-where. We were brand-new Boy Scouts—very much the tenderfeet—and this seemed a proper project. It would teach us the art of survival.

Building a raft was a far holler from bathing, but I assure you there is a connection.

We chose birch trees for our logs because they were straight and true. We chopped them down with our new Scout axes, about eight inches in diameter and ten feet long, and tonged them with rawhide which we had cut from the hide of a dead cow.

We built the raft alongside the Uncompahgre River, which at that time, I remember vividly, was fringed with ice. When it was finished we packed on the provisions we had hoarded, most of it swiped from Hiram's mother's cellar. Then we cut two long poles to propel and guide our craft and, finally early Saturday morning, we put on all the clothes we owned and prepared for the first leg of our journey. We had not told anyone we were going for fear of being forbidden.

We shoved the raft into the river and were a little troubled that water came almost up to the tops of the logs. We were concerned for our provisions, especially the crocus sack full of cornmeal with which we planned to make pancakes.

Hiram, being larger than I, held the raft steady while I stepped gingerly aboard. To our astonishment and chagrin, particularly mine, the craft yielded at my weight, and the side I stepped on sank. I lost my balance and went kerplunk into the icy water. We learned the hard way that green birch trees are not buoyant.

Hiram built a fire and I took all my clothes off—the two coats, four shirts and three suits of long underwear—and dried them. In retrospect it seems to me the drying took all day.

We never did get under weigh.

History Lesson

O.K. Stephens, the South Laguna sage, reminds me of the story, now almost lost under the dust of time, of the Indian woman who, deserted, lived alone for twenty years on San Nicolas Island, west of Santa Catalina. This female Robinson Crusoe was rescued by a distant relative of Captain Nidever and several companions, including four Indians who came upon the woman attired in a garment made of shag and rabbit skins. Her matted hair was the color of burnished copper. When found she was engaged in stripping the blubber from a piece of seal skin, using a knife made from a barrel hoop. Her rescuers report that as she worked she talked incessantly to herself in a singsong voice.

At sight of the men she sprang to her feet with a cry of fear and "put a hand to her breast as if to calm her heart."

Her rescuers squatted on the ground around her, anxious to hear the tale of her strange adventure, but try as they did they could not understand her. The mainland Indians had a hard time translating her lingo. They prevailed upon her to accompany them to Santa Barbara. Upon reaching the city her delight was like that of a child at a circus, but not even the

Mission padres, familiar with several native dialects, could understand her speech. By the use of signs they learned she had been left behind on San Nicolas when a raiding party of Alaskans, on an otter-hunting expedition, killed all the men on the Island and took the women and children as slaves—all save this lone girl who had concealed herself. One account says she was left behind because she went back to get her child and another says she hid.

She lived only six months after reaching Santa Barbara, dying of a stomach disorder. She was buried by the Mission padres, who sent many of her trinkets, as well as a feather dress, to Rome.

While on the subject of our islands, Catalina once was a dumping ground for Mexico's most hardened criminals. They would be shipped thither and left to fend for themselves or die. Most of them eventually got to the mainland in balsa canoes.

CHAPTER 13

The Telltale House Dress

Working as a newspaper reporter in 1934 on the now-defunct *New York American,* I was instrumental in causing the arrest of a man who killed his wife and burned her body. The body was found near White Plains early one Sunday morning, a fine time for news-hungry Monday morning newspapers.

The only clue to the young woman's identity was a piece of house dress, that portion which, lying under her buttocks, did not burn. It was a cotton print—yellow with blue forget-me-nots.

While the photographer assigned to the story with me distracted the policeman guarding the body in the coroner's back room, I tore off a bit of the cloth and took it to the managing editor. The print was reproduced on the front page in the bulldog edition which hit the streets about six P.M.

I was hanging around the White Plains police station after ten P.M. waiting for somebody to identify the corpse when my editor called to tell me that a woman had telephoned saying she recognized the print. He gave me the name of the woman and her address in Yonkers. Without saying anything to the detective assigned to the case, I hailed a taxicab and went thither.

It was a duplex. The middle-aged woman who had called lived upstairs. She said her neighbor, who lived on the first floor, called her attention to the photograph of the cloth, saying, "Isn't that the material you used to make your daughter a house dress?" It was indeed. She still had some of the scraps of it in her sewing basket. She had bought it at Wanamaker's.

Her daughter was married, she told me, but was separated from her husband and living in a rooming house on 148th

*"We have a surfer living upstairs.
I wonder if that has something to do with it?"*

Street. I took the mother to White Plains to identify the body and headed for 148th Street, arriving about midnight.

The sleepy landlady told me that her roomer had gone out Saturday afternoon with her husband and had not been back since. It seemed her husband wanted a reconciliation, but she was determined not to go back to him.

The landlady and I found the husband's address on an envelop in the girl's room. He lived in the Bronx. The house stood in the middle of a block. No one answered my knock, but I had the extra-sensory feeling that someone was just inside the door and very much awake. I spoke, calling the man by name.

"Your wife's dead," I said. "We want you to identify her."

Some time went by in silence, and I began to doubt my hunch. I also suddenly became frightened. He probably had a gun. I knocked again, and a man's voice said, "Who is it?"

"The police," I said. "We want to talk to you."

The door was opened. "Come in," the man said.

I looked back at the cabby, his face outlined by the dashlight, caught a shallow breath and stepped into the darkness.

My host switched on a light. He was rather short, freshly shaved as if he had been expecting company and fully clothed.

"Where's the gun?" I asked. He took it out of a pocket and handed it to me. When I said, "Come on," he moved meekly enough. I saw that he preceded me through the door.

On the way to the White Plains police station I asked him what had happened, and he tearfully blurted out the sordid story of how they had quarreled about her coming back to him. When she started to leave he shot her, put her body in his car and drove it into the country where, after drenching it with gasoline, he set it afire.

His name was Peacock (during the trial we referred to him as Dementia Praecox). He got a life sentence and may still be in Sing Sing.

Don't You Cry for Me

Spent last week and am spending this one in the purlieu of Hollywood, specifically Culver City, laboring with pencil and pad on what Aaron Rosenberg, the producer, and I hope will be a definitive, meaning classic, "Western" movie. If what we are preparing turns out well and lots of people go to see it, a precedent will have been set. In our story, based on the Donner Party tragedy in California history, there is not one Indian raid, men do not stalk each other with six-shooters and a man actually kisses a woman.

You can see that this is going to raise hob with the old formula. Cowboy-and-Indian pictures were among the first films ever made, and, in the years since, the story hasn't changed much. The cowboys are always honorable, romantic, glamorous figures, while the Indians are treacherous, bloodthirsty and lecherous. In every picture in which covered wagons appeared there invariably comes in the third act a scene in which the encircled wagons are besieged and surrounded by screaming Redskins shooting from horseback.

I remember that this was very exciting when I was a child, but through repetition the scene had lost its power for me. As I grew older I learned that our western history was not quite like that. I learned that the pale face was not always noble and right and that the Indian was not always treacherous and blood-thirsty.

"The whole idea of the cowboy," Harry Golden wrote in *The Carolina Israelite,* "is based on a myth. He flourished for only a short period in the history of the West, maybe twenty years at the most—the cattle drive from Texas up into Kansas. The coming of the railroad ended his short career, yet he remains a figure of romance."

It is of interest to note that his modern counterpart, the itinerant farm worker, has never even come close to achieving this status. On the contrary, the itinerant farm worker who follows the crops from the Mexican border to the Dakotas is held in low esteem.

Bat Masterson wrote about the "romantic" cowboy, and what a vagrant bum he really was, but not even Masterson, who was there, could stem the onrushing tide of legend and romance. People wanted it the romantic way. That the cowboy was often a thief, a drunkard, a vagrant and that Indian girls were taught to run screaming when they saw one coming has had no effect at all in erasing this legend. The end of the story was always the same. The cowboy has cleaned up the town; he has said goodbye, ma'm, to the beautiful girl; the whores in the Last Chance saloon have voted to contribute half their earnings to the new school house; and there he goes, our hero, riding off into the sunset with no involvement, no possessions to tie him down, no notes to pay, no rent, no mortgages, no responsibilities.

Well, that was not the western Rosey and I were concocting. His company had bought the movie rights to my novel *Don't You Cry for Me* and it was to be distributed by MGM. In it there is a plethora of characters, men, women and children which head out together to cross the prairies, mountains and rivers from Independence, Missouri to California in covered wagons, the year 1846. We had to condense the film to three hours while telling the experiences of the entire kit and kaboodle. This did not come easily. After six months we were still developing the three principal characters. As it was we had a mosaic of stories, which was the way I had plotted it, but Rosenberg and his co-producers wanted someone like John Wayne to lead the coterie and a beautiful actress like Loretta Young to add romance.

By the time we had finished the screenplay MGM was in production of a western migration film entitled *How the West Was Won* and the moguls decided not to produce mine. It has never been produced. I lost the better part of fifty thousand dollars.

"As near as I can figure it, he's some big name in the winter theatre."

CHAPTER 14

Michael Jackson, 1955

Mike Jackson has moved his humor from the pages of this sterling journal to the more widely circulated pages of the *Los Angeles Examiner.* He has been hired by the Hearst organization which is paying him more money. It is cause for local weeping. Among those for whom we feel sorry are out-of-town *Post* subscribers such as Nan (Mrs. Walter) Huston in New York and Caddy Fitzsimmons in Chicago.

It was only a question of time before Mike would be discovered. Talent such as his is too rich and rare to be confined in a small town and it is fine that his audience has been enlarged.

Although he has written for other media, including two novels, he had never done any newspaper writing until shortly after Katy and I acquired the *Post.* He brought in some scribbling and asked if we would be interested in running something like it every week. We said we would and he made a stipulation that we not reveal his name. As a pen name he used Jesus de Pancho. I quote an example of his talent from his first column.

> Writing a book? First learn to be a speedy typist, says Saroyan. "No," Hemingway says. "The typewriter is the enemy of careful composition." Take your choice.... Lots of books these days on diet. People don't want to face the simple fact that the way to lose weight is to cut down on fattening foods. Exercise doesn't take off pounds, only moves them from here to there.... If you walk up Bluebird Canyon note the tree in front of Bob Sheppard's house. Looks like it might fall down some day soon. Won't though. Bob has it propped up....

•

The reason Mike did not want his name used is that he was afraid the venture might be a failure.

I was so impressed by his work that I sent his first twenty columns to King Features in New York, which syndicates newspaper features. They were returned without comment. I'll bet a dollar no editor there read any of them, or if he did, that he has gone back to digging ditches for a living. I persuaded the managing editor of the Costa Mesa *Globe-Herald* to run a few columns. It was through his pieces in that paper that Mike got his break. It happened in a circuitous way.

Few days later Mike's phone rang. It was a call from Arizona. A man named Pegler said that a friend had sent him a copy of the *Globe-Herald* and he liked what Mike had written. He asked Mike if he had ever considered having his column syndicated.

"It would be nice," Mike replied.

"Well," Pegler said, "I think I can help you. I'll see what I can do."

Mike asked Pegler if he were any relation to Westbrook Pegler, the famous journalist, and Pegler replied, "I am Westbrook."

Nothing happened for some time, then Randolph Hearst, son of William Randolph and publisher of the *Los Angeles Examiner,* telephoned Mike and asked if he would come to Los Angeles and have lunch with him. Mike said he would be delighted. It was a polite fib. He hates big cities and is uncomfortable in the presence of big shots.

Hearst and his managing editor gave our hero the red carpet, took him to Perino's, the most expensive restaurant in the city, and treated him as if he were a celebrity. Their pitch—would he write a five-day-a-week column for the *Examiner*? Terms were agreed upon and the next day Mike was on the *Examiner* payroll.

Talent

One of the most promising young writers I know is David Iredell, sometime play reviewer for this sterling journal and son of noted painter Russell Iredell. Only trouble with David is: He appears to be allergic to the pen, won't apply himself to it. Example of his cleverness was the Christmas card we received from him—photograph of him sculpting a head of his father. The caption:

Picture of old block being sculped by chip-off has absolutely no connection with Christmas.

Deadbeat

They say it takes a moocher to recognize one. I used to think I was a pro in the field and a fair judge of the breed until last week when I met the Grandaddy, the guy who wrote the book, and learned I'm strictly an amateur.

However they come, whether as old friends you haven't seen for years who are down on their luck, the technique of moochers is the same. They come for a cup ("happened to be passing by") and stay until your patience is exhausted.

The deadbeat I met last week signaled his approach by a letter from Copenhagen. A mutual friend, he said, had given him my address, told him to look me up. He was flying to Hollywood from Denmark via the North Pole on his way to the South Seas, he wrote and wanted to talk with me about a book he was planning. He also needed to buy a car. I being a Ford dealer, the latter interested me. He put in a clincher by saying he was a fan of mine, had read all my books and thought I was the best little-known writer in the language. Whether that's a compliment or not, I'm not sure, but always eager for praise I took it as such.

I should have smelled at least a small mouse, but my drooling ego cut off all sensitivity. I wrote and told him to let me know when he was to arrive and I would meet him.

I went to the airport and brought him home—a big,

handsome fellow in a middle-aged, flabby sort of way, with thinning hair. Our house being for the moment loaded, I engaged a deluxe hotel room for him and invited him for drinks and dinner.

I was so interested in what he had to say about my work I did not even get suspicious until he had lapped up almost a fifth of our best whiskey.

He was a constant conversationalist, told us he had been all over the world as actor-producer and was now engaged in hush-hush work for the State Department. He ate everything TLW put before him, guzzled the wine and added brandy to coffee.

The next morning he telephoned and I went to fetch him for breakfast. He brought some of his soiled clothing and asked to use our washing machine. Katy did it for him.

When I went down town to the dealership he came along. Seems he needed to cash a check, didn't have any U.S. money, only Danish kroner. I endorsed his check and, inasmuch as there was no place in Laguna to exchange kroner, bought a few of his seven to the dollar, that being what he told me they were worth. He did not mention buying a car.

We made a trip to the Danish consulate in San Diego to get some travel papers cleared and I took him to lunch. That evening we went to the Victor Hugo restaurant for dinner. He was in the men's room when the check was presented.

I suggested he get his next morning's breakfast at the hotel to save my coming from South Laguna for him. It was the only meal he bought the three days he was here.

I drove him to the airport the third afternoon, but when he suggested we go into a bar for a drink pending the departure of his plane, I refused. I watched him sail off with vast relief. I learned he had not paid his hotel bill. My bank sent the kroner to Los Angeles for exchange and got ten to the dollar, not seven as he had claimed.

Any day now I expect his check to bounce.

String Around My Finger

It's terrible to be forgetful. I wake up in the middle of the night remembering something I failed to do the day before.

Only way I can remember is to write myself notes. I end up every day with a pocketful of them: *Jim Talbert—Frank Baker—Pick up chair—Go Santa Ana—Blair Edwards—Dr. Ott.*

Sometimes I can't remember what the notes mean.

I have the hardest time remembering names—especially of people I don't like. Fortunately there aren't many of them.

On the other hand, I can remember practically everything that happened long ago when I was a cub reporter in New York. I can remember what a suicide's body looked like after it had fallen thirty stories (it didn't look as if it had any bones in it, especially the legs; and when it landed the shoes flew off). I can remember what a gangster's widow looked like wailing at the scene of her husband's death (he was shot from a passing car). I can remember a pretty girl I saw briefly on Fifth Avenue in New York thirty years ago. Never have seen her since. I can remember Irving Berlin, the song writer, in his magnificent apartment on Sutton Place in New York, sitting at his piano and telling me how it was that Arnold Rothstein was killed. (He was shot because he welched on a poker debt of $175,000. He claimed he had been cheated.) I can remember the look of anguish on the face of Franklin D. Roosevelt when he had taken a few steps in his braces. I remember a Negro bootblack on Broadway across whose face a huge scar ran; when I asked about it he said, "Feller shaved me too close," and added, "He's dead." I can remember the night Lindbergh tried to run over me when I attempted to flag down his Franklin. That was in New Jersey. He had been on his way home from visiting Anne Morrow.

I remember rock candy, horehound drops and licorice sticks, when raisins were considered a cure-all and were bought for five cents in a little red box. That was when a nickel would buy many things, even a twelve-ounce glass of beer and a free lunch. I remember street cars and pocket watches, the speakeasy ("Joe sent me"), Texas Guinan in her night club and Helen

Morgan sitting on a piano singing "My Bill." I remember seeing Bob Hope's first Broadway show *(Roberta)* and drunks sleeping on sidewalks in the Bowery. I remember the sachet bag and button shoes.

I even remember the joke about a mother-in-law who, having been reported to the missing persons bureau, was found playing second base for Sacramento.

I have a mind cluttered with trivia and nonsense, unrelated events and people, but I keep forgetting important things like anniversaries and people's names.

Beachfront

Virginia Nixon, wife of the eminent psychiatrist Norman, lived on Marine Drive in what I consider the most beautiful house in Laguna. (It is presently owned by Nancy and David Bushnell.) Next door is one of the finest pieces of beachfront property in our town. Interested in acquiring it, I went to see the lady who lived there in a jerry-built cottage. Her name was Katherina Wickman. She was ninety-two and vastly rich. She told me she had been offered a quarter of a million dollars for the property but had scoffed at the idea.

"What good's money?" she says scornfully.

She knows whereof she speaks because money has never been a problem for her. Born in Frankfort, Germany, she, as a young girl, went to live with her grandmother in Hamburg. A relative came to live in the United States, and Katherina begged her grandmother to let her come with her. "I will send you all the money I make," she told her grandmother, and the old lady gave in. Katherina was thirteen. She and her relative first came to Chicago.

There she got a job as a nursemaid to two children of a wealthy family. Every month she would send the money she made to her grandmother in Hamburg.

The wealthy family to which she became attached had a mansion in Pasadena and thither they moved. The gardener whose name was Wickman was a German and he and Katherina were married. The man for whom Wickman worked was a banker, and in 1929 he went bust. Unable to pay Wickman for his services he asked the gardener if he would accept instead some vacant land—about three acres—located in a remotely rural place called Santa Fe Springs. Wickman would.

It wasn't long after the transfer of the title that oil was discovered in this area and the Wickmans became inordinately rich. Even so, they did not change their simple way of life—except in one respect: he bought a beach house in Laguna.

Nearby was the beautiful point Mrs. Wickman owns today (Mr. Wickman has long since passed away). Here she used to go to watch the restless sea. She yearned to own it. In fact, she told me, it was the only thing in this world of a material nature she ever really wanted.

One day she learned it was to be sold by court order, so she hied to City Hall and, as it turned out, was the only bidder.

What she paid for it she can't remember—surely not much, perhaps less than a thousand dollars. She doesn't even remember when she acquired it. When one gets to be ninety-two events have a way of fading, I suspect.

Real estate agents are always coming around trying to make a deal for the place, Mrs. Wickman tells me, but she says she'll never sell it. It will be left to one or more of her twelve grandchildren.

"I've got no use for money," she says. "Never did have. It's what's here," she added, rapping her head, "that's important." And then she said, "You know that money I sent my grandmother in Hamburg?—Well, when she died it all was in a bag—every last dollar of it. and on the bag was a note saying, 'This belongs to Katherina.' It was disappointing to me that she hadn't gotten some happiness from it." She made a wry face. "Money!—Bah!" she said.

Today the beachfront property I wanted to buy is owned by Mrs. Wickman's grandchildren. It is worth several million dollars.

"With this painting you get this record so you can actually hear the pounding of the surf on the rocks."

CHAPTER 15

Lindbergh Ransom

Guy Glassford, son of General D. Glassford, has moved to Laguna with his wife, Marjorie, and their two children, Lynn and Guy, Jr., and has become associated with me in the Ford car business. One of the rules of our dealership is that all employees must read this column as soon as the paper appears every week and praise it for its rhythm, syntax, good sense and wit. Guy was very quick to catch on. He had been with me for a few days when he read that I had "covered" certain aspects of the Lindbergh baby kidnapping and the subsequent trial of Bruno Hauptmann.

Reminded him, he told me, of an experience his father had. At the time of the kidnapping, General Glassford was head of the Washington, D.C., police. Along with other police chiefs in the area, he was alerted and asked to be on the lookout for the kidnapper.

One evening about eleven o'clock, a vice-president of the Washington Loan and Trust Company phoned and asked General Glassford to come at once to the bank, that he had something startling to impart. When Glassford arrived the V.P. was stacking ten- and twenty-dollar bills—one hundred thousand dollars worth of them, it turned out. The money was to be a loan, the bank officer said, to Evelyn Walsh McLean, owner of the *Washington Post* and the Hope diamond. She was putting the diamond up as collateral.

It was a mystery why she wanted the money, the V.P. said. He thought it might have to do with the Lindbergh's baby being kidnapped, then hot in the news. Perhaps it was ransom money. Surely it was unusual to want so much money in cash and particularly in small bills and more particularly at night. "I stalled her until tomorrow morning," the bank officer said," so I could contact you."

The General called on his son Guy to deliver the money to Mrs. McLean in a suitcase—and follow her wherever she went with it. He did so. Eventually she made a rendezvous with a man who proved to be Gaston B. Means and turned the suitcase over to him.

Seems that Means had told Mrs. McLean he was in touch with the kidnappers, that he had seen the baby and that the kidnappers had agreed to return him for one hundred thousand dollars. Mrs. McLean, an extremely gullible gal, handed over the dough.

A few days later the baby's body was found. He had been dead since the night he was kidnapped, proving that Means was a liar. Charges were brought against him and he was convicted of extortion and sentenced to a federal penitentiary, where he subsequently died.

Part of the hundred thousand dollars was found in Hauptmann's house and was the principal reason he was found guilty.

Travelogue

Our friends Rosemary and Wendell Finley invited TLW and me to fly to La Paz, Lower California, with them in their four-seated Stinson and, although TLW is not overly fond of flying we jumped at the chance to see this famous town at the lower end of the peninsula.

From Orange County Airport we flew two hundred miles south of the border and put down for a picnic lunch, landing on a dry lake at one end of which was a crashed plane. Sight of this wreckage did not heighten TLW's appetite but she managed to take nourishment. We swam in the Gulf, then took off for Bahia de Los Angeles, where we spent the night. Here in a beautiful setting live about eighty Mexicans who make a precarious living fishing for giant turtles. They have to travel a week by burro to get supplies in Ensenada. They fed us well—the main course being turtle steaks which tastes like veal, only richer.

Next day we flew further south over the mining towns of Santa Rosalia and Mulege, landing at Loreto to get fuel. The Tabors, who own the Loreto Hotel and dispense aviation fuel when available, were in the States on holiday. The caretaker refused to sell us any fuel, but Wendell managed to talk him out of some automotive gasoline. Then Wendell, by himself, took the plane up on a trial spin to make sure the gasoline was not contaminated. We made it to La Paz—flying over rugged country.

La Paz has a population of about seventeen thousand—up considerably since World War II. The airport has contributed heavily to the town's growth. It is a fishing paradise but in recent years its economy has shifted to cotton. Today much is being grown on the southern end of Baja and ground is being cleared for more.

Comparative prosperity has come to this area, though when I said as much to a local resident, he said, "I don't call it prosperity when the daily wage for a grown man is only eight pesos." Eight pesos was worth about sixty-four cents.

Money, I was told, is hard to borrow in Mexico. Banks want twelve percent a month, and when a man invests in a project he expects to make three hundred percent on his investment in one year.

Obviously the government is going to have to raise wages in Mexico if they ever expect to have prosperity.

We stayed at Los Arcos Hotel, which is run by Bob Elias, a gracious host with a fine sense of humor. In our room was this notice:

"Please don't think we're boasting when we say we have hot water in the rooms. It's a rather funny diesel-burning job, slow but sure. Please don't get discouraged. Let the hot water tap run quite a while and eventually hot water will come—that is, if the man who tends the heater didn't have too much fiesta last night."

In the lobby is this notice:

"Since our little hotel has been in operation we've never had a case of theft. However, if you wish to deposit cash or valuables for safekeeping, you may do so at the desk. As for locking your room every time you go out—you needn't bother because no one will touch anything. We are proud of our employees and can vouch for their honesty."

On our way home we got gas in Santa Rosalia, flew over "the Lost Mission" recently found by the Dana Lambs of Santa Ana. We also got a bird's-eye view of what I believe is the only onyx mine on the American continent. It is owned and operated by Ken Brown's father. Ken is the San Diego Gas and Electric Company's manager in San Juan Capistrano.

We spent a festive night at Hamilton Ranch, which is now owned by Margo Cesna-Henkle. Hattie Hamilton, who used to own it, now lives in Laguna Beach. Margo had invited a couple of tax collectors to dinner and did not want to be bothered by guests, but she put us up. She locked the kitchen about midnight and the next morning we had to fly all the way to San Diego for breakfast.

Baja California is a beautiful place and one day, when atomic power is abundant and man has contrived a cheap way to freshen sea water, it is going to be a paradise. Everybody has suggested the U.S. purchase Baja California from Mexico. It is really a peninsula of Upper California, and its ownership should have been negotiated when the Treaty of Guadalupe was signed.

Suicide

A friend of mine is having a hard time and, I suspect, is contemplating suicide. I want to do what I can to help him through this period, but don't feel that I can speak to him about it directly. He doubtless would deny it, so I'll approach it from here.

My friend, Norman Nixon, a psychiatrist, tells me that the urge to take one's life comes from a surfeit of melancholia, a hopeless illness, financial reverses or unrequited love, but that its seed is planted in us in our conception. "It is a concomitant of life," he said. "Strong and amazingly tenacious as life is, it hangs by a cord and each of us can snip it at will. It is the most important facet of freedom with which we are endowed—a safety valve to be opened only when leaving life is better than living it."

I am an overly hopeful person. It seems to me that each of us, regardless of his or her station in society, has been accorded a rare franchise, a privilege to share a strange and wonderful journey. We should all realize how lucky we are, that we've been chosen by some unknown god from among millions of other sperm, carefully nurtured through the gestation period and squeezed through a tiny orifice onto the earth.

From the moment we are born we are guided through a maze of mishaps and illnesses, any one of which might have sloughed us into the hereafter, but here we are, going on and on, having not the slightest idea whither.

My friend said, "Do you realize that every day we live we are the chosen ones, that we are unique, that we have characteristics, peculiarities, traits and talents no one else has in the same combination?

"Do you realize that, despite the fact we know little if anything about who we are and why we're here, we are all integral parts of what must be a great whole?

"You may not like the experience and want to get out. Take your life, what does it gain? What do you lose? You lose the big one—the battle for yourself. It is amazing how many times failure has been turned into success by those who learned the lesson failure was designed to teach.

"If nothing else life is a test of courage and a chance to learn. None of it—for the sick and well, the rich and poor—is easy, but life is such a tremendous experience and such a fantastic privilege that it is stultifying to leave of one's free will—unless your living days are numbered."

Real Estate and Social Notes

The John McLaughlins (he's a marketing consultant) have bought the Betty Pierrong house in Emerald Bay, plan to refurbish it. It is there that Joan Irvine and Russell Penniman were living when their marriage went keerpoof. It was a bust-up reported around the world, she being one of the owners of the famous Irvine Ranch.

The Marcel Langlois, erstwhile owners of the Victor Hugo Restaurant, sold their beachfront house on Camel Point while on their way around the world by freighter. They returned by air to pack up, move out.

Ode to the Childless Couple

TLW and I are childless. As such we can only suspect what, in the thirty years we've been married, we've missed. As we watched 1968 come in over the hills of Taxco, Mexico, Muriel and Larry Reynolds, who have two beautiful daughters, sympathized with us on account of our poor childless lives.

There's nothing sadder than the childless couple. It breaks the heart to see them stretched out relaxing around swimming pools in Hawaii, sitting all suntanned and miserable on the decks of boats, trotting off to Europe like lonesome fools. It's an empty life. There's nothing but more money to spend, more time to enjoy and a whole lot less to worry about.

The poor childless couple get so selfish and wrapped up in their own concerns that one has to feel sorry for them. They don't fight over the child's discipline. They don't blame each other for the child's most nauseous characteristics, and they miss all the fun of doing without things for the child's sake. They go along in their own dull way, doing what they please and loving each other. It's a pathetic picture.

Everyone should have children. No one should be allowed to escape the wonderul experience attached to each stage in the development of the young. The happy memories of baby days, the alert nights, coughing spells, doctor's debts, diaper doings, burpings, baby sitters, saturated mattresses, spilled food, tantrums, emergencies and never-ending crises. Then comes the real fulfillment as a child grows like a little acorn into a real nut. The wonder of watching your overweight ballerina make a fool of herself in a leotard. The warm smile of the small lad with the sun glittering on five hundred bucks worth of braces, his teeth ruined by peanut brittle. The frolicking, merry, carefree voices of hysterical kiddies at a birthday party.

How dismally vacant is the home without the childish problems that make for a well-rounded life and an early breakdown. The tender, thoughtful discussions when the report card reveals the prodigy to be one step below a half-wit; the close-knit family gathering around the fireplace to roast hotdogs; the end of the day reunions with all the joyful happenings like well-placed blows to the temple.

Children are worth it all. Every moment of anxiety, every sacrifice, every complete collapse pays off as a sturdy adolescence is reached. The feeling of reward the first time you took the boy hunting. He didn't mean to shoot you in the foot. Remember how sorry he was? How disappointed that you weren't a deer? These are the times with a growing son that parents treasure.

Think back to the night of romantic adventure, when your budding, beautiful daughter eloped with the village idiot by whom she is pregnant. What childless couple ever shares in the stark realism of that dream? Aren't you better for having lived it? It was the cause of that tic in your left eye.

Could a woman without children touch the strength and heroism of your wife as she tried to fling herself out the bedroom window? It takes a father to attain the stature of standing by, ready and resolute to jump after her. The climax comes when you two become real close in the realization that, after all, your baby girl is a woman with a mind and morals of her own.

The childless couple lives in a vacuum. They fill their

lonely days with golf, vacation trips, civic affairs, tranquility, leisure and money. There is a terrifying emptiness without children, and the childless couple is too comfortable to know it. You just have to look at them to see what the years have done. He looks boyish, unlined and rested. She's slim well-groomed and youthful. It isn't natural. If they had kids they'd look tired, gray, wrinkled and sagging...in other words, *exhausted.*

CHAPTER 16

Farewell Is a Lonely Sound, 1959

After more than eighteen years in one house, TLW and I are moving. We've sold the chateau on the ocean front and have bought the old Snyder place on Diamond Street. Moving is an emotional experience, especially after living in a place for a long time. We're going to miss Roscoe Arbuckle, the pack rat. He has stolen many a thing in our kitchen.

Over the years Roscoe and I carried on a long-ranging barter game, which he consistently won. He dearly loves the bright, the new and the shiny and has appropriated many a screw, bit and drill—leaving for payment a variety of orange peels and bits of paper. In another incarnation he must have been a used-car dealer, because he takes such delight in getting the better of me.

We're going to miss Ambrose, too. He is our mouse. In fact, Ambrose is several mice. They have lived under our sink since first we came to Pelican Perch. I'll bet I've used twenty pounds of Tillamook over the years trying to trap him and his—without success. He has the cutest ears and the most exasperating way of getting what he wants and then scurrying down a drain pipe to the safety and darkness of that netherland under the kitchen. He's far smarter than Disney's Mickey Mouse.

Yes, we're going to miss Ambrose, but I have a feeling he is going to miss us even more—on account of the cheese.

Then there's the blue jay, Josiah J. Littlejohn, named for one of TLW's uncles on her mother's side. We shall miss him with certain reservations. A more unpleasant, raucous, thieving rascal never drew the breath of life, but in the long, arduous years of our association I have come to hold him in a certain

Phil Interlandi

affection, as a father loves a wayward son. We'll miss him in the same way we'll miss the week-end beachcombers who leave their lunch wrappers, beer cans and milk cartons on "our" beach.

Myrtle, the garden snake, will always have a place in our hearts. She's a better mouser by far than any trap ever made. She lives in the misembryanthemum and is quite shy. I think she has an inferiority complex, which is strange considering the respect we have for her. I'm afraid she may become a nervous wreck if the family which moves into Pelican Perch has children or dogs. Having neither, we sort of adopted Myrtle and tried to give her confidence. Of late she has shown marked improvement. I feel that we are abandoning her at a crucial moment in her nervous life, but alas it cannot be helped. We're not going to take her with us.

Probably more than any other inhabitant of that cliff-side bluff, I am going to miss Moe, the squirrel. We have been buddies for years. Moe had a sister named Less; but Everett, the eagle, caught her one day when she was en route from the dripping faucet to their home in the hydrangeas. That was a sad occurrence indeed, but Moe doesn't seem to have lost any weight grieving. He is a fat, sassy, cute little plague carrier with the most aware eyes I've ever seen. When we first came here in 1941 he was startled almost out of his wits to look up and see me at my desk watching him instead of working.

As time went on he got rather used to me and I to him. I came to look for him every morning as I read the newspaper. He became so friendly in fact, that he would stay and gnaw on the ice plant, expertly peeling the pods with his teeth, while I talked to him of the momentous problems of mankind. During these sessions Moe always gave me his undivided attention. His little bright eyes would blink knowingly when I made what he considered an especially good point, such as maybe we could teach children in their homes by TV instead of building so many schoolhouses. And once I thought I heard him say to me (though perhaps I imagined it) something to the effect that "if Kruschev and Bulganin want to come over here and talk about peace, why, for Heaven's sake, let 'em. Even if nothing comes of the talks they would be highly entertaining. A good laugh these days," he said as he spat out a piece of pod, "isn't to be eschewed."

Yes, we're going to miss Moe, and we're going to miss the pelicans and the gulls, which come crying every morning for breakfast scraps. And we're going to miss the whales and the porpoises swimming past.

But there are a couple of characters around the old house we're not going to miss, and they are Timothy and Esmerelda, the skunks. They've lived behind our stairway, in the vicinity of the wood box, for lo! these many years, and though we've tried everything we could think of to get rid of them, nothing has been effective. In this long-drawn-out contest, they'll be the winners. It is we who are moving.

Our Friends the Morthlands

Connie and Andrew Morthland, who live in Laguna, are up to their gills in the commercial fishing business. They have three tuna ships which ply the waters of the Galapagos, off the coast of Ecuador. This seems to be tuna territory and all the ships from San Diego and San Pedro high-tail it thither.

Fascinating endeavor, this business of tuna fishing, and Drew Morthland, who was a commander in the Navy, got wind of it during the war. Smelled good. So come peace he shipped on a tuna ship as navigator. He learned the ropes so well that after a few trips he bought a ship of his own and turned into a tuna tycoon.

The way his crew works is this: Drew gets half the catch, the crew the other half. Crew may be as few as eight and as many as fourteen. Veteran crew members get as much as a whole share, while new men generally get a quarter or half share. There are two captains—a navigator captain and a fish captain. They get two shares each. Ships cost as much as half a million dollars, are floating refrigerators. One of the Morthland ships, the *Royal Pacific,* was built to their specifications in Seattle, has a capacity of two hundred tons of fish.

The owner stocks the ship with provisions for ninety days. If the capacity catch is made before that time it is considered lucky; if not, it puts into a port and is re-provisioned. The food is the finest available. Mostly the tuna ships are manned by Portuguese-Americans because, Connie says, they have been fishing tuna for generations. It is strictly a gambling business, but when they're lucky it pays off whoppingly. Thirty tons of fish is the break-even point for expenses. Everything over that is gravy—usually at several hundred dollars a ton.

The Morthlands have a fish cannery in Puerto Rico and ships take their catches through the Canal to that U.S. island for canning. The Morthlands do this because the Government currently waives income tax for those who invest in a Puerto Rican industry. If their luck holds out they will be more than rich. Couldn't happen to nicer people.

The Good Earth

Good example of how Laguna Beach real estate has jumped in value in recent years was told me last week by LeRoy Childs, owner of the Pottery Shack. In 1942 Roy could have bought three houses and seventy-five feet of frontage on Pacific Coast Highway adjacent to his famous shack for $8,500. He happened to be away at the time with the Sea Bees in the South Pacific, but when he learned the property was available he wrote his wife, Dorothy, to buy it. By the time the letter reached her someone else had bought the three pieces for $10,000. In six months the buyer sold the properties for $20,000—to Roy. He also bought the next twenty-five feet for $20,000. The third twenty-five feet is not on the market, but it is valued in excess of $20,000.

He and Dorothy are remodeling their Pottery Shack, propping up some of the older bat-and-board walls which have little foundation. "All that's been holding 'em up," Roy says, "are termites."

The Pottery Shack is one of our town's outstanding attractions and Roy and Dorothy Childs are among our town's finest people.

Greetings and Salutations

I am in bed at my usual hour (9:30 P.M.) when an old pal calls from Los Angeles to say, "I'm at Perino's restaurant and the maitre d', Roger Boddaert, told me one of the best chefs in the business is opening a restaurant in Laguna. Thought you ought to know about it."

He was referring to Lucien Brack, whose Old Brussels Restaurant at 2007 Pacific Coast Highway opened last Friday. This, as old timers well know, is the location once occupied by Mona's of pleasant memory. Brack and his wife have purchased the historically rich property and remodeled it with Belgian architecture and atmosphere.

Brack has been in this country for five years, speaks English well, as does his wife. He had a restaurant in Denver, sold it to help found Franscatti's in Los Angeles. Later became second chef at Romanoff's in Beverly Hills. He is only thirty-six but has been in restaurant work for twenty years. His brother is the proprietor of one of the outstanding restaurants in Antwerp, The Astrid.

Lucien says, "My wife and I came here because we fell in love with the town. I think it is one of the most charming places in the world."

Isn't he somewhat apprehensive about founding another restaurant in a town that's full of them?

Lucien says, "California is growing and Californians are learning to appreciate and enjoy the good things of life. I feel confident Lagunans will like us and our cooking."

Welcome and good luck, say we.

Epitaph

I want to tell you about my friend, Alex Drohomer, who was killed in our garage last week when a car under which he was working fell on him.

Alex was a fine and rare human being. He took fierce pride in his work, and when he did a job you knew it was done as well as was possible. Indeed, he was a mechanical artist and the utter core of integrity. He used to say he was the most fortunate of men because his work and his hobby were one and the same. He truly loved to fix cars, to help people.

Alex and his wife Stella did not have any children, but he sort of adopted a few young men of the town—those interested in automobiles. After hours and on Sundays he would work on their cars for them, often gratis, and teach them about engines and such.

There was not any honorable thing he would not do to help anyone. And this kindness and generosity were not confined to any race or creed. He was a thorough believer in the brotherhood of man, and it was not surprising at his funeral to see people from all walks of life come to pay their respects.

He was a great man—a phrase I do not use lightly.

The Lord disposes, I know, but to me it is a shame to have deprived the world of such an outstanding gentleman in the prime of his life, to have erased forever such generosity, kindness, skill and knowledge.

Mystery Story

You've pounded the typewriter for years, struggling to perfect your craft, to tell a story, straining for bread and bed. You've got a trunk full of manuscripts and rejection slips. It's been a hard life. Every now and then—just often enough to keep you plugging away—you've sold something—maybe a book for which you have great hopes. The book may get good reviews, and one or two isolated voices may hail you as you hoped to be hailed, i.e., as an artist. But nobody buys the book. Nobody, that is, outside your family, and a few of your friends. Some expect you to give them copies, which when you do, they don't read. It's a funny thing.

In time you entertain thoughts of doing something else to

make a living—that or cut your throat. You don't know much besides words and how to use them. You figure any fool can run a chicken ranch, so maybe you should give that a try. You could sit on the front porch with a mint julep and watch the feathered friends multiply. Might even be able to get in a story once in a while, maybe even a book—between egg collecting, that is.

You talk this over with The Little Woman and she remonstrates: "But darling, you're not going to give up your art! You're the best writer in the world."

So you go back to the typewriter, to waking up every morning and facing that blank piece of paper, the while thinking to yourself, "Is there a harder way to make a living?"

Then one day, out of the blue, one of your works catches fire and begins to sell. People want to read it. You get so much publicity even your friends notice you. The book is rewritten into a play and motion picture companies bid for the screen rights. People invite you to dinner. You're a lion. And yet, this book was written by the same hand as the dozens which proceeded it. The others had much the same quality, the same care. Why is this one magical? Why does it sell? What caused the stone wall against which you've been pounding for lo! these many years to break?

It's hard to figure. Maybe it was your wife's faith. Maybe it was timing. Maybe it was luck.

Let me hasten to add, this good fortune has never happened to me. But I've seen it happen to other writers, painters and actors, and I'm still hoping.

Pride, Pomp and Snobbery

You have to be socially geared to want to own a Rolls-Royce. It is a status symbol first and a means of transportation second. I have never needed that kind of opulence. It would embarrass me to drive up to a friend's house, a hotel or a gas station in a Rolls because it says too much and it says it too loudly.

What a Rolls says is: This is a rich person who wants you

and everybody to know that he and or she is extra-special and is high not only in the money marts but in the social and achievement worlds as well. So, it keeps on saying, "Give the owner-driver your respect," whether he or she deserves it or not.

I don't think a Rolls says much else, unless it has a flat tire and you, the owner, are standing distressed beside it off the highway. Then the onlooker, passing by in a much cheaper car, will feel a certain sympathy, a sympathy that somehow is stronger than if you, the stalled person, had been driving a Ford or a Volkswagen.

I tell you this because a friend, Rae Axtell, who lives in that high-rent district known as Rancho Santa Fe, recently won in a drawing the use of a brand-new Silver Cloud Rolls-Royce for a year and he is in a quandary because he feels about Rollses the way I do and wouldn't be caught dead driving it. He asked me, "What the hell am I going to do with it?" He doesn't even want it to sit in his garage for fear his neighbors might see it. I suggested he rent it and contribute the fee to charity.

What Rae had done was buy two tickets to the drawing ($100 each) as a gesture to charity, never dreaming that he would win first prize. There were at least a thousand ticket holders. The Rolls-Royce sells for $207,000, including tax ($12,000) and license ($2,000).

At a committee meeting the other morning at Scripps Memorial Hospital, where I happened to be, Rae offered the car to any of the committee members for free. However no one accepted the offer, so the car sits in his garage covered by canvas.

"We're thinking of moving down here, but I'm not sure whether it would be good for George."

CHAPTER 17

The Column that Almost Put the Post Out of Business

Seems to me the Ten Commandments, as delivered on the Mount by Moses, are sadly outmoded and that we need a new set of moral precepts. Today everyone honors his father and mother, even when they are not admirable characters. This commandment obviously was thrown in as a sop to the elders at a time when there was little law enforcement. Another commandment which has become superfluous is the one which says you must not bear false witness against thy neighbor. That's got rabbinical whiskers on it. Today if you accuse a person falsely, nine times out of ten he or she will sue.

The first commandment is all right: We should have no other God but God.

But the second—You must not carve any god-like images or pay homage to them—is silly, because if you accept the first commandment it precludes the second.

The third is solid enough: Do not take the name of the Lord thy God in vain. That's blasphemy, but I don't think His Nibs would give a hoot.

The fourth is outdated. It has to do with working six days a week and resting on the seventh. Today we work five days a week and there's a movement on for four.

The seventh, about adultery, is difficult to define. *Webster's New International Dictionary,* which is the last word, says it means sexual unfaithfulness of a married person, but today, when there are so many legal separations and other odd situations in marriage, it doesn't seem sinful.

And the tenth—the one which says thou shalt not covet

thy neighbor's home, nor his wife nor his ox nor his ass—that doesn't hold water. The American standard of living has been keeping up with the Joneses. As for coveting a man's wife, when a man quits looking at a beautiful woman he needs a psychiatrist.

The Ten Commandments as Moses told them to the children of Israel are sadly out of date, but there are a number of modern offenses which might be included in a rewrite. For instance:

Thou shalt not think ill of thy neighbor because his political beliefs are not yours.

Thou shalt not be stingy, greedy or gluttonous.

Thou shalt not be timid or over cautious. Far better to be audacious.

Husband and wife should not quarrel either privately or in public.

Thou shalt not be snobbish.

Thou shalt not brag about thy children.

The day after the above appeared, twenty-five percent of the newspaper's subscribers canceled, and a number of people wrote letters which the paper printed. The following is typical of the letters:

Publisher, the Post

This is a definite and sincere protest against your article in your paper about the Ten Commandments.

Such an attempt to pull down by cheap ridicule the very foundation of the Christian faith is inexcusable and cannot leave thinking people unconcerned—especially when these ideas are put forth by one who should know better.

Most people realize that the Bible must be interpreted in its spiritual meaning, and all of the good things you presume to suggest are included in the Ten Commandments.

My special plea is for the young, who look up to the publisher of a newspaper as a person to be admired and will mistake inanity for sophistication.

You, John Weld, are much too smart a man to have written this without knowing it would create a stir—and I deplore this misuse of your talent.

Sincerely,

(Mrs. B.W.) Gertrude P. Thayer.

I wrote and thanked the lady for her criticism.

A traveling preacher, one like Billy Sunday, rented a vacant lot on Pacific Coast Highway in South Laguna, put up a tent, got two hundred chairs from Abbey Rents and hung a bannered sign: COME HEAR THE CHASTISEMENT OF JOHN WELD. Katy and I did not attend the service, but a goodly crowd did. Reverend Hauser, the Episcopal minister in Laguna Beach, also berated me in his Sunday sermon.

I wrote a column apologizing. To my surprise subscriptions to the paper increased and so did the "Letters to the Editor" in my defense.

Bishop Hears Call, Abandons Flock

The *Los Angeles Times* runs church news in its Saturday editions. Recently the following paid advertisement appeared there:

FAREWELL

To all Apostolic brethren:

Due to the abundance of earthquake warnings from God to His converts, the congregation of the Gospel Church of Arieta will be leaving California this Saturday. Because of the short notice, we will not have time to notify all of our brethren of our departure, especially the congregations of Rev. McDaniel, Rev. Gregory, Elder Hoss and Bishop B. Cantu. I'm not sure where we will be but will let you know.

[signed] Bishop and Founder, B.C. Galvan.

•

Dear Bishop Galvan, wherever you may be:

I wish you and your Apostolic brethren well. You did not say where you are going, and perhaps the Lord asked that you not reveal your destination. Only He, I guess, knows where on this whirling world you will find a haven from earthquakes and other turbulences. Not in the Holy Land, surely. Not in Africa or Europe or the Orient. Not in South America or Alaska or Saskatchewan. One place seems to be as fraught with the dangers of cataclysms as another.

What disturbs those you are leaving is that you are doing so abruptly. Did the Lord warn you not to tarry? You are a man of the cloth and therefore filled, I assume, with the milk of human kindness. It is hard for your followers to believe that you are more concerned with your own welfare than you are with theirs.

You say that "Because of our short notice, we will not have time personally to notify all of our Apostolic brethren. . . ."

Apparently you got right on your horse and skeedaddled. When your Apostolic congregation showed up for service Sunday you were long gone. Here it is the middle of November and the only calamity that's hit these shores has been the election of a Democrat, Alan Cranston, to the U.S. Senate. (A disaster only in Orange County.)

Your hasty departure reminds us of the man who, seeing a cyclone sashaying across the prairie, ran to escape it, only to have the danged thing change course and swallow him. Had he stayed where he was, chances are he'd have been saved.

I remember at the time of Pearl Harbor, a thoroughly frightened man locked his house on the oceanfront at Wood's Cove and fled toward Kansas, figuring he would be safe from the Japanese submarines which, he was certain, were going to shell our shores. It grieves me to report that en route he was killed in an automobile accident.

I know a man whose wife was such a shrew that his life was miserable. She was forever upbraiding and scolding him. Unable to bear her abuse any longer, he fled to another city, changed his identity and began a new life. In no time at all he was living with a woman who turned out to be even more of a termagant than his lawful wife.

The moral is obvious, Bishop Galvan. There is no rest or safety for the fearful.

Unlike Noah, who had a similar message from on high, you appear to be unconcerned with posterity. You apparently did not take any birds or beasts with you. Noah went around imploring his fellows to heed the call of the Lord; he took the time to urge them to join him. But not you, sir. The Lord spoke and you took off, abandoning all of us poor infidels to our miserable fates.

If you find a place on this earth, dear Bishop, which is safe from "earthquakes and destruction" I beg you to send us word. Chances are you will gain a goodly congregation.

How to Get into Egypt

TLW and I are about to take a journey, and one of the countries we plan to visit is Egypt. To get into this member of the United Arab Republic, there being a state of war between Egypt and Israel, one has to give evidence that one is not a Jew.

Such evidence generally is in the form of a letter from the church one attends. Unhappily, TLW and I, while members of the Episcopal Church, are not regular churchgoers. This does not mean we are not pious folk. I think we are. But we certainly do not attend church as often as we might.

Last year, before we went to the Mediterranean, we secured letters attesting to our faith from Rev. John H. Hauser, the minister of our church; but when we returned, I, thinking we never again would have need for such, discarded them.

Now, faced with the identical problem, I was somewhat shy about asking Mr. Hauser for copies. My trepidation sprang from the fact that Katy and I had not attended our church all year.

Oh, as sightseers we've been in lots of churches, mosques and temples of various faiths (and even had an audience with

Pope Juan Two Three), but we had not set foot in our church. And I had the uncomfortable feeling that on this account we had been wayward and remiss.

So I suggested offhand-like to Katy that she stop by the church office and ask Mr. Hauser's secretary if she would kindly make copies of the letters issued us last year and have the minister sign them. I'd pick them up later.

This was sneaky of me, because she would get the brunt of any criticism. But I have always been a coward, and I simply can't bear being placed in an indefensible position.

Some time later that day, when I thought the coast was clear, I breezed into the church office and asked Mrs. Balzer, Mr. Hauser's secretary, if Katy had stopped by and spoken about the letters. She had. Well, then, were they ready? They were, Mrs. Balzer said, on Mr. Hauser's desk, and he was in his office.

I drew on my shallow courage and went in. The handsome rector, attired in his clerical garb, was seated behind his desk. "I suppose there is some doubt in your mind," I said, dredging up a hollow laugh as I extended my hand, "that we are members of your congregation." He smiled rather gravely, I thought. "Well, I must admit," he said, "I have not been favorably impressed by your attendance record."

I was properly apologetic and looked at the letters lying before him—one for Katy and one for me.

"In all good conscience I cannot sign these letters," the minister said. "However, I understand you require them today, and I shall do so on one condition: that you promise to attend church at least once before the year is out."

I promised. "Furthermore," I said, "I promise to do so more frequently than I have done in 1960."

Forthwith he signed the letters. I breathed a sigh of relief and took them to Elmer Brown at his travel office so he could send for our Egyptian visas, and began feeling better right away.

True to my word, Christmas Eve Katy and I got all gussied up and went to the midnight service. This was something of a sacrifice because it meant leaving a fine Christmas tree-trimming party at which delicious black velvets were being poured. However, this gave us the proper feeling of sacrifice.

The theme of the service, naturally was the nativity. There was singing and prayer, and Mr. Hauser told the story of Jesus' birth. It was a beautiful service, and we enjoyed it very much. Did us lots of good, I think.

The October Wail

As people grow older they begin to treasure the fast-moving days. Thereto they had taken them for granted. Even before one is three score and ten a person should have learned that anger, vexation, wrath and fury harms everyone involved and that complaining, protesting, remonstrating are self-demeaning. By the time one gets on life's downward slope he or she should have learned that it is better to swallow disappointment than to bewail it.

What brought this sermon to mind was seeing Elmo Young trudging droop-shouldered on the beach. He was the picture of despondence, of a man who had given up the struggle for fame and fortune. His every step was carrying him closer to his grave.

Knowing that recently his wife Gladys had died, I felt a pang of pathos for him. For years he had run the race for gold and glory and along the way had won a dib and dab of both. He was a musician-composer and over the years had written a number of songs, a symphony and a comic opera, but only a few of his works had won the public's fickle fancy. As time went its inexorable way he had worked as a piano salesman. Meanwhile younger musicians had come along and written successful songs he considered inferior, while his had gathered dust. He considered this unfair, but it had happened so often he had ceased to protest. Then something unforeseen happened. His wife, throughout their lives together his one enthusiastic fan, died. She had been his joy and inspiration. With her went his reason for being. The lights had gone out.

As he came between me and the sea I whistled and he came and slumped down beside me. I said, "I heard about your bad luck. How are you getting on?"

"Not well," he said, and, eager to talk he went on: "She was a wonderful woman. I never thought I'd lose her. Husbands are usually the ones to go. It would have been better that way. She didn't depend on me as I did on her."

I said, "Wives sort of expect to become widows. They figure on just picking up the insurance money and start traveling. How about you? Are you going somewhere?"

"I got nowhere to go."

"How about your children?"

"Oh, I can go see them, but they don't want me hanging around. They both live in Arizona, are married and have kids. With Gladys' insurance and my ASCAP royalties I'm free of responsibilities and obligations, able to buy what I need and I don't need much. I've got more clothes than I'll ever wear out. I'm still able to read and the library is close by. I've got that car you sold me, but I don't use it very much. I walk a lot. My trouble is: I'm lonely. At home I talk to Gladys, hoping she'll hear me. I tell her how much I love her, how much I miss her and say I hope to be with her soon."

"Does she answer you?"

"No. But every now and then I see her smiling face."

Christmas

Dear Santa:

For Christmas this year I'd like a new, tailor-made, all-wool-and-a-yard-wide character. The one I have is threadbare. I'd like one with a built-in, eighteen-carat confidence, particularly when I speak publicly.

I'd like a few personality qualities such as congeniality and graciousness; I'd also like a modicum of meanness, enough so people won't say of me, "I never heard him utter an unkind word." When I think somebody is a double-barreled dastard, I want to say so.

Please be sure, dear Santa, to put in an upgraded perspicacity, so I'll be able to tell the false from the true, and give me a greater capacity than I have now for wine, women and song.

If you can find any, I'd like a modicum of intolerance. Mankind has become too forgiving, and I'd like to counteract this weakness. Don't, for Heaven's sake, put into my character any more virtues.

While you're going to all the trouble, Santa, enlarge my sense of humor gland. Make me see through the hogwash, the hokum and the hooey. As far as I am concerned, you can leave me conscienceless. And while you're leaving things out exclude the segment of hope. To me hope is the first of the seven sickly virtues. I'd like a strong faith in myself, only a smidgen of charity.

If you don't mind, I would like a restraining order keeping me from attending parties during which people show slides of their travels or at which young children are present.

While I'm asking, I'd like you to give me some protection from sportswriters' cliches. I'd also like you to make me blind to the scribblings of financial writers who dream up reasons why the stock market rises and falls. Include a pair of earmuffs so I won't have to listen to campaigning politicians berate one another.

Inasmuch as I have been circumspect this past year, I feel these requests are modest. If you grant all of them I promise not to beg you for anything next year.

Yours gratefully,

More Christmas

Greetings. This is the time of year to proclaim "Let there be peace on earth! Peace! Oh, peace! Don't let peace cease!"

Not the Muscovite kind of peace, but true peace. The tranquility kind. Quiet, harmonious, free from international bickering and name calling. It is the time of year to expose the heart and extend the hand in friendship and affection to all Homo sapiens who inhabit this restless, inexplicable earth.

Hence I herewith send greeting to such unlikely bed fellows as Nikita Kruschev and Winston Churchill, to Ike and

Adlai, to friend and foe, to high and low, to Carmine De Sapio, an unlikely name as ever I heard; to David Ben-Gurion and Abdel Nasser; to Princess Margaret, who still carries the torch, and to Peter Townsend rocking on his front porch; to Hugh Gaitskell and Anurin Bevan, spade-caller Adenauer and his counterpart in East Germany whose name I cannot recall...good will to those folks, all.

Oh, sing out with joy to Susan Hayward and Jil Jarmyn, to Red Saunders and Jess Hill, to Pope Pious and Nebuchadnezzar, to Sidi Mohammed ben Youssef, Hadj Thami El Glauci and their relatives....

Peace, peace, oh, gentle peace, gentlemen.

To Mr. Ford and Mrs. Chevrolet, peace, I say.

To everyone listed in the Laguna Beach telephone book, hail!

To Dow Finsterwal and Dow-Jones, to Y. A. Tittle, who sounds like a clown, to Tallent Tubbs, Aramis Dandoy and Leif Ede, to Sid Gluskin and Hugo Winterhalter, salute.

To Halldor Kiljan Laxness, who works hard for the United Nations, to Seydou N'Jimolloh Njoya, which is the unlikely name of the leader of the French Cameroons, raise the curtain and let the sunshine in.

Lift the cup to the ill and lame, the crackpot, the halt, the blind. It is a season of cheer, of live and let live. To those who cannot pay, to those whose minds have lost the way, to the poor and needy, the rich and kin, to those who're living in sin, greetings.

To the drab and dreary, the gay and bold, to the soon to be born, to the young and old, let us sing a song of harmony.

Bury the hatchet, the axe eschew, let us call on the angels few; let us hearken to the dove and resign our long-term lease on her. On every ranch plant an olive branch.

Let's decry the language called profane and confine our tones to the sweet and sane—let's outlaw the pounce just for the nounce.

It would do all of us good to say something nice for a change about Secretary Anso Grange.

Oh, hail, my fellows, oh hail, oh, hail! Let's catch this year by its shortening tail—what the heck—wring its neck. The ensuing quiet will be peaceful, I 'speckt.

Old Home Week

Our neighbor Palm Springs has always been a place I could take or leave alone, like opera and afternoon tea. It has a phony sophistication sometimes referred to as glamor, and by and large the weather there isn't as good as Laguna's. As a place to live I think it is for the coyotes.

TLW and I spent New Year's Eve weekend there and I never had a better time, even when I was single. We had so much fun I've still got a hangover. Most of this pleasure was due to our hostesses, Joan Bering and Edna Rothbart, ladies known far and wide, from Chicago to Timbuktu, for their gracious and lavish hospitality. Thanks to them we were up to our navels in celebrities.

Hobnobbing with the rich and famous always gives me a giddy, breathless feeling. I enjoy it immensely, but it also increases my natural feeling of inferiority. If I shake hands, as I did with Conrad Hilton, and he says to me, as he did, "How do you do?" I become tongue-tied.

My trouble is that I want to make a good impression so that celebrities will think I am an outstanding man of wit and wisdom. But my tongue at such times has a way of becoming somewhat knurled, and by the time I get it untied it spouts words like an unmanned fire hose spews water.

All I was trying to do was tell him about the time we were ensconced in the Nile Hilton, in Cairo, and room service sent up our breakfast at three in the morning when it had been ordered for nine o'clock.

Mr. Hilton, a handsome old man who squires pretty young ladies and has his life-size portrait hanging in every lobby of his hotels, was not in the least interested. All the time I was talking his attention was on a pretty newspaper reporter, Joan Winchell. I suppose people of his importance have to be rude; otherwise they would have to listen to all kinds of drivel from nonentities.

I did manage to hold Paul Whiteman's attention for a little while by reminding him of the time he had the fat cut off from around his ample girth. I guess it's true that everyone likes to talk about his operation.

William Powell was his urbane self, full of good humor and what are commonly referred to as off-color stories, and we reminisced about a mutual friend, Mayo Methot, who became Mrs. Humphrey Bogart. He gave me a minute or two but I let him do most of the talking.

Harpo Marx was introduced to me merely as Harpo, and I asked, "Harpo who?" and everyone thought I was being witty.

Mervyn LeRoy seemed bored by my telling him we started in pictures about the same time, away back yonder in the early twenties (actually he started in 1917, he told me)—he as a prop boy and I as a stunt man. I don't think he took it kindly when I said I probably could have become a director, too, if I'd married money as he did (the daughter of Louis B. Mayer).

Helen Kindleberger, wife of the famed Dutch, late president of North American Aviation, reminded me of the time Henry Ford II and I came to their house on Pacific Palisades and partied up a storm. I was flattered she remembered me and kissed her on a cheek.

We came across some old friends during that gay weekend—Fieldsy Lang, wife of movie director Walter Lang, and probably the kindest (next to Maggie Ettinger, who was with us) and surely the funniest woman in the world. Fieldsy, who was the late Carole Lombard's best friend, and I were members of the Ambassador Hotel swimming team in the 1920s.

We ran into Earl Blackwell, who developed Celebrity Service into such a fine business that he had become a celebrity himself. The association between Earl and me goes back to our youths when my mother and another generous woman, Lillian Terry, took him under their wings.

All in all, it was old home week in Palm Springs, and I

came away feeling like a celebrity. Even toyed with the inebriated notion of hiring a press agent.

"On the dinner you get soup, salad, rolls, coffee, dessert, one vegetable and a portrait sketch."

CHAPTER 18

Travel Note, 1960s

Next time you plan a trip to Mexico don't fail to include Alamos in your itinerary. Situated about thirty miles east of Navajoa at an altitude of about twenty-five hundred feet, Alamos is an old (over three hundred years) silver-and-gold mining town. Much of its past grandeur lies in ruins today, and, where once thirty thousand persons lived, now but a bare three thousand dwell. Here is to be found the true charm, the other-world feeling, the throat-closing pathos of Mexico.

We were in this ancient town last week with the Wendell Finleys, traveling thence in their airplane, and a rewarding experience it was. There we met Americans Alvin and Darley Gordon who operate one of the finest and most unusual hotels in all of Mexico, Casa de los Tesoros. The hotel is a reconstructed hacienda, one of the many grand mansions of a long-gone era, doubtless once the house of a silver king.

When the Gordons took the place over it was in ruins, only its magnificently beautiful arches and a few odd adobe walls intact. With the courage of naivete and the enthusiasm of fresh love they set about rebuilding it—this without any knowledge of architecture or construction and little skilled labor. The procurement of beams alone (to say nothing of tile, brick and glass) was almost enough to discourage them.

But they persisted, and what they finally wrought is beautiful—a house of traditional fidelity and hospitality. Every room has a fireplace and in each to greet the weary traveler is a freshly laid fire of sweet-smelling wood. The only bows to modernity are electricity, running water and a swimming pool in the patio.

Having built the hotel, the Gordons were faced with the problem of securing a cook. One Chinese they found who knew about cooking refused to submit to a physical examination, others—a German, a Mexican-American and a second Chinese—proved unsatisfactory. So finally, Al Gordon, something of an amateur chef and certainly a gourmet, undertook to do the cooking himself. For travelers to Alamos this turned out to be a most fortunate circumstance. Here in this quiet, faraway, charming place one finds food that cannot be surpassed. One of the drawbacks to the traveler in Mexico is getting good food, and it is therefore a doubly rewarding experience to sit at Gordon's table.

I give you a sample recipe:

LOBSTER TESOROS

Cut lobster meat into chunks. In a saucepan melt butter and garlic and simmer. Add salt, pepper and a handful of walnut or pecan halves. Add lobster. When hot, add a generous shot of sweet vermouth and lemon juice. Hold lid on for a few minutes. Serve in the center of a rice ring.

Have that with a bottle of Almaden Rosé, and, brethren and sistern, you're living.

At the Casa de los Tesoros everyone eats at a common table. Service is hand-painted blue Pueblo ware, amber mouth-blown glass, individual bottles of wine, candlelight from antique candelabra. After dinner there are liqueurs—"on the house"—around the fire, with story-telling of course. Newcomers to Alamos get to know veterans and are taken into "the family."

Alamos is for the traveler who seeks the quaint, the historical and the unusual. It has the same atmospheric quality as, say, Virginia City, Nevada—but with life emerging Phoenix-like from ruins, thanks to the Gordons.

The mines are to be reopened soon by an American we were told, and more and more travelers who take the new highway from Nogales, Arizona, to Mexico City are finding it rewarding to deviate those thirty miles. Hunters of birds, deer and other game find it a paradise with no season, no limit and no fences.

Alamos is about seven hundred and fifty miles south of Laguna. Best way is to stay overnight at Tucson or Nogales, thence to Alamos the next day. Rooms with meals at the Casa de los Tesoros are about eight dollars U.S. currency (1955) a day. No tipping is allowed.

I realize the foregoing reads like an advertisement, but I assure you, dear reader, it comes from a much-traveled connoisseur.

Alamos, in the state of Sonora, Mexico, might well be renamed Phoenix, because this ancient silver-mining town is rising from the ashes and dust of its former glory. Once one of the most important cities of Mexico, it has, since the turn of the century, declined. But now Americans are discovering it and practically everyone knows what that means.

They are purchasing the ruined homes of formerly important personages of Mexico and are not only restoring them and their beautiful arches, but are adding electricity, gas and running water.

It is a fascinating town. We stood in the street watching masons working to straighten an arch. A very small American woman in her sixties was standing nearby, obviously very interested in what was going on. "Your house?" I asked.

She nodded. "Just bought it," she said. "I came down here to spend two days. Now it looks as if I'm going to be here for the rest of my life."

Her story is typical. Some sixty Americans have bought property in the town in the past few years, most of them on impulse, and forty have restored or are restoring the buildings.

Former Laguna resident Walter Franklin is restoring what had been one of the most beautiful homes there. It was the summer home of Bartolome Almada, one of the silver kings. When it, its guest house and twelve acres of garden are completed it will have cost between forty and fifty thousand dollars (American) but it will look like a million.

TLW, Muriel Reynolds and I were looking through a gate when the lady of the house came out. "Muriel!" she cried. Turned out she was Mrs. Owen Churchill, an old friend, who lives part time at the Balboa Bay Club. Her husband is one of America's outstanding yachtsmen.

The architecture of Alamos is colonial, with the arch dominating. Windows are grilled, walls are three to five feet thick and plastered, ceilings are twenty feet high and beamed, and floors are tiled. Patios have palms and bougainvillea-bordered swimming pools.

The town has been named a National Colonial Monument by the Mexican government and as such it can never be changed; that is, its narrow, haphazard streets will always remain cobbled as they are and if one wishes to rearrange a stone he must get permission from the government.

But you can make over a house, just so you follow the original lines. And it is possible for Americans to acquire title to properties there. Indeed, foreigners can get title to small properties almost any where in Mexico save along the border or ocean.

A ruined house, with some walls and arches standing, cost anywhere from two to ten thousand dollars, according to its state of preservation, location, size, etc. One needs one's own diesel plant because the town's electricity runs only from six P.M. to midnight. For water one sinks a well. There is city water, but sometimes the city wells dry up.

There is an airport in Alamos suitable for small planes and in much better repair than when we and the Wendell Finleys landed on it three years ago.

Masons get seventy-five dollars a month, helpers between one and two dollars a day, and both are excellent. Construction, however, is slow, for the masonry walls are thick and the pace of the country is leisurely.

Maids get fifty cents a day, a mozo (male cook) one dollar. Most Americans have men servants because maids pose a problem if left alone with the man of the house. Either they will bring their mothers and sisters to chaperone them or, the first time their master calls, they will head for the highest hill.

A Canadian company has resumed mining in the vicinity and the operation is proving profitable. The mine, which was being worked by Indians in 1519 when Cortez came to Mexico, had not been worked since 1906. The problem then was lack of water—still a bugaboo, but this has been solved by an ingenuous method whereby water is used over and over again. And the Canadians have brought to the mine a new process for extracting ore from rock.

The old method of mining was to hand pick the best pieces of ore, discard all the rest. The new operation crushes these tailings, of which there are thousands of tons, and extract the silver therefrom.

They are taking some twelve hundred dollars in silver a day from the tailings, and Don McLean, the engineer in charge, says there is every reason to believe that there is a great deal more silver in the mountain.

New Year's Resolutions

It's getting so years follow one another fast. They seem to whip past. This year I'm determined to make a resolution and keep it.

I'm getting to that time in life when the sinews don't have the snap of yore and bones begin to creak. I've been in such a hurry all my life you'd think His Nibs the scythe cutter was hot on my tail.

Well, I'm going to quit hurrying.

Know what I'm going to do? I'm going to buy a "Magic Massager," which I see advertised in the *Los Angeles Times.* Converts your favorite rocking chair to a vibrator. Only $14.95.

A vibrating chair is just what I need.

The advertisement goes fascinatingly on: "The Magic Massager stimulates circulation, relaxes muscles, improves breathing, eases tension, quiets nerves and promotes sleep."

The one thing I want my favorite chair to do is vibrate. I spend a considerable part of every day in an automobile and a squeaky swivel chair, and a chair that shakes is just made for the likes of me. I can come home nights and keep right on shaking.

I can see it now. TLW will bring my slippers, my favorite book and a bottle of sarsparilla, and I'll curl the old carcass up in the chair and turn on the Magic Massager.

Then I'll sit back and shake.

I've heard tell that we Homo sapiens are not as stationary as we appear. Truth is, certain theorists aver, we're spinning like the earth, spinning so fast that we only seem to be stationary.

As for the Magic Massager, I think I'll buy two and attach one to my bed so that I can shake as I sleep. That way, come morning, I'll be relaxed and calm and my circulation and breathing will be immensely improved. Maybe my writing too.

Blue Jay

Laguna is a haven for birds.

There are scads of them around our house, those which are here the year around and those which migrate. Many use our birdbath daily, either to bathe or drink. The most beautiful one is a Scrub Jay which nests in our hedge. His head, wings and tail are a rich blue, his back a pale brown, his underpants pearl gray and he has a white jabot on his neck and chin. Pretty, but tough. Wow! He runs the neighborhood like an eagle.

We have named him One Punch because of the way he commands his fellows. When he wants a bath, and there are other birds—white-crowned sparrows, red-winged blackbirds or black-eared bushtits—in the pool, he'll fly in with a flourish and, though dripping wet, the others will hastily scatter. He is so courageous that he'll fly from a nearby perch and peck a kernel of corn or a nut from an outstretched hand.

He thinks he owns the oak trees in the neighborhood and is master of their acorns which he plants methodically in our garden. He's very good at it, but he must be absent-minded because he often can't remember where he buried them. Sometimes they sprout.

The other day I saw him sitting on a limb with his plain-garmented lady-friend, and I imagined him saying: "You are a lucky female."

"Why?" she asked demurely.

"Because I'm your mate."

"Oh, yes. That's right. I *am* the lucky one."

To see what would happen, I put a mirror on the patio where One Punch often perches and from inside watched his reaction. It took him a little while to see it, possibly because he is always on the alert for adversaries and cats. When he did see his image, he gave it a double-take, as if to say, "Now who on God's earth is that?" His third look said, "What the hell are you doing here?"

Because there was no reply he was puzzled. Suddenly he lunged at this image and *wham!* fell backward, stunned. After shaking his head to regain his senses, he fluttered to his feet and struck again, though not so forcefully, and this time he landed on his feet instead of his back. Pacing up and down he noticed that the image in the mirror moved precisely as he did. When he opened his beak to say, "Wise guy, eh?" so did the bird in the mirror.

Suddenly and with marvelous agility he darted behind the mirror to take his adversary by surprise, but was surprised to find nothing there. He hopped around and around the mirror, trying to flush the image and solve the mystery. Nonplused, he looked around to see if other birds had noticed his befuddlement and, seeing none, drew back to reconsider the situation. He decided to bypass the ornery dastard in the mirror. At this juncture his mate flew down and joined him.

"What are you doing?" she asked.

He pointed his beak at the mirror and was astonished to see that now there were two birds—a male and a female—where there had been but one male.

"What's the trouble?" she asked. And added, "That's us."

She lifted a foot and touched his ribs playfully. "You know what that is? That's a hub cap. One of those shiny things that reflects your image."

"Oh," he said, relieved.

She flew back into the pine tree where there was perched another female Scrub Jay. I couldn't hear what they said to each other but can guess. After having seen what had transpired, her friend probably said, "Just like a cock-a-doodle—always preening himself."

Know Thy Neighbor

"What prodded you to become a bullfighter?" I asked William Hedrick, twenty-eight, the Lagunan who two weeks ago performed in the bullring at Tijuana.

"I was on holiday in Mexico," he replied, "and some friends took me to see a bullfight in Colima. It is near Manzanillo. I was fascinated by what I saw and became at once an aficionado. Thereafter I attended every bullfight I could get to and read every book I could find on the subject. Eventually I went to Spain, attended a bullfighting school and fought four times in Barcelona."

The sport challenged him and so did the danger and the opportunity to be a cynosure, to show off. But more than that, I gather, he wanted to prove something to himself.

"My mother says I am a thrill seeker," Hedrick told me. "And I guess that is how it looks. But the answer to my interest in bullfighting is more complicated than that. Through the ages men seem to have wanted to dominate and master, not only other animals but the animal that is within themselves. I think he comes closest to doing this where danger is concerned."

Hedrick is attracted to other dangers. His business, as differentiated from his vocation, is deep-sea diving commercially (that's with full diving gear) for abalones—no child's play. He does this four or five hours a day off San Clemente Island, makes a good living from fifty to seventy-five dollars a day.

His hobby, aside from bullfighting which comes closer to a fixation, is surfing, and the higher the waves the better he likes it.

He looks like a good athlete—about five feet ten, lean

and hard with taut lips and a fine competitive gleam in dark blue eyes. He was a Marine and spent three years in Korea.

This hitch in the service may have set him back irretrievably in his bullfighting ambition. Two more years fighting as a novillero (novice) are before him ere he can become a professional and entitled to the honorific title matador. He will be thirty. He says that's pretty old to be getting started.

He's saving his diving money to go back to Spain. There he will fight first on the ranches to get his "hand in," and then in the big rings as a preliminary attraction. He leaves the first of the year.

Bullfighters, he says, are like movie actors in that they get fan mail, are lionized by the public, are besieged by autograph seekers and are paid high sums for their draw at the box office.

Señor Hedrick believes very strongly that he has what it takes to become a star in this esoteric profession—all he needs, he says, is luck.

"Luck is very important in bullfighting. Mostly it has to do with the bull. If the bull has nobility it can be a good show. If he has none the performance will suffer."

Nobility, he explained, is the true fighting spirit and the urge to charge directly. Bulls are bred for this. The fighting bull gets courage from his mother and nobility from his father.

What does his family think of his becoming a bullfighter?

"My mother hates it," he said.

Neither she nor his father have ever come to see him fight.

"They probably never will," he said.

El Toro

There are many bull throwers in Laguna, some of whom we hold in affection. However there is another *bona fide* bullfighter. He is Patric Kennedy, who lives at 385 Flora Street with his mother, Mrs. J.R. Kennedy. Pat is only twenty, but he has been fighting bulls for five years. He may become a great matador. Indeed, he quite frankly and simply, without braggadocio or bravado, says he will.

His introduction to the cape and sword occurred in Venezuela, where he went in 1950 with his father, a construction engineer. A friend was an apprentice bullfighter and he taught Pat the rudiments. After three years of fighting young bulls in a barnyard, Pat made his first appearance in a bullring.

Was he afraid? "Well, not exactly, just nervous. When you go into the ring you have to have the proper mental attitude. You mustn't worry about getting hurt, you worry about doing well. As an apprentice, I fought young bulls—only three to four years old, of seven hundred and fifty pounds. When you are a full-fledged matador you fight older bulls of a thousand pounds or more."

So far he has made five public appearances in bullrings and each time dispatched his bull. The first bull he fought gashed his thigh with a horn and the scar is still there. It happened when he first tried inserting the banderillas; the bull raised his head at precisely the wrong moment. "I'll never make that mistake again," says Pat.

How does one go about getting a job fighting bulls? "You have to have an agent," Pat said. "I have one in Mexico City. He is promoting my career. He tells me the time is ripe for an American matador. All of Mexico will come to see me if I am good enough," he says. "But there is the build-up—the publicity and the experience. It takes time and money. I need a sponsor—someone to stand my expenses while I am coming along. I have to eat. Once in Mexico, I went three days without food. Americans cannot work at anything in Mexico without a permit. I can do nothing there except fight bulls.

"The magnificent costumes of the matadors can be rented for ten dollars a performance. Shoes are the pump type, with no heel, a slightly pointed toe with a bow and very thin soles to allow dexterity. Entering the arena all bullfighters are nervous, but after the third pass the nervousness is gone. Everything is split-second timing. You work as in a dance, with each movement precise and exact. The tension is great. Once the fight is over the nervousness returns. You feel utterly wilted. After a fight I cannot hold a cup of coffee without spilling it."

Pat fought two five-year-old bulls—the big ones—last January 14th in Santin, Mexico. His performance was so good he was awarded one of the bull's two ears by the judges. One ear is good, two ears is excellent. Sometimes a fighter is awarded both ears and tail—that is perfection.

"I figure I will be a bullfighter for ten years," Pat said. "I want to become very good so that I can make enough money to take care of my mother and father. My father is not well and he can't work much longer. He's a bookkeeper. They have sacrificed much for me and I want to make it up to them. I want to do well to represent my country. As an American I am subject to more criticism than if I were a Mexican. Who knows, I may become the greatest bullfighter in the world."

Beach Scene

"Do small, silvery fish actually swim up onto a beach and do a wriggle-tail dance in the moonlight?" a visiting fireman from New York asked me the other day.

I assured him that such was indeed true and invited him to accompany me on a grunion catch. "First we have to get a fishing license," I said, and forthwith led him to a bait-and-tackle store. We paid our four bucks and pinned the badges on our hats.

We didn't need any equipment, only a gunny sack and a couple of flashlights. The law stipulates that the grunion must be caught by hand.

"What time's the tide high?" my friend asked.

I consulted the town's sterling journal and learned that night it came at eleven-thirteen.

"Well, let's get a batch," he said.

It was a nice evening, warm for the south coast, and the swells as they curled under and spewed across the sand, splashed a Wagnerian crescendo. Along the beach we saw lovers locked in passionate embrace and there were a few strollers at the far end of the cove. We sat down on a rock and I passed my friend the jug.

"What's so fascinating to me," I said, "is the delicate and exacting adjustment the grunions make to the tidal cycle. The eggs require two weeks to ripen in the female and two weeks to hatch once they've been buried in the sand. The spawning takes place only at night and at the turn of the highest of three tides. By depositing her eggs after the tide has turned, the female grunion minimizes the chance her eggs are washed into the sea. Two weeks after the eggs have been laid, the next series of high tide waves will free the eggs from the sand, the babies will hatch and will be carried back into their natural habitat, the sea."

"Very enlightening," my friend said.

"Absolutely incredible," I said and retrieving the jug, took a swig. The soft strains of a ukulele drifted wistfully on the prevailing zephyr. "The grunion is found only along the California shore," I went on. "With its cousin *Hubbsiella sardina* it's the only fish in the sea to have such unusual spawning habits."

"Wish they'd hurry up," my friend said.

"The first fish we'll see," I said, "probably will be males. They'll come in to test the waves—to see that they reach far enough. Spawning will commence shortly thereafter. Each female will be followed by one to eight males. As the wave recedes she will stand on her tail and wriggle herself into the sand up to what would be her belly button, if she had one. She will then lay her eggs while the males arch around her and discharge their milt."

"Their what?" my friend asked.

"Milt."

"Oh," he said, and took a swig.

I snapped on the light. The beam swept over the sand, moving along the water's edge.

"Won't be long now," I said. "The digging in and laying takes about thirty seconds, although grunion have been known to stay on the beach for several minutes before a merciful wave sweeps them back into the sea."

We kept tabs on the time and remarked eleven-thirteen.

"They'll be coming in any time now," I said. "It'll be the damndest thing you ever saw."

Well, we kept looking until midnight, but nary a grunion did we see. And as the minutes ticked off and nothing happened I sensed my friend's growing skepticism.

"I have a suspicion you don't believe a word of what I've told you," I said,

He laughed and said, "You Californians play elaborate practical jokes."

To this day that guy thinks I was pulling his leg.

festival of arts
Phil Interlandi

CHAPTER 19

With Apologies to Pepys

Up betimes and congratulate The Little Woman on her good fortune to be married to one so handsome and full of joy and say isn't it wonderful we have a nice day to spend together on our secluded "estate."

Words hardly out of mouth when phone jangles. Nerves are somewhat tender from late party night before. Girl Scout asks if we would purchase cookies. Refrained from telling her it is bad salesmanship to call prospective customer at such an early hour.

Washing teeth when man comes with matting for carpet.

Barely seated at breakfast when Jules Marine, the boniface, drives up in his new VW. With him are his son Junior and Gene DuPont, the syndicated artist-naturalist. Jules is seeking information anent an adjacent lot Roy Childs has for sale. Jules tells us he has rented his White House saloon to Bob Mikels for two years. Reason: He and his Mrs. want to be free to travel. Obstacle: Their fifteen-year-old stepdaughter is in love with a horse.

Reheat tea and return to newspaper and Mike Jackson's column. Barely seated when Girl Scouts come to front door with cookies. Buy batch and discover they are not the girls who telephoned.

TLW and I are laying carpet matting when two of our favorite people, Ruth and Jack Davis, of Bloomfield Hills, Michigan, arrive with daughter Tink, son-in-law Ted Cartwright, and four grandchildren. They are laden with hamburgers and beer. Hooray! We can get rid of the cookies. Children head for pool. One, named Tray because he was number three, jumps in, can't swim. Father has to go in clothes and all, pull out. Phone rings: wrong number.

Ralph Bell drives up to measure garage for new doors. Girl Scouts who telephoned arrive to deliver cookies. Barbara and McKee Thompson, of San Marino, drop in: McKee wants to know if I'll go on a fishing trip to Cabo San Lucas with him. Barbara wants to know why Myford Irvine killed himself. Muriel Reynolds calls to report progress of husband Larry and John Antrobus, en route by car to Mulege, Baja California. They had gotten as far as Los Angeles Bay on Baja's side and had dined on turtle steaks.

Johnny Cartwright keeps tugging at my sleeve to share what he refers to as a secret. The secret: Will I take him to see sea lions. Man arrives from Spigot with beer. Johnny and I compromise on the Buffalo Ranch. Tray falls into pool again, drenched father fishes out. Pauline Beck, the upholsterer, calls to say the couch she has recovered is ready.

Trying to gulp hamburger when man drives up, is on wrong road. Terry Cartwright is trying to show me how to work an Alaskan yo-yo when a lady calls to ask if I would write something about Jesse Hayden's upcoming bridge party, a benefit for the hospital and would TLW take a table. Another couple of Girl Scouts, one very tall and one very short, come to sell cookies. While I'm trying to explain to them as how we've got a cupboard full, real estate agent Peggy Taylor calls, wants Katy to see a house. I have hardly hung up when a man calls to know if I'm still in the Ford business (haven't been for over a year). Johnny Cartwright challenges me to race him to the beach. Before we can start the phone rings. A lady is selling subscriptions to this sterling journal. I tell her I am the co-publisher, get copies for free.

Look at watch: 2:15. While I'm wondering whether or not I'll make it through the day, comes a knock on door.

It was Girl Scouts.

One of the joys of living in a small town is strolling the

street and saying hello to friends. Other day I started at Pacific Coast Highway and progressed down the left-hand side of Forest Avenue, said hello to Hal Coward and Bill Draddy in Bank of America, to Miriam Smith and Bea Jack in the real estate office next door, to Roy Marcom, the insurance broker, to Carl Klass in his appliance store. Drifted past the Forest Avenue Market where I stole a grape, Trotter's Bakery, Hayes jewelry shop, Bushard's Pharmacy, Shield's Hardware, spoke to Bud Green a black man in his shoeshine "parlor," waved at the ladies in the Live Wire Cleaners, paused to look at the new suits in John Peter's Men's Store.

In Trotter's I saw a number of familiar characters—Bill Lambourne, Clarence Young, Peg Henry, Melba Dreyer, Ida Trotter—lined up at the soda fountain settling the weighty topics of the day and exchanging the latest gossip.

As I went along I passed the time of day with Charlie Branham, who, I subsequently learned, is leaving Laguna for Palm Springs, for shame. He is one of our finest citizens. We will miss him. A nickel says he'll be back within a year. Had a word with Vic Andrews, who tells me Sammy Wong, the Cantonese chef who owns the Chinese restaurant, is going to have a hernia operation, but intends to wait until the South Coast Community Hospital opens in July.

In the parking lot of Paul Dodd's and Charlie Haskins' Security First National Bank I met America and Ned Griffith, America enmeshed in the latest color of blue. Her blue stockings are particularly fetching. Her "little brown car" is a Rolls Royce.

Promises of New Drugs

If those of us who are considered "over the hill" (past fifty) can hang on a little longer we may be able to attain immortality. The new advances in drugs and surgery promise to lengthen our lives and make them happier.

George R. Stone, general manager of the J.B. Roerig Company, before a meeting of the Pharmaceutics Manufacturers Association, forecasts a "heart disease drug" and a "series of other drugs" by the year 2000. He says they will help cure mental, nerve and other diseases as well as the common cold. He promises by then a cure for cancer and an important breakthrough for arthritis. He did not mention a cure for the common hangover, but that may be in the offing, and along with it a drug to sexually arouse old men—a sort of pepto-gizmo.

Surgeons today are transplanting kidneys and eyes. Early in this century the Vienna surgeons once transplanted monkey glands into elderly men, since then it has become common for surgeons everywhere to transplant human hearts.

All of this portends that mankind is on the verge of a heavenly era. No more ulcers, gout or athlete's foot. The time may not be far away when any part of the human body can be rebuilt, like the Model T Ford, with parts culled from otherwise healthy accident victims. Everyone will be handsome and intelligent and witty and charming and everyone will have good taste and there won't be any poverty.

What I would like first, doctor, if it's all the same to you, is a new brain—a computer that is incapable of prejudice, one that can spell correctly and translate languages; I'd like one that understands modern art, the Kabuki theatre and appreciates rock and roll.

I'd like a computer that will be able to think up fresh ideas for this space, one with a sharp and penetrating outlook on life and mankind of the Mark Twain or Lewis Carroll mold.

Agua Caliente

Many of us Southern Californians had the great good fortune to have known Agua Caliente, the fabulous hotel and gambling resort of the 1920s and early '30s south of Tijuana. It was closed in 1935 by the Mexican government when moralistic President Cardenas outlawed public gambling throughout the land. It was the forerunner of Las Vegas.

An hour and a half drive from Laguna, one approached the hotel through the squalor and dust of odoriferous Tijuana.

It was like passing through Purgatory to Paradise. One arrived at mission-style buildings magnificently landscaped where one was supposed to sleep in the daytime.

No one asked whether or not you were twenty-one or if you were married. Here in this romantic Arabian Nights setting, with its wishing well and swimming pool, its Mariachi music and colored lights, there was no moral code. Here was freedom in a foreign land, far from the scrutiny of neighbors, and the sky was the limit.

It was a magical world. One was intoxicated by the freedom and exhilarated by the atmosphere. One rubbed hips at the "mile-long" bar and gambling tables with movie stars and moneyed moguls. It gave one a feeling of worldliness and irresponsibility.

The food and wine were superb and inexpensive. With the dollar dinner there was a floor show of native talent and dancing to a first-class band. The house often served free highballs, and if you bought one the cost, as I recall, was 25 cents.

There were two gambling rooms—the main casino and the "Gold Room," the latter geared to plungers. There, chips cost a minimum of $25, I watched a movie producer win $15,000 one night, and remember it vividly because I was broke and owed a month's rent ($25).

Another time I went with my sister Elinor and her husband, Bill Webb. As we walked into the main Casino, Bill dropped a silver dollar on the number 32 spot while the wheel was spinning. The number came up and Bill collected $35. We ate and drank that night "on the house."

Caliente was an outgrowth of Prohibition. It was built by Baron Long, who owned the Los Angeles Biltmore Hotel, and was so successful it is said he got his investment back the first year.

Jack Dempsey, the Manassas Mauler, thought to duplicate Caliente's success by building the Hotel del Pacifica in Ensenada, some seventy miles to the south. His big miscalculation was: Americans bent on gambling and transgressing would not drive the extra miles to Ensenada, even if the road had been good, which it wasn't.

The Del Pacifica, a beautiful and costly hotel, lost a ton of money. It stands empty on the beach at Ensenada, a mute symbol of a gamble that didn't pay off.

As for Caliente, the main building is still there and is a school with all of the morality that implies.

Farewell to Jack

Panting Father Time finally caught up with Jack Norworth this week and dispatched him to Saint Peter. One of Laguna's famous, Jack died last week and in celebration of his arrival in Heaven you can bet the angels are clapping their wings and tapping their bare feet on the golden streets. It was fitting that he died at harvest time and I hope he went singing his most famous song, "Take Me Out to the Ball Game."

Many of us go through this life the hard way, but not Jack. "I've always been lucky," he often said. And it's true; he lived an enchanted life. For almost eighty years he milked this world for the best it affords. He had all the fame a man could hope for, never wanted for money, had friends as numerous as a Pope's and good health to the end of his days.

Maybe it was just luck, but he never pressed it; he took things as they came, the good and the bad, and looked at everything through eyes which were always glistening. Fate tried to spoil him, but he remained a vaudevillian. After his first wife and partner, Nora Bayes, died, he suffered the loneliness of bachelorhood. Then one day he asked me: "Do you think I'm too old to get married again?"

There was this lady in Texas, widow of his old friend Bert Swor, also a vaudeville veteran. 'Twas not long before Jack went south and returned with Amy. She had his gay spirit, saw things as he did, that is from the sunny side. He couldn't have found a more delightful companion for his twilight years if he had had his choice from the world's harems.

"Just luck," he said.

But you don't have that kind of luck unless you're that

kind of person. We all agreed the other night at the wake that we had never known a happier, more loving couple.

Jack's father was a prominent doctor in Philadelphia, where Jack was born. Jack knew fame so early it seemed to him something everybody got, like the common cold.

One night, just after he expired, I wandered into his study with Amy. The room was cluttered with memorabilia, souvenirs of hundreds of events. His great miniature collection, autographed photographs, gags, plaques, loving cups, books, newspaper clippings and a copy of his unpublished memoirs. There was his joke file, his correspondence file and his memorandum pad, and a sheaf of letters he intended to answer "mañana."

Delightful Adventure

If you want to spend an unusual holiday go to Stockton, rent a houseboat from Havalark, Inc., and spend a week on the inland waterways of the California Delta. That's what the Victor Andrews, the Larry Reynolds, Katy and I did last week. We had an enchanting time.

So you didn't know there are over seven hundred miles of navigable rivers and channels branching out from the Sacramento and San Joaquin Rivers? Well, neither did I. Nor did I know that for $280 a week one could rent a houseboat which sleeps six and meander through this vast and fascinating area.

The first night we docked at Locke. It is a quaint little town near Walnut Grove which is inhabited primarily by Chinese-Americans, descendants of those who came to California during the gold rush or later as laborers to build the 1,400 miles of levees which hem in the rivers and sloughs hereabouts.

Among those who live in Locke is a man who has managed successfully to circumvent the law governing the sale of firecrackers. He is Chinese and lives in a store-home, one of the old paint-thirsty shacks which line the levee. An elder citizen of these United States, he is supported to an extent by the Social Security system.

But the meager sum he receives each month from that governmental agency is not sufficient to keep him in the style to which he has become accustomed. It covers the essentials all right—food and lodging—but it is not enough to keep him in rice wine or to pay his losses at fan-tan. So he has a business on the side. Every year, proceeding July Fourth, he sells firecrackers.

Where he gets the bangers which make up his stock I don't know and he is not about to tell. Chances are they are made in Macao, that tiny Portuguese colony on the mainland of China south of Canton; and he probably gets them through Mexico, perhaps Tijuana.

He knows that selling firecrackers in the U.S. is against the law, but doesn't know why. In his opinion firecrackers should be accessible to celebrate the birth of this great nation for which he has such fervent devotion.

The reason Ah Mee, which is our hero's name, knows that selling firecrackers is against the law is because the fourth day of every July he gets arrested for selling them and has to pay a fine. The fine never varies. It is $100.

Fortunately, the $100 fine is a deductible expense. Or, if it isn't, he takes it anyway. Otherwise his Social Security would be jeopardized. According to the law, as a Social Security beneficiary he is permitted to earn only $1500 over and above what the benevolent government pays him. So during that one week of the year he sells firecrackers. The rest of the year he fishes the rivers and sloughs thereabouts, basks in the sunshine or plays fan-tan. He does no advertising, but is so well known for his firecrackers that people come from as far away as San Francisco to patronize him. And every year, after compiling a profit of $1600 he closes his store and puts up a sign GONE FISHING.

When the sheriff, a kindly man who puts off arresting Ah Mee until he has made his nest-egg, sees that sign on Ah Mee's front door he descends upon the store and takes the Chinaman into what is commonly referred to as custody. But custody is hardly the word for what happens. Custody means guardianship or imprisonment. But the sheriff and Ah Mee are good friends and in truth they simply take a walk together to the courthouse where Ah Mee pays his fine, shakes hands all around, including the judge's, and then goes back home.

"Of course they're locals—see the high-water marks!"

CHAPTER 20

Know Your Neighbor

Adolph "Papa" Kroch is one of the best known and most successful booksellers in the United States. He is chairman of the board of Kroch's and Brentano's in Chicago, an institution which is to the book business what Marshall Field's is to the department store business. Since Papa retired to Laguna six years ago, his son Carl is the company's active head.

Known to everyone as Papa, Adolph Kroch could have been the prototype of that cartoon character, Foxy Grandpa. And in character he is not unlike Foxy, which is to say he is extremely astute, wise, kind and generous. Hale and hardy at seventy-seven, he is a perfect example of the uselessness of physical exercise. He has confined his calisthenics to sitting in chairs and reading books, and probably has read as many books as any man alive.

Books fascinated him from childhood, and he began collecting them at an early age; they have remained his hobby as well as his means of livelihood. Born in Austria, Adolph lost his mother shortly thereafter. When he was nineteen he and his banker father had a disagreement and, as a result Adolph sold his precious library and set sail for the "land of opportunity," the U.S.A.

In that day it was necessary, before being admitted to this country, that an immigrant have at least fifty dollars—proof that he would not become a public charge. Before reaching Ellis Island, one of Adolph's fellow passengers asked him for a loan of fifty dollars "just until I can get through immigration." Wonderfully naive and always the humanitarian, Adolph loaned the man the money, though he had precious little to spare. He never saw the man nor his money again.

With what little resources he had left, Adolph bought a railroad ticket to Chicago, where he expected to find an uncle; but when he reached the mid-west metropolis he learned to his acute disappointment that his relative had moved to New York.

Unable to speak English, the young man sought employment at a German-owned bookstore. He did not get a job, but the proprietor told him to keep in touch, that if there was an opening he could have it.

From the want-ad section of a newspaper, Adolph learned that a bookkeeper was wanted in Milwaukee, the population of which was largely German, and thither he went. He was not certain what a bookkeeper did exactly, but felt sure that if the job had to do with books he could perform it satisfactorily.

The job proved to be in a sash and door factory. Upon learning that Adolph could not speak English, the proprietor set him to work, not on the firm's books, but as a helper in the factory. Here he labored for several months—until the Chicago bookseller, whom he pestered, wrote that there was an opening for him in his store.

The store was run in a very old fashioned, ultra-conservative way, and whenever Adolph made a merchandising suggestion the owner would tell him in effect to mind his own business. Adolph did just that. And when he had saved a few dollars he opened a store of his own—a very small place on a side street. In time he bought out the book seller who had told him to mind his own business.

Adolph minded his business so well that, though bookstores are notorious for financial failure, his became profitable and he became a dominant figure in the book industry.

In the 1930s, during the Great Depression, the Brentano bookstore chain, with stores in New York, Philadelphia and Chicago, fell into financial trouble, and Papa was engaged to bail them out. That he did so with a spectacular performance is a bright chapter in the history of the book business.

Papa has advised many of the principal figures of his era on the acquisition of rare books. He has known most of the important authors of the last half century and has helped many of them to best-sellerdom. He gave Irving Stone, the biographical novelist, his first big boost. On his way to Europe to buy rare books for his clientele, Kroch read Stone's "Lust For Life" and was so enthused about it he wired the publisher an order for one thousand copies—an unprecedented order for a book by an unknown author. The book, a novel based on the life of Vincent Van Gogh, became a best-seller and since then Irving Stone's name has become known throughout the world.

Since Papa Kroch has come to Laguna he has continued to help promote books which he thinks have merit. Publishers still flood him with their output, seeking his opinion. It seems that all that is necessary for a book to get on the best-seller list is for Papa Kroch to put his stamp of approval on it.

The Literature Epoch in Paris

The following little essay can be considered an unpaid-for advertisement. A new book by your faithful correspondent—me—has just been published. It is entitled *Young Man in Paris* and is about my experiences as a fledgling newsman while working for the *Paris Herald* during the late 1920s and early '30s. It has been published by Academy Chicago and sells for $14.95.

The publisher thinks it's going to be a BS (best-seller) and that in time an autographed copy of the first edition will be valuable. Moreover, according to my friend John Huston, who read the manuscript, it is "utterly fascinating."

Paris between the wars was a dazzling gathering place of writers, painters, musicians, publishers and just about anyone interested in the arts. James Joyce was there, F. Scott Fitzgerald, Ernest Hemingway, Ezra Pound, Eugene O'Neill, Ford Madox Ford, Elliot Paul, Sinclair Lewis, Andre Gide, Jules Romains, Gertrude Stein, Paul Claudel and of course Pablo Picasso and musicians Darius Milhaud and George Auric. It was, as Huston, who was also there, says, the most extraordinary cast ever assembled on that wonderful stage.

To whet your intellectual appetite, I quote from the book's opening pages:

> During the 1920s, I and other aspiring young writers were strongly influenced by Ernest Hemingway's *The Sun Also Rises.* We thought that wandering through Europe living on free love and wine—what could be a more perfect existence? The American intelligentsia had taken the position that the United States was a tasteless, materialistic, boorish country where artistic endeavor was stifled. Sophisticated people went abroad or had been abroad or were going abroad; debutantes were being 'received' by the Queen of England, rich American mothers and widows were looking for titled sons-in-law or husbands.... Everyone who was anyone was going to Europe.

Henry Stansbury and I both worked as cub reporters on the *New York American* and shared a small basement apartment on West Ninth Street, just off Fifth Avenue. We were both twenty-one and had been working on the *American* for a year. We were ready to go to Europe and work on novels. We also thought that with a year's experience we were ready to become foreign correspondents. Hank's father was the head of Hearst's International News Service in Europe. His office was in London. We thought if we needed them he would give us jobs.

We made plans to sail on a Belgian freighter bound for Antwerp. The day before we left, Charles Lindbergh announced he was going to enter the great air race. A wealthy Franco-American hotel owner named Raymond B. Ortiz had offered a prize of $25,000 for the first non-stop flight from New York to Paris. I had been covering this race. The weather had been unsettled that spring. Admiral Richard D. Byrd and his crew with one plane and Clarence Chamberlain and Bert Acosta with another were at Roosevelt Field on Long Island waiting for the weather to clear so that they could take off. When Lindbergh, a tall, skinny guy whom nobody had ever heard of, flew in from

Saint Louis and announced he intended to fly alone everybody thought he had lost his marbles. He was still there when Hank and I set off on the freighter.

Halfway across the Atlantic our captain received a wireless message to all-the-ships-at-sea saying that Lindbergh had taken off in an attempt to fly to Paris by the Great Circle route, asking all along his course to watch for his plane. Thereafter for several days we spent a lot of time craning our necks and looking at the sky.

I had covered Lindbergh's arrival in New York from Saint Louis and, as it turned out, would be with him many times thereafter. Somehow I got caught up in his tailwind.

Almost everyone yearns for fame. It is one of man's secret hungers. While most of us can satisfy our appetites for food and coition, fame is tantalizingly elusive and unpredictable.

It descended upon Lindbergh the moment he landed at Le Bourget Airport. Instantly he became the most famous man in the world. Indeed, in all of history no one had been so acclaimed. He had expected publicity but did not realize that fame grants her favors nymphomaniacally. He suddenly found himself in a different world, a world of renown. He hated it.

Hank's father, head of International News Service, hired Hank and me to "cover" the *Lone Eagle.* Lindbergh had become a guest of U.S. Ambassador Myron Herrik at the American Embassy. It was our job to report everything he said, what he ate, how he liked his eggs, what he put in his coffee (one spoonful of sugar). Most of what he said was trivial, but I dutifully wrote it all down. Overnight he had become a legend, as well known as Napoleon.

I stayed with him until he left for New York. The next time I was swept up in his draft was while he was courting Anne Morrow, the girl he married. I had returned to New York and was working on *The World.*

The Morrow family lived in New Jersey and I, along with as many as twenty reporters and photographers, were at their gate every day for a month during Lindbergh's courtship and were there when the marriage took place.

Then when their child was kidnapped and killed I was assigned to the story and reported it for weeks. I was even assigned to the Richard Hauptmann trial. It was as if I were born to follow the *Lone Eagle.* It was a job I did not relish.

He abhored publicity.

Keeping Up with the World

Did arise and go out into the rain to fetch the daily newspaper and did cogitate the miracle that every morning it is on our walkway at 6:30, usually in a plastic envelop so that the rain or the sprinkler system won't douse it. In its many pages is all the news of the previous day, including reports of sports events which might not have ended until just before midnight.

How all this gobbledygook gets from typewriters, computers and presses to our house so early in the morning is a miracle. It not only has to be collected, written, edited and pressed, it has to come by truck to Laguna, dumped, picked up, folded, placed in plastic bags or string-tied, driven more miles and dropped at hundreds of thousands of houses.

Did think, as water dripped from my nose, that daily newspapers are an amazing institution. They are all connected by wire systems—the Associated Press, the United Press-International and their correspondents and stringers around the world. The news from everywhere is funneled into their offices as the events happen. The stories are then edited, evaluated and positioned in the various sections.

Did wipe off dripping face and take paper to the breakfast table. Did give Katy the first section and chose sports. This is customary. She is more interested in international, national and local news.

Did come to the conclusion that sports writers have improved considerably in my time. Today they write more imaginatively and poetically than they did when I went to work as a cub reporter on the *New York American* in 1926. Today they puff up pieces, sometimes several columns long, about athletes, fishermen, jockeys and horses, these to fill up the blank spaces between the advertising.

Did wonder what the sports sections of today's newspapers did for advertising before computers came along. I remember cigarettes and liquor, but these have become taboo.

Did spend the usual hour and a half at breakfast table sipping tea and perusing. TLW reads more quickly than I. Her favorite part, after the front page, is the women's section. It covers news of arts, "society," dressmakers and designers and advertises ladies attire. It also has Dear Abby's column. I don't read Abby as religiously as Katy does, but sometimes she is very funny and Katy brightens my day by reading one of her items to me.

Next to sports and business, my favorite part of the paper is the want-ad section. There can be found a collection of stories. This morning did read under "personal message" the following:

"David, I understand why you left me. I love you, Alice." That's all. No phone number, no address. Wonder how many Davids and Alices there are.

Another caught my fancy: "Anyone having knowledge of the estate of the late Joseph George Isaacs Sr., directly concerning his son, Ronald, please correspond to Gene Sandayo, POB 211, Youngstown, N.Y. 14174. Discretion and consideration upheld."

I don't know what "consideration upheld" means, but thought I'd write Mr. Sandayo and ask. It's a good beginning for a novel.

You want to get a divorce? Go into bankruptcy? Are you being evicted? Listed in the ads are people who will help you. There are ads for surrogate mothers but none for surrogate fathers. One cheerful person bought a one-line ad which probably cost about $7.50 to say, "Have a nice day, Charlie."

A Metamorphosis

A discerning lady, who lives in Blue Jay, California, called to criticise me recently for writing so much about myself. She said she and her mother had counted thirty-seven first person singular pronouns in one of my pieces.

Today for her sake I am going to be objective.

This story has to do with Katy Johnson, her husband Stan and a young lady who used to work for them as a children's nurse. Katy is David Iredell's half-sister (they had the same extraordinary mother, different fathers) and Stan is the well-known film editor. They live in Laguna and, indeed, have just built a fantastic house overlooking Bluebird Canyon.

A couple of years ago the Johnsons and their three children were in Germany, where Stan was engaged in film work. There they hired a young German girl, Karola, to take care of their children, to teach them German and to help generally around the house.

Karola turned out to be a twenty-one carat jewel. Such a delightful person is she that, when the Johnsons returned to the United States, they brought her with them.

"We had to go through a lot of red tape," Katy says, "but it was worth it."

That was two years ago. Karola was twenty-one. As far as looks go she was plump and slightly frumpy in the stereotypical German peasant mold. But from the moment she reached America she started to change. It was truly magic. She took to American mores and customs as a duck does to corn. While teaching the Johnson children to speak German, she learned English from them and was soon speaking like a native Californian.

Whereas in Germany she had not paid much attention to her appearance, she suddenly began to take pride in it. She dieted, or rather she just stopped eating so much bread and potatoes. The result was that she slimmed down to a stunning figure. She quickly learned to dress in the American manner and how to take care of her hair. She learned the art of make-up (to use less instead of more), the correct posture, how to care for her nails—so that, all of a sudden, she became a beauty.

As Katy Johnson says, "I never saw such a transformation in my life. It was like a movie." She watched all of this with some misgivings, because she could foresee that it wouldn't be long before some ardent swain on a white horse would come by and carry Karola away. She kept her at home for the most part, but eventually had to give her a vacation. To do that she enlisted the help of her brother, Bill Fassett, who operates the famous Nepenthe Restaurant at Big Sur. She sent Karola to be with him and his wife. They would return her to Laguna.

That was the latter part of August.

Alas, the best laid plans ... Karola had not been at Nepenthe an hour, I understand, when it happened. One of the young men at the bar came over to where she was standing at the fireplace and asked if she would honor him with a dance. And from that moment, although they did not know it, the Johnsons were in need of a nurse.

The young man, it turned out, is in the insurance business in Portland and is very successful. Success in the insurance business, I believe, is based to an extent upon persistence, and this the young gentleman, it appears, has in abundance. After a few days, when Karola returned to Laguna, he wrote, telegraphed and telephoned her at least twice a day.

"He never let her out of his mind," Katy Johnson says wistfully.

Stan gave the bride away October tenth, thus ending a whirlwind courtship. But the denouement came as Katy, on her knees helping Karola into her wedding dress, accidentally caught one of the bride's elbows in an eye. Arriving at the church she had an uncomely shiner.

"Believe me, it wasn't hard to cry a little," Katy said. "Sure hate to lose that girl."

"They ought to change the sign to 'Home of the Festival of Potholes'!"

CHAPTER 21

Shipwreck

An expression often misused, usually having to do with someone who wins a large sum of money from a lottery or a slot machine, is: "It's a dream come true."

Dream is the wrong word. Dreams are almost always full of anguish and torment. You are in danger, are trying to escape; every step you take, you somehow slip back two. You're falling out of an airplane or having to jump from a burning building.

I spent what seemed to me a good part of last night in a shipwreck. It is a recurring nightmare and almost always the replica of an experience Katy and I had off the coast of Japan in 1961.

We set out from Los Angeles late in January on a Danish freighter with friends June and Victor Andrews. The night we left it was cold and raining and the weather didn't get any better for two and a half weeks. Crossing the Pacific, we went through eye after eye of storm after storm. The waves were so mountainous that the ship's captain frequently had to slow the vessel to five knots from the cruising fifteen. Because of this we were days late approaching Japan.

The morning of the sixteenth day, the weather for the first time began to clear and in the afternoon we caught glimpses of blue sky, enough now and then to make a pair of the proverbial wide-beamed Dutchman's breeches. By four o'clock as it was going down the glorious sun broke through the clouds, brilliantly highlighting the purple, jagged skyline of Japan. After it set, a dark night took over and the cold wind increased.

When the ship's clock struck four bells signaling six

o'clock, the Andrews and we, the only passengers aboard, gathered as usual with several of the ship's officers for dinner. It was always a gay time. Lightheartedly jesting, we had progressed through the soup and fish courses when we were startlingly surprised by a short blast of the ship's whistle. This signal was followed by two, more distant blasts.

Although we in the dining salon did not know it, our ship and another were on collision course. But we knew something important was happening and stopped eating to listen expectantly. Suddenly the ship shuddered and there was a horrendous sound of crunching steel. Almost immediately the throb of engines ceased and the lights went out. What had happened, we were to learn, was that the prow of the other freighter had peeled our ship open as if it were a can of sardines and tons of water were flooding the engine room.

Within seconds came the piercing, chilling sounds of mouth-blown whistles and men's frantically shouting voices.

We passengers groped our ways through the darkness to our cabins to get life-jackets. By the time we got on deck there was intense activity. Crewmen carrying flashlights were running along the main deck. Katy and I had been assigned a lifeboat on the starboard side but we quickly learned that the two there had been sheared away. Already the ship was listing badly. Victor and I joined crewmen in an attempt to launch one of the port-side lifeboats, but although there were twelve or fourteen of us leaning into the task with everything we had, we were unable to do so.

Flares whistled upward through the cold wind and exploded overhead, then drifted down, glowing like giant fireflies and suffusing the night's blackness with a pink sheen. By now the stricken ship was listing so it was difficult to stand. The captain came by and took me aside to whisper, "It's hopeless. Abandon ship."

At first I did not get the full import of the message. Abandon ship? How? What should we do? When the horrible meaning penetrated I thought of the film I had shot. All marvelous footage of storms I had photographed, all wrapped for mailing.

Katy, clinging to a railing begged, "Don't leave me!"

"The film! I've got to get it! Be right back." As I entered the superstructure I heard the terrifying tumbling of furniture, glassware, bottles, dishes and cargo. A chair had fallen against our stateroom door, but I managed to force my way in and crawl on my hands and knees to reach the built-in desk. The film and a packet of letters to be mailed were in a drawer. I stuffed the letters into an overcoat pocket and spent precious moments trying to force the package of film into the pocket on the other side. The untied life jacket kept getting in the way and the package proved too large, so I tucked it under an arm, frantically found a camera in its case and slid back to the door. Groping through the darkness, one foot treading the deck, the other the superstructure, I saw in the faint light of the still-burning flares Katy and the chief steward's wife hanging onto the ship's railing directly above me. I put the camera between my feet and the package of film between my thighs and braced myself.

"Katy!" I cried. "The ship's sinking! We've got to leave! Let go!"

The two women dropped simultaneously. I attempted to break their fall but their weights upset me and the three of us collapsed in a heap under the stairway. Camera and film went askew. By now the ship's stern was under water and the bow was rising. As we scrambled, trying to get to our feet, it seemed that we were about to be engulfed by a gigantic wave; actually the ship was on her way down. I gave Katy a push to help her clear the stairway, then grasped Mrs. Simonsen's hand, but the water closed over us and she was wrenched away. In the split second before the sea swallowed me I took a deep breath, all I could inhale, well aware it might be my last.

During the first of those watery moments I swam furiously, flailing and kicking, impeded by the soaked overcoat; but it soon became evident that I was making little progress and that my chances of survival were decreasing with every stroke.

Suddenly something uncommon occurred; it was as if a spring in me had snapped. The cold water had something to do with it. Euphoria set in. Chest pains and ear pains ceased. I felt exalted. I was not floundering in water; I was afloat in rarefied air. One moment I had been clinging maniacally to life and in a split second was welcoming death as a long-sought friend.

I thought that man goes through life concerned with oncoming time, and suddenly it occurred to me that I had no future. Whatever happened thenceforth was no concern of mine. Like chalk hieroglyphics on a blackboard, all of my obligations and responsibilities were being wiped away; intentions and aspirations were being sucked down a drain. It was a glorious feeling. I was truly free. My only regret in bidding the world goodbye was that I would not have the joy of being with Katy. My core shrank at the thought she might be drowning too. I prayed for her deliverance....

Obviously we managed to survive or I wouldn't be here complaining about the misuse of the word "dream." Surely my shipwreck dream is not an experience anyone would want to relive.

Politics, 1963

Dear Mr.Goldwater,

I have at times admired you, sir, for several reasons:

For one thing, brought up a rich man's son, you did not become a playboy, but instead, like John F. Kennedy and Nelson Rockefeller, turned your hand to the public's welfare.

You have been astute enough to hire a good writer to express your ideas in a newspaper column. The fact that these ideas are sometimes lacking in balanced judgment has at times shaken my faith; for example they have all been willy-nilly against the Kennedy administration's policies, whether those policies are good or bad. This is typical of a two-party system. It seems to me that, if you would temper the steel with a little heat-absorbing alloy, your sword would be less dull.

I have admired your promptness in speaking out on any subject. Apparently the finger has been put on you, meaning you seem to have been touched by the hand of God, making you the spokesman for that respectable group at the far right.

This is not an easy role to play—this canine-like part which calls for yapping at the heels of those in authority in the hope that you can undermine them. But you have performed it well and loudly, if without feeling, and I went along admiring you for your tenacity.

The other day, Mr. G., you lost me as an admirer. When you publicly proclaimed that we should be willing to take the chance of war over Cuba I could hardly believe my ears. How, I asked myself frantically, could a candidate for President be so lacking in judgment?

Just what is there about Cuba and Castroism that you believe is worth one soldier's pint of blood? We are aware, of course, that Castro is a communist and that his administration is communistic. But do you believe it is worth a war to be rid of him?

Might it not be more reasonable, rational and far less costly by several billion bucks to let that character cut his own throat?

It seems to my simple mind, Mr. G., that (1) Castro is not doing us harm by not selling us sugar; (2) the potential harm he might do us is relatively small; and (3) in all likelihood he will hang himself if given the rope.

Is it not possible, sir, that we have a precious opportunity here to show communism up for what it is, i.e., an unnatural, inhuman and unworkable theory, one that, as practiced in Russia and Cuba presently, won't work?

In fact, going in and slaying Castro now would tend to make of him a martyr throughout Latin America and would do more to perpetuate him and his communism than anything I can think of. But if we leave him alone the chances are overwhelmingly great that his form of government will die of its ineptitude and he will go with it.

Mass Hysteria

If you are looking for a new and profitable business to go into, I suggest you start a mob supply agency. By this I mean a sort of Central Casting Office to furnish crowds for those who need them—politicians f'rinstance.

Your principal part-time employees would be teenage corybantics and ladies and gentlemen who like to be seen on television.

Say Senator Goldwater is coming to town and calls you on the telephone: "I need ten thousand assorted hero-worshippers to meet me at the airport. How much will they cost me? Now, go easy. Remember, I am a conservative."

"Oh," you'll reassure him, "for you, Senator, we'll make a special price. How about three dollars a head."

"That's an awful lot."

"Our usual price is five dollars, Senator. But you're so popular it'll be easy to trot them out. For another buck we can have them wearing Goldwater ribbons."

"I want them all to holler, 'We want Barry' when I step off the plane."

"We usually charge extra for hollering."

"Our budget can't stand any more than three bucks."

"Okay, we'll throw it in then."

"What about a band?"

"We can give you a good one of thirty pieces for two thousand—and in uniform to boot."

"How much would twenty cost?—and the hell with the uniforms. All I want them to play is the National Anthem and our campaign song."

"What's that, Senator?"

"We want Barry!"

"They'll have to learn it. I'm afraid that'll be a little more. The unions, you know."

"You're damn right I know unions; and I aim to curb them once I'm elected."

"To play the campaign song the band'll have to have another five hundred."

"Well, I don't want them unless they play We want Barry!"

"Send me the sheet music; I'll see they play it—and for only three hundred."

"Very well. So we'll have ten thousand hero-worshippers and a 20-piece band."

"How do you want the mob?—Young, old? Men? Women?"

"Mix 'em up. But get lots of pretty girls. The photographers love 'em."

"Yes, sir."

"Well, I guess that's it."

"I'll need a check in advance, Senator."

"Why? Don't you trust me?"

"It's not me, Senator. It's the mob. They'll want their money as soon as they show up."

"Seen the ca...?"

CHAPTER 22

The Male Menopause, February 28, 1963

The distinguished opinion analyst, Elmo Roper, was in Laguna Beach recently. He had flown from New York to lecture in Beverly Hills and came to Laguna for a reunion with members of his family and because he wanted to reevaluate the community as a place to live. He probably couldn't have chosen a more biased person to ask about the town and I filled him full of the old smaltz.

Elmo is about to cut himself free from the market and opinion sampling firm which bears his name, and he and his wife Dorothy are considering what they should do with the rest of their lives.

This is a door through which every man must pass if he lives long enough, and it opens to the most difficult period of his life. It is the male change of life.

Passing through this portal a man ceases to pursue that which has motivated him for many years. All his life he has struggled toward a goal, one which would give him and his family financial independence and gain him a place of respect in society. Now the need to attain these ambitions no longer exists.

Perhaps his performance has been good, as in Elmo's case. He has fulfilled himself and accomplished all he set out to do. The time has come to settle for the status quo, whatever that might be. The play is over. The curtain is about to fall.

As a rule, this is not a problem women have to face. Indeed, women can only sense it in their husbands, and they are often puzzled because men obviously have a difficult time adjusting to it.

"Dorothy can't see why I just don't shrug, turn my back and walk in another direction," Elmo told me.

It is not that easy. The struggle to attain fame and fortune keeps a man on his toes. Competition in the world of men is intense, and quite different from what it is among women. Don't show any weakness or the competition may jump on you like a pack of jackals.

When suddenly a man finds he doesn't have to live intensely any more, that he can relax his guard and ignore responsibility, it's bewildering. All of a sudden he has to face the fact that he has passed his prime. It can be humiliating.

By prodigious hard work and self discipline Elmo has attained a high place in our society. He is on the boards of twenty organizations, some of them highly important to the welfare of our country. His business, built up over the years, is thriving under his son's management, and Elmo feels that he should step out of it.

What to do? "I don't want to retrogress," he said, speaking of a fear every man feels who comes to the "retirement" door.

Elmo and Dorothy live in Connecticut and plan to keep their house there, but they are looking for a place to go for the winter months.

"I want to come to Laguna or the desert," Elmo says. "But Dorothy wants to take a place on an island in the Bahamas."

That problem will be resolved. But it isn't the important one. What's important is—what is he going to do when he gets there?

Travel? "Yes," he says, "but I tire of it. I can be happy in one place."

Fortunately he is a talented writer and lecturer and doubtless will keep up these activities. But what he really needs, as do most men who retire, is to find a charitable goal toward which to work and thereby keep from going to seed.

I suggested he take up lawn bowling and he laughed.

Musical Note

All my life I have yearned to be the life of the party, to speak to the waiter in French, to be admired by my fellow man. As a boy I answered every advertisement which promised to improve me in any way. One was a tonic calculated to hasten my manhood called Dr. Willoughby's Tasty Elixir.

I took a memory course which had something (I can't recall what) to do with Mr. Addison Sims of Seattle, and sent away for a copy of Emily Post's book of etiquette so that I could learn what was wrong with a guy walking down the street with a pretty girl on either arm. I subscribed to a mail order to build muscle and bought a set of books which, when read for fifteen minutes a day, was guaranteed to give me a college education.

Out of all this endeavor, I am sorry to report, nothing noticeable came.

One of the things I was told—I forget by whom—was to take stock of myself and recognize my weaknesses. So I looked in the mirror and there was the same skinny, clumsy, awkward, self-conscious, lantern-jawed nincompoop. Far from having made any improvement, I seemed to have become dumber than ever, besides which a batch of pimples had broken out on my face.

What I needed, I decided, was some identifying symbol, some accouterment which would immediately establish me as a man to be reckoned with. It was about that time that I came across an advertisement which read: THEY LAUGHED WHEN I OFFERED TO PLAY THE SAXOPHONE. It seemed to me a direct message from Heaven.

Identifying myself with the hero of this advertisement, I envisioned the consternation of Amy Ames (the prettiest girl in town) when I suddenly whipped out a horn and played "Love for Sale." She'd be putty in my hands.

I sent away for the saxophone, but its cost proved to be more than I could afford, so I settled for a bugle. This proved to be a mistake on two counts: 1) Mother forbid me practicing in the house and 2) a neighbor, Mr. Herzog, came over one Sunday morning while I was blowing in the backyard and gave me a dollar to cease and desist. Those were the words he used—cease and desist.

This rejection of my artistic aptitude may have been the cause of my inferiority complex. I became convinced I had no musical talent. The only thing I learned to play was reveille, which is French for get the hell out of bed, and ever since then I have been shy about tooting the horn. Thus, for lo these many years I have been a frustrated musician.

Painfully aware of my musical yearning Katy recently gave me a guitar for a birthday present. If she had bestowed upon me an honorary Lit.B., she couldn't have pleased me more.

It is a beautiful instrument with six strings and a whole slew of frets. I haven't the faintest notion how to tune it, but when I plunk all the strings at one time it sounds remarkably like music.

The book of instruction was written in such an obfuscating way that I can't understand it, so I bought one of Segovia's records (he's the world's leading guitarist) thinking that might help, but this has only added to my disconcert.

All I've learned to play so far is "Hand me down that gin, son, 'fore I tan your hide" on one string.

I'm sure I could have done better with a ukulele.

Reader's Digest, June 28, 1966

Recently in this space I wrote of the *Reader's Digest* and the column somehow found its way to Pleasantville, New York, where the offices of that profuse publication are located. I have a letter from Mr. Willard R. Espy, one of the editors to wit:

"We enjoyed your May 17 column in the *Laguna Beach Post*.

"I have a suggestion: Why don't you try to develop one of the article's topics (such as 'Will We Ever Get to Pluto, and If So, Why?') and send to us. It might be just what we are looking for."

Thus encouraged, I forthwith knitted my brow. The first thing that occurred to me was that there's nothing I know less about than the planet Pluto; it therefore seemed a fit subject for my somewhat florid style. To tell the honest truth, which is so much franker than the ordinary truth, I didn't even know where in the scheme of things Pluto is. But turning to the encyclopedia, from which I crib much of my material, I located it between Pliny the Younger and Pocatello, a city of southeastern Idaho—slightly closer to Pliny than Pocatello.

According to the encyclopedia, Pluto is the outermost known member of our planetary system. It requires two hundred and forty-eight years to make one complete circuit of its path, which means that it moves very slowly, doubtless thereby giving all Plutoneans a good view of the passing scenery. Its diameter is estimated at about one-half and its mass at about one-tenth the size of the earth. Its orbital plane is inclined about seventeen degrees, which keeps it from intersecting Neptune, its closest neighbor. You can imagine what would happen if they collided. The effect would be felt through all the planets, and our north pole might move down to the Tropic of Cancer.

While I was thus thinking about it, I looked up my horoscope and found that I have Pluto descending, which, an astrological book tells me, explains my ignorance, lack of imagination and perversity.

So much for Pluto's size, location and my horoscope. Now the question is: Will man ever reach it?

I don't think there is any doubt that he will—if he can survive an atom bomb he will find a way to visit a planet, and if he visits one he's going to want to visit them all. He is like that.

When man does go to Pluto he'd better be well suited, because that planet is said to be plenty cold—probably about minus two hundred degrees Centigrade, according to the book. It doesn't say what our intrepid brother will find there, but somewhere in outer space is the answer to what life's all about, and it could be on Pluto as well as anywhere. He may find out why we're here and where we're going, perhaps even where we came from.

What man will do with the knowledge I don't precisely know. Considering his curious, creative character, he will want to produce a universe of his own. Bridey Murphy or no Bridey Murphy, I wouldn't want to be around when he makes the mock-up.

I hope that on Pluto there is a law that no man's name may start with an initial (J. Willoughby Blasengame, for example), not even if he's a preacher. And I hope that there are no titles, such as doctor, just because one has studied the body or earned a Ph.D.

I hope all honors and titles are out. I hope that if one is talented or generous or otherwise distinguished from his fellows, it doesn't call for pinning a medal on him. Pluto is so small it is likely everyone knows everyone else, and I hope they've learned long ago that no man is without some virtue and failing.

I hope the wearing of lapel buttons is forbidden.

I believe that on Pluto there is only one religion, that it is linked to love and divisible by two.

Another riddle I hope our friend finds answered on Pluto is where grunion learn about the tides on earth (so they can lay their eggs in the sand at high tides).

According to the book it's pretty dark out there where Pluto is, so there may be no way of knowing whether a person is light or dark, black or white. That might eliminate racism.

CHAPTER 23

Lagunans Proposed to Help Mr. Richard Nixon, Dec. 1968

Along with several early Christmas cards and some junk mail, I received a letter yesterday from President-elect Nixon. He wants my help. Apparently I am not the only one to whom he has made a petition. Doubtless a copy of the letter was sent to everyone who is listed in a biographical book entitled "Who's Who."

"You, as a leader," the letter said, thereby elevating my spirits, "are in a position to know and recommend exceptional individuals ... men and women who by their qualities of youthfulness, judgment, intelligence and creativity can make significant contributions to our country."

I was delighted to hear from our upcoming President. The last time I communicated with him was here in Laguna. He was staying at Lillian and Harry Willats' Riviera Hotel. It was shortly after he had been chosen General Eisenhower's running-mate. We talked mostly about the weather, which was good, and how much he has always loved Laguna.

When he wrote the letter to me Mr. Nixon probably was not aware that I did not attend the recent $100-a-plate dinner to raise funds for his campaign at Anaheim Convention Center. I had been invited but pretended to have another engagement. When I first read the letter I had a heady feeling that at last my talents had been recognized and that it was I who was being summoned to Washington—perhaps to run the Post Office department about which I have a strong belief that it can be operated at a profit.

But the letter was not drafted to enlist me in the affairs of

"Something near the beach, but not too fancy; with a view, but not too high; nice, but not expensive. As near as I can figure, what you want are three houses."

State; rather it was to request that I suggest people who might so serve. Applications were included and I had no hesitancy in making a first choice.

It so happens our community is deep in the kind of talent that the President-elect is seeking. Few communities our size can boast of a per-capita talent pool such as we possess. And my first recommendation to Mr. Nixon is that he find a place in his administration for the man who managed his campaign in Orange County, Victor C. Andrews. Through Mr. Andrews' effort, Orange County gave the President-elect the greatest proportion of votes of any county in the nation.

Mr. Andrews is of cabinet stature. What he has done from the kindness of his heart for the public weal has been nothing short of Herculean. I'm sure Mr. Nixon knows of Mr. Andrews' virtues, but just on the chance no one has pointed them out to him, I feel I should. Mr. President-elect, you could go far and not find a better man. Inasmuch as you may have already chosen your Cabinet I suggest that you appoint Mr. Andrews ambassador to Lebanon, the land of his ancestors, and I hereby apply for the job as his secretary. Love that Lebanon.

Another person from our community I recommend to the nation's new leader is Roy Childs. Roy has more savvy and integrity and balance than almost anyone I know. His civic generosity is well known. And he would keep the Nixon administration on an even keel with his marvelous humor, an ingredient that is always in short supply in Washington.

Dr. Vincent Carroll, Harry Lawrence, Bob Peacock—they would all acquit themselves well at whatever assigned. Dr. Norman Nixon (no relation) would be a fine asset to any administration. Ditto Carl Miller, Don Teetor and John Lawson. For ladies: Muriel Reynolds and Dibbie Teetor are outstanding examples of creative administrative talents.

Some of those I have mentioned might be precluded because of their politics, but all are vital people of good judgment, young in spirit and eminently capable. Call me, Dick, and I'll give you their 'phone numbers.

Christmas Curmudgeon

Every December I begin to get my annual depression. The reason is I'm going to have to fork over a bunch of kale to purchase presents for a number of people, mostly young. I detest spending money and time to select gifts they may not like. This year I took a look at my psyche and discovered that I am parsimonious. Stingy is a better word. I'm a miser, a skinflint, a tightwad. I don't like to spend money for anything except food and drink.

Penury is a disease, like alcoholism, and I seem to have been born with it. Friends call me a curmudgeon. Perhaps it comes from my childhood. Born into a family that was purse-poor, I learned the value of a penny. The Civil War had left my great-grandparents all but destitute; their plantation, silver and slaves were gone and nothing trickled down to us.

Today though, I'm fairly well-to-do and, in other respects than stingy, a nice fellow. Still don't like to turn on the air conditioner, even when it is uncomfortably warm or shiveringly cold. I am a turner off of lights and a saver of paper, string and rubber bands. Christmas is a holiday that should bring out the best in me; instead it brings out the Scrooge.

Money is funny and people handle it in different ways. Some are misers, some are spendthrifts and there are many opposite variations. Generosity and penury are characteristics. Some use money to buy friendship, love, applause, respect and esteem. Some save it to leave to their children, and when the children get it they often squander it.

I know an extremely wealthy lady and, like me, a scrimper. She hates to let go a nickel. Even the pennies interest her. The classical phrase for her is "Penny wise and pound foolish." She gives money to charities (to keep it from going to Uncle Sam) and is generous to her children, but she doesn't like to buy anything unless it's a bargain. If it's a bargain she can't resist buying it whether she needs the thing or not. Her house is full of stuff she bought cheap and has no use for.

I know a wealthy man who is generous to relatives and

charities (all write-off-able) but suffers aches and pains when he has to shell out any of his spondulick to Uncle Sam. The IRS is his bête noir.

It pleases me that I am not alone in my penury. There are others, maybe some even worse. I hope so. In fact, the disease of penury might be widespread, though according to the ancients, hoarding money is not profitable. I've been reading *The History of the Decline and Fall of the Roman Empire* by Edward Gibbon, and came upon the epitaph of Edward Courtney, Earl of Devonshire. Inasmuch as it is apropos I quote it:

What we gave, we have;
What we spent, we had;
What we left, we lost.

Maybe this Christmas I'll turn over a new leaf and spend cheerfully.

Pressures

How do you react to the pressures which life foists upon you? Some habitually bite their nails. Others have a tic. We all know people who crack their knuckles. I know a woman who talks all the time. Another woman continually redecorates her home. I also know a man who is addicted to lawn bowling.

A psychiatrist tells me insecurity is at the bottom of many quirks. Sometimes it is a lack of money, sometimes ill health. I know a man who worries about earthquakes. Earthquake insurance is expensive, so he hasn't any on his house and spends a lot of time worrying about it collapsing.

Loneliness perhaps is the most poignant insecurity of all. A woman I know has a pet chicken—Plymouth Rock hen—which follows her everywhere. Dad-blasted union I ever saw—that clucking hen following that lonely old lady around. Believe it or don't, the hen is housebroken and understands, or seems to anyway, what the woman says to her. They carry on long conversations, the hen holding up her end with a series of "Cawrrrr, cawrrrr clucks." And such affection this widow showers on that chicken! The lady's husband has been dead several years, and judging by the way she reveres his memory he must have been quite a guy. She has conversations with his spirit from time to time. They go like this:

"Joe," she will say, "you've got to advise me, tell me what to do. Should I go visit Cousin Gertrude in Colorado or shouldn't I?"

And if she wants to go to Colorado, Joe will say, "Take thy chicken in thy basket and go on back to see your Cousin Gertrude," and if she doesn't want to go Joe will tell her to stay home.

Once I heard her say, "Joe, you've got to tell me how I should invest my savings." At that time she had three hundred dollars which, because she distrusted banks, she kept hidden in a coal scuttle under the anthracite.

Joe answered, "Take thy money in hand and go on down to the Post Office and buy some United States savings bonds," which she promptly did. She swore she had never heard of United States savings bonds before Joe told her about them.

We have a friend who has a maid who won't take a day off. Doesn't want to leave the place. She's uneducated, can't read and is afraid she might get lost in the great, indifferent world outside.

Came the time, though, when our friend grew tired of having the maid under foot and insisted she take a vacation. The maid's passion was animals: she had goldfish, a cat, a canary, a turtle, which, praise Heaven, she kept in the back yard on a leash. My friend thought the best thing to do for her would be to send her to San Diego to see the zoo. She engaged a San Diego hotel room for a week, pinned several notes on the maid's clothing in case she got lost and put her on a bus. She was back in six hours. "Got lonely," she said,

"Didn't you go to the zoo?" my friend asked.

"Oh, yes, ma'm,' the maid said. "And I saw the funniest-looking animal you ever saw—a big monkey with great pink spots on his behind. Somebody's beatin' him bad. I couldn't stand it, so I came home."

Why January 1 Is the New Year

Every day, of course, is the beginning of a new year, but January 1 is the one most celebrated the world around. Why the calendar-makers didn't chose a spring, summer or fall day for the celebration is a mystery; but they didn't, so we are stuck with January, which, weather-wise in the northern hemisphere, isn't a particularly pleasant time. On the other side of the earth, however, it is summertime, so January 1 is prime time.

What we celebrate, of course, is the world's birthday. The old ball has managed to whirl another year, the champagne flows, people stay up too late dancing, drinking, kissing, hugging and singing *Auld Lang Syne.* Unlike other holidays, such as Christmas and Thanksgiving, they don't eat as much as they imbibe. The rich hie to the south, where there is sunshine, and the Chinese pay their yearly bills.

Many people make resolutions which, after a few days, they forget. I don't make resolutions anymore. Was never good at keeping them, anyway, but save a few traffic violations, am law-abiding. I don't over-eat or over-drink, my annual physical examination tells me I'm hale and hearty, so there is nothing I can think of to swear off.

I realize I could be more tolerant of people who don't approve of what I write, but everyone should have a defect or two.

TLW and I have formed a club to celebrate New Year's Eve 1999. Anyone over sixty-five may join. There are no dues. All one has to do is promise to be at our house for the big party. It is fifteen years away, but that isn't long if you look back. Somehow, as one grows older, time accelerates. Seems like yesterday that TLW and I were celebrating the beginning of 1984.

New Year's Eve 1999 will be sensational. Beginning a new century is loaded with hope. By the time it rolls around, there will be several billion more people to celebrate. A cure for all cancers will have been found; indeed, the medical profession may have compounded a sure cure for the common cold. Even the national budget may be balanced. Or is that too much to hope for?

By the year 2000 the people in Africa may have learned to feed themselves, and apartheid in South Africa will have died. Unbelievable as it may read, maybe the Moslems and the Jews will have become friends.

No matter what, it's going to be a fine celebration. The twentieth century, which we'll be commemorating, was phenomenal. There has been nothing like it in the history of mankind. Just look at what has come about during the last ninety-five years! Wireless communication, automobiles and airplanes, freeways and airports, radio and television, the pill, artificial insemination, heart transplants, the development of genetics, supermarkets and frozen food, to say nothing of computers, robots and Cabbage Patch dolls.

By the year 2000 there may be a device, other than turning the set off, for eliminating television commercials. There probably will be a four-day work-week and month-long vacations. Wages surely will be higher, high enough for almost everyone to have a second home or take a cruise around the world. Like professional athletes, TV commentators and newscasters, all people will be astronomically overpaid.

We in the Century Celebration Club foresee by the year 2000 a much longer and healthier life for everyone. Want to join? Just give me a ring and I'll put your name down. (So far I have two dozen.)

Travel: "Where The Grass Is Greener"

For those who want to get away from it all and live cheaply in a climate such as ours, I know of a far-away place where one can. How does twelve dollars a week, room and board sound to your penurious ears? This figure includes afternoon tea in the British fashion (one gets thin sandwiches, crumpets in season, tarts and perhaps a dollop of sherry).

I'm not referring to Eagle, Alaska, or Little America. I'm extolling an island where sport fishing is as fine as it is at the Gulf of California.

It's away the heck-and-gone out yonder in the south Atlantic—the island of Saint Helena—where Napoleon Bonaparte spent his last years brooding in exile (he died there in 1821). Use your magnifying glass to find it on the map. It is ten and one-half miles in length, six and one-half miles wide and boasts a mountain two thousand, six hundred and eighty-five feet high. It lies sixteen hundred and ninety-five miles northwest of Cape Town, South Africa, and is seven hundred miles from Angola, the nearest continental landfall.

St. Helena is a British possession and English is its language. Thanks to the southeast trade winds its climate is moderate throughout the year. Its summer season is December to April, and a more salubrious climate would be hard to find outside of ours. The days are bright and warm, the evenings clear and cool, just like Laguna's. The only hotel is The Consulate. It is situated in the island capital, Jamestown, and it is here that you get the twelve dollars a week accommodations. You can rent a gig suitable for two anglers, complete with crew of three and free fresh bait, for seven dollars a day [1956].

Only recently regular steamship service to the island has been inaugurated. The Farrell Line has two ships—the *African Enterprise* and the *African Endeavor*—which ply between New York and Cape Town. They make regular calls at Jamestown. One of the ships leaves New York every five weeks. Fares range from four hundred dollars per person, three to a cabin, to six hundred and fifteen for exclusive use of a cabin.

St. Helena was discovered in 1502 by a Portuguese admiral on the birthday of Helena, mother of Constantine the Great. The island was uninhabited but verdant. The Portuguese, realizing the value of the island to the trade with the Indies and the spice islands, managed to keep its position secret for eighty-six years, though rival maritime powers constantly searched for it. When the British and the Dutch finally learned of its position they used it as a base for piratical operations. They would allow the Portuguese and Spanish ships to sail to the Indian Ocean unmolested and then attack and loot them on their return voyage.

First inhabitant of the island was Don Fernando Lopez who sought military sanctuary there after having his right hand, the thumb of his left hand and his ears and nose cut off as punishment for deserting to the Indians during a battle at Goa, a former Portuguese colony on southwest India. In this day and age the punishment seems severe, but on St. Helena Lopez found solace and peace. He lived there for thirty-two years, finally being pardoned by the King, whereupon he left the island.

Native St. Helenans are of mixed origin, varying from pure European to a minority of Africans—fifteen hundred and fifty-seven of them, according to the last census. All are courteous, polite, gentle people.

So, if you must go somewhere, you could do worse than hie yourselves to St. Helena. Don't blame me if you get homesick.

1967—A Long Time Since I Was a Dealer

I have a new car. It's a Thunderbird and has so much power (that of 196 horses) it can go straight up. I'm trying to settle on a name for it. Seats two comfortably, three in a pinch, so I might call it Cuddles on that account. It has power steering, power brakes, power seat and power windows, so maybe I should call it Herky (short for Hercules).

Haven't had a new car for so long I'd forgotten what a pleasure it is. Feel the sin of pride when people stop and gawk. It has the delicious odor of fresh-baked enamel, and I'm careful getting in and out not to muss the leather upholstery. It has an automatic transmission, a tachometer, whatever that is, and a plastic top that comes off and can be left in the garage.

Trouble is: We have but one garage and TLW's old car, Hugo, sleeps in it. She's not about to let me take it over, Thunderbird or no Thunderbird. She knows ocean air ruins metal and chrome, wants to preserve Hugo. Maybe I'll call mine Cuckoo because it has no nest of its own.

There's hardly enough room in the Thunderbird's rear compartment to store a spare tire, so maybe Chintsy would be a good name to yclept it. In fact, it is so small I am reminded, riding in it, of the Englishman who was shoved into a crowded New York subway car next to a pretty blonde. When finally he managed to extricate himself he gave her his card, saying, "Here's my name and address in case anything comes of this."

TLW calls her car Hugo because one of her favorite expressions is "You go, Hugo." The car she had before was called Benjamin, for Benjamin Button, the F. Scott Fitzgerald character who was born an old man and died an infant. Last car I had I called Cuff because that's how I bought it. I don't really own the Thunderbird; it belongs to the Bank of America.

"Pssst! Want to see a good buy?"

CHAPTER 24

Haircut

One of the joyless chores of this life for a male is having to go to a barber shop. When I was a lad, even before I had learned to use a straight razor, I paid my first visit to a barber to have my fuzzy whiskers shaved off, figuring they would then grow quicker and thicker. I was eager to have a four-o'clock shadow. I had tried shaving with a straight razor but had put a number of bloody nicks in my tender visage, so, although a barber shave cost a quarter, decided to splurge and have one. It didn't take the barber long to scrape away the down, and when he finished he bathed my face with sweet-smelling lotion. He said it made me smell sexy.

Thereafter I'd only get a shave when I got a haircut, which was about once a month. Haircuts cost fifty cents. In those days barbers took advantage of youths by selling them other services. I was a pigeon. A barber sold me a "mange cure," a "Bonilla" facial (some kind of mud smeared over the face) and a shampoo. The whole mess cost six dollars and seventy-five cents—all I had.

As I grew older and less gullible, I learned to shave with a straight razor; shortly after that a genius invented the safety razor and thereby saved me from a lifetime of nicks and notches. I still went to a barber for a haircut, but he started raising the fee so I switched my patronage to a barber college where one could get a haircut for a dime. By now I had begun to understand the value of a dollar, which means that the penury in me was blossoming.

When the haircut went to two dollars the barber college went out of business, so I began to look for another. Couldn't find one in the vicinity, and driving to the city, where there was one, was too costly. On a sudden inspiration I asked TLW to cut my hair (she was complaining it was too long). This was brave of me. I didn't know but what she'd cap me with a bowl and clip around it. We had been married for several years, the honeymoon had passed into the limbo of domesticity and she had lots of other things to occupy her time. But she, kind as always, consented to give it a try. Fortunately she is remarkable in that she can do anything she sets her marvelous mind to.

Right away she bought hair-cutting shears ($9.95), a special comb ($1.10) and a small brush ($6.98). I cringed to see her invest so heavily, fearing the experiment might not work out. But it did. It worked out fine. That was years ago, and she has been cutting my hair with the same scissors, comb and brush every two weeks ever since. I think I have saved about $5,000.

Not only does she cut and style my hair superbly, better than any twelve-buck hair-cutter in Beverly Hills could, while she does so she regales me with gossip and social news. One of the things I used to dislike about barber shops was the loquaciousness that abounds in such places. I prefer to doze while I am having my hair cut, but barbers always kept me awake with small talk about politics, athletes and athletics or corny jokes they had learned from unfunny guys who preceded me in their chairs. When Katy does it she goes on about the trials and tribulations of friends and neighbors, but when I doze off she stops talking.

Another good thing: While she is clipping and snipping, the phone will ring and, because I am strewn with hair, she will go answer it, thereby saving me. This morning while she was engaged on my head the thing rang twice. One was a wrong number.

By having her cut my hair I not only save the four dollars I'd have to pay a barber, I save time and gasoline.

There is another important advantage to having Katy cut my hair. When she finishes trimming the thin, diminishing locks she gives me a kiss, right on the lips. Wakes me up.

Grandmother Teaches Me Manners

My greatest dislike as a child was being constantly told what to do. Usually the lessons were about manners and my tutor was my maternal grandmother. Her name was Anne, but she was called Nana. She was a dyed-in-the-wool, twenty-four-carat, very elegant Southern lady whose family (her father was a doctor) had lost its fortune—a North Carolina plantation and slaves—during the Civil War. Though poor, she was genealogically proud and considered herself an aristocrat. When I came along, the first male in three generations, she set out to make me aware of my nobility.

Before I was old enough to comprehend, she told me: "You're the gentry and don't forget it. See that you conduct yourself accordingly. You're going to grow up a gentleman. To be a gentleman you must have good manners and I'm going to see to it that you do."

I don't know whether what she taught me is in common practice today. I sorely doubt it. The children I encounter today, boys particularly, don't seem to be brought up as we were in Georgia in the early years of this century. By and large they are ungracious; they look out for themselves, paying little attention to the wants and needs of others. Not having a tutor like Nana, they haven't suffered as I did; on the other hand, they are not gracious and charming, as I turned out to be.

Nana really molded me. She knew Emily Post's book of etiquette by heart. Every day for several years during my childhood she pounded into me the nuances of social politesse.

She started with table manners. The first thing she taught me was not to try to pick up peas with a knife. (I'd have learned that anyway.) She went on to teach me not to take a bite until everyone was served; not to talk while chewing; not to put an elbow on the table; not to lean my knife or fork on my plate; not to be the first to take a piece of bread or cake but to pass it to others; not to talk with my mouth full; not to leave the dining table without politely excusing myself, even if I had to hurry to the bathroom.

These and other dining rules were drilled into me day after day, and eating with Nana wasn't any fun.

So much for the table. Now let us move into the parlor. When a "lady," i.e., female, came into the room, I was taught to rise; and if there was no empty seat, I was to offer her mine. Not only that, I was to assist her to sit by pushing the chair under her behind while her two hands smoothed her skirt. I was taught to open doors for ladies and let them precede me through them. I was taught not to walk ahead of a lady and on sidewalks to walk on the curb side.

That last nicety came from way back before that procreator of manners, Queen Victoria, was born, as indeed most of them did. Then streets were unpaved and horses and wheels splashed mud, thereby spoiling the long skirts ladies wore.

It took me years to learn that these polite, self-effacing functions always favored females. They were treated with respect, catered to and assisted in every way. Ladies still call it a man's world—and it may have seemed so to them before they got the pill—but in those days they got most of the benefits.

I recently wrote a letter to a godson:

> Dear Christopher:
>
> I am writing this on your fourteenth birthday. And while I know it is not polite to pontificate, particularly to you young people who know so much already, I make so bold as to proffer a glimmer of knowledge earned through prolonged experience in the hope it might be of some value to you.
>
> When I was a child my grandmother (your great-great-grandmother), a very socially conscious lady, was ambitious for me to become a great man so that I would reflect credit on her and the family, so she gave me a lot of advice.
>
> For example, she was forever nagging me to keep my shoes shined and my knickers pressed. To her, these were among the most important reflections of good character. Indeed, she thought that neatness in dress was

about half the key to any kind of success.

But where she led me astray I think, was in prodding me to stand up straight. "Throw your shoulders back," she constantly commanded me, "and face the world unafraid."

I took all her precepts to heart. They became adhesions. Whenever I met someone I would throw my shoulders back and ramrod my back. It has taken me almost fifty years to learn that is wrong. As I am constituted, my hips are thrust slightly forward, and when I try to stand up straight it not only looks awkward, it throws me off balance.

The best way to stand, I have discovered after all these years, is relaxedly: for me this means with a moderate stoop.

As I analyze them now, most of my failures have come from trying too hard. I know, for example, that's the reason I was never an outstanding athlete. I probably could have become one of the world's great golfers if I hadn't tried to hit the ball so hard. I've got one of the sweetest golf swings you'll ever see, if I do say so myself, but I simply can't refrain from putting that extra punch into the pill which sends it anywhere but down the fairway.

I probably would have been a great businessman, a tycoon even, if I hadn't stretched my resources so thin. My failures as a writer (I've trunks full of unpublished material) can be traced to my desperation and Grandmother Nana's advice.

My strongest desire in this world is to be liked, to be admired and esteemed. I've wanted appreciation and fame much more than I've wanted material things.

My trouble has been that I've been too eager to please, too anxious to impress and too quick to take bows. And just as sure as God made little crabapples these characteristics are connected with Grandmother telling me to throw my shoulders back. Somehow doing so has made me artificial, a falsetto. People have come to see me as a strong facade with nothing to back it up, like a movie set or a barking Chihuahua.

And there is another piece of advice my fond, well-meaning grandmother, bless her memory, gave me which has backfired. That is, looking persons straight in the eye.

I've tried for fifty years, but I've never been able to do it without losing track of what he or she was saying.

Well, Chris, that's about all for this year. There must be a moral in it somewhere. Perhaps it is that old coots, like me, shouldn't try to give young people advice.

Love,

The Handkerchief

Come, dear ones, and let us shed a glysery tear to the passing into limbo of the handkerchief; let us combine to chorus it farewell. For this doughty bit of linen which has served us so importantly in our past is fast going the way of the lace cuff and the spat. Tissues have taken the handkerchief's place.

'Tis sad because the handkerchief has played an important role in our history and the saddest aspect of its demise is that we are deprived of an outstanding Christmas gift. Who has not tried to think of what to give Aunt Mabel or Grandmama and come up with the brilliant idea of handkerchiefs?—of imported linen—monogrammed of course.

The history of the handkerchief is somewhat shrouded in the mists of time, but apparently it was born in Central Europe sometime about 1530—at least that's the first time the word was ever used, according to the Oxford dictionary. Apparently some royal personage had the snuff habit and often when he or she sniffed they would sneeze. This not only necessitated drying oneself, but often caused others to need drying. Sneezing also served to spread colds and other respiratory viruses. Hence the handkerchief.

The genius who picked out that name for it is not recorded, but it obviously comes from the word hand and the sound of a sneeze. Actually kerchief comes from a cloth used by women to cover the head, but I like the sneeze derivation better. The object was generally tucked in a glove (by ladies) or into a gentleman's cuff.

Some of us ancients can remember when it played a part in romance. No lady would be "caught dead" without a dainty bit of lace in her hand to "accidentally" drop to attract a man she wanted to meet. How many marriages and children have resulted from the dropped handkerchief I cannot accurately estimate, but both may run into the millions.

Women rarely carry handkerchiefs any more. Kleenex or some other tissue is more sanitary and disposable and they don't need washing and ironing. Today ladies have no need to carry one for dropping purposes. Women are not coy, naive or shy as of yore. The custom today when they want to attract a man is to smile and ask him the time of day.

Of recent years men wore handkerchiefs in their breast pockets. It was the fashion to wear the linen fluffed up and with a corner dangling, that indicating a dashing cavalier. This style gave way to one in which the corners of the handkerchief were starched and evenly spaced protruding from the pocket. Today the style is to wear the handkerchief unobtrusively—folded square and with only a thin line of it appearing above the pocket. But men rarely use handkerchiefs any more. Indeed, a man who wears a clean handkerchief every day is subject to criticism. "I get sick and tired of washing and ironing the damn things!" a wife will say.

"No, no, stupid! It's before except after !"

CHAPTER 25

Paris, 1960

Back in this beautiful city where I spent several years as a newsman on the Paris edition of the *New York Herald-Tribune* I came upon the following want-ad:

"Armenian writer needs work-and-living apartment, preferably on Seine, with good view and lots of light, for three, six, nine or twelve months in exchange for two or three of his original manuscripts. Will pay money if absolutely necessary. Love,"

It was signed William Saroyan.

Not having seen Bill for twenty years, I called him up and he invited me to come for a drink. He had become an expatriate, he told me, because he owes the U.S. Internal Revenue Service $60,000.

"I can't afford to live and work in the United States," he said, and added: "The worst part about getting behind is that I not only have to pay interest on the money I owe, I have to pay interest on the money I pay. To pay off the $60,000 debt I would have to earn $180,000, and there's not much chance of my doing that. So you see, I am in a hell of a fix."

By moving to France he hopes to keep enough tax-free money to reduce his indebtedness. To this end he has written three plays for European production. One, called *The London Story* or *Sam, the Highest Jumper of Them All,* opened last month in London to unanimous repugnance. However, at this writing, some two weeks later, it is still running.

"The critics," Bill said wryly, "seemed to expect to find some hidden meaning in it, and they all sounded angry because there is none." He said the criticism did not bother him, but it obviously did.

The second play, entitled *The Paris Story,* was bought by Darryl Zanuck, the American motion picture producer now living in Paris, who had it translated into German. It opened recently in Vienna to rave notices and big business. It is now playing in Berlin. Both Saroyan and Zanuck stand to make some money from it.

"Fortunately for me," Saroyan said, "he is paying me in monthly installments, so I am able to live."

Seems that Zanuck wanted a scenario for his friend the French actress, Juliette Greco, and asked Saroyan to write one. "I said I'd have to meet her," Bill told me, "so I could see what kind of person she is." After knowing her for a few days he wrote a story outline on a sheet of paper and Zanuck bought it. Its title is *The Moscow Story.* It has not yet been produced, but if Zanuck can figure out some way to get paid in rubles, it may get a Moscow production.

"How about producing it in New York," I asked.

"A successful play would put me in a higher income bracket," Bill said. "I'd be getting ten cents on the dollar and paying it in interest on my debts."

Saroyan has a trunk full of manuscripts which in all probability are worth a small fortune. One of the manuscripts is an autobiography. "I wrote it during my fiftieth year," he said. "I wrote every day for three hundred and sixty-five days and it runs about a million words. It will make several books, but I can't afford to have them published."

Saroyan surely is one of the most humorous writers of our time. He sees life as one sees it in amusement-park mirrors—lopsided, squat, elongated and hilarious. Yet underneath his zany humor is a strong and tender criticism of man's faiths and foibles. He is a hard worker and profuse producer and what he offers the world is delightful.

When I asked him why he did not borrow the money and pay the government, he said, "Banks don't have faith in writers. To them we are the most unstable people in the world, worse even than actors."

I was reminded of what James Joyce told me: "Every writer needs an angel."

O, Politics! O, Ferment!

By next Tuesday night all of the oratory, name calling and viewing with alarm of the current political campaign will have come to an end. Newspapers will return to other crimes, divorces and obituaries and radio stations will resume broadcasting recorded music.

It will be a vast relief. Until the voting is over and tabulated we shall be on pins and needles contemplating what will happen if William Knowland doesn't win the California governorship. From what I've read and heard the State will go straight to the dogs, by which I mean dope peddlers will ply their trade unmolested, other crimes will increase drastically, labor bosses will call the turn, spending will become profligate and taxes will have to be raised catastrophically. Knowland's wife says, "Our beautiful state will be all but ruined."

Aside from these dire predictions, Knowland has declared that if he loses, he never again will run for public office. This is sad because from what I've been able to observe he is a good and dedicated man. He is inclined to be stubborn and I think he has resorted to a little more desperation in this campaign that he should have, but considering all in all, he would make a good governor. I'm sort of sorry Mrs. K. got into the act. Good as her intentions must be, I don't think she helped him.

I have always wondered where we get our political opinions. What makes us Republicans or Democrats—and some rabidly so? God knows. We don't inherit these convictions, because quite often one does not vote as his father does. And apparently one cannot be educated to vote one way or the other. One's political opinions seem to be very personal beliefs held deep in one's core.

Sometimes we tend to forget that in our two-party system one party is as important to our way of life as the other. All Democrats are not spendthrifts nor are all Republicans reactionaries. There is much common good in both parties. Despite the noise you've heard in the past weeks, both have the same objective, i.e., to administer and to govern so that the greatest number will be benefited.

I guess there will always be more Democrats than Republicans, because the basis of the Democrats' philosophy is liberality. They have something for almost everybody—even the rich. And the basis of the Republicans' philosophy is conservatism—let us save what we have gained and not go gambling it away on half-cocked theories.

The philosophy of the Republican party is to keep the money in the bank, cut taxes and don't rock the boat. Sometimes this makes them look stuffy. Sometimes they are stuffy; but oftentimes this is the course to follow.

If Republicans have their way we probably wouldn't have some of the social gains of the last few decades—social security, anti-trust laws, lower tariffs. But if it had not been for the Republican brakes we'd probably also have socialized medicine and government-paid funerals.

Not that these last measures don't have merit, but, with our national debt what it is, it is just as well that we are not saddled with them. If we could ever get off the military spending spree we could have them and maybe free martinis too. But Russia's political ideology and ours are so juxtaposed there seems little chance of this. We'll just have to continue to carry the military budget like a goiter until it (1) sloughs off through improvement of international relations, (2) chokes us to death or (3) we learn to live within our means despite it.

Bacchus, Take a Bow, August 30, 1962

There is a great deal of nonsense spoken and written about wine. The subject is high on the snob list—on a par, say, with painting. Nevertheless, wine, like art, is an important part of man's life and has been since the beginning of human history. It is the oldest intoxicant known and probably was the first medicine.

Wine is very important to the economy of California, and every year sixteen bibbers of the southland are invited to judge the wines of California by the Los Angeles County Fair authorities. I have just returned from a four-day session of wine tasting at Pomona and if my mouth appears to be puckered you know why.

Harold Richardson, the Whittier attorney and bon vivant, is chairman of the wine judges, and Laguna has always been well represented on the panel—at various times by historian-novelist Idwal Jones, by writer William Wister Haines, by inventor Richard Campbell and by yours truly.

Judges this year included columnist Fred Beck, chemist William Converse and epicure Philip Gabriel, all members of the Wine and Food Society of Southern California; physicist Paul Lloyd of Rancho Santa Fe, Thomas Rees, State Assemblyman, 59th District, and Art Nisson, Santa Ana attorney.

What goes on at these sessions?

We arrive at the deserted Fair Grounds (the Fair doesn't open until next month) at 9:00 A.M., which is an early hour, you will allow, to face a bottle of wine. The sixteen judges are divided into four panels of four. Panel No. 1 will judge one group of wines, cabernets, say, while No. 2 will judge the burgundies, No. 3 the zinfandel and No. 4 the pinots, the gamays or the clarets. Then we will proceed through the other reds to the whites, the fortifieds and the brandies.

The bottles containing the wine which have been entered for judging are masked in paper sacks so that no part of the label can be discerned. Wine from bottle A is poured into a glass marked A, wine from bottle B into glass B, and so on. There will be as many as fifteen wines in a category, so there may be fifteen samples to taste.

The wines are judged for their character, their taste, their bouquet and for their body. Among the factors taken into consideration are acidity, sugar content and to what degree the wine is true to its type.

The judges do not swallow the wine. After sloshing it about in their mouths, they expel it. Nonetheless, some of each mouthful manages to get beyond the palate, and after eight hours of tasting one is inclined to be somewhat wine soaked.

When a judge has tasted all of the wines submitted in that class he will grade them. If there are eight wines in the category, the one judged best will get eight points, the next one seven, and so on down the line. In the judging one taster does not confer with another—each comes to his conclusion separately.

Then, having made their decisions, the panel caucuses—that is, the members get together and compare opinions. The wines will be rated according to the number of points they receive, and the awards will be made on this basis—gold medal, silver medal, bronze medal, honorable mention or, in many instances no award at all.

It is hard work, this tasting wine for eight hours a day, but it is fun, too. There is a lot of camaraderie, jollity and wit, but no nonsense. Everyone performs seriously, because the decisions made are very important to the vintners who have submitted their wines for judging.

The judging itself is a game and it is surprising the unanimity of opinions amongst the judges. Snobbery aside, there are wide differences in wine. I have learned a great deal about wine and its culture in the six years I have been a judge at Pomona, and I've found that in learning to taste wine I have learned to taste food. Thereto, I'm ashamed to say, I had merely eaten it.

This year, it is good news to report, every class of wine I tasted, it seemed to me, has become upgraded. The burgundies, especially, are beautiful and so are the cabernets and the pinots. And the California wine makers are making a light, sprightly rosé which tastes like a Moselle—to the joy of mankind. I salute them.

How to Become a Wine Judge, July 1965

It's easy. Just read my dear friend Fred Beck's new composition, *The Wine Book.* It is published by Hill and Wang, and is a richly satisfying guide to California wines and wineries.

Franciscan padres brought grape vines with them when they came to California to convert the heathen "Indians" to Christianity. These wise gentlemen would go anywhere to carry the word of God and, along with the Cross, they always managed to tote a few grape cuttings. A person can stand almost any hardship, including loneliness, if he can fortify himself with a Bacchanalian brew.

In the years since the padres planted those first vines California has become one of the world's greatest producers of wine. The rich yield of the grapes at the Missions, particularly those at San Gabriel and San Fernando, attracted in 1824 an American vineyardist, one John Chapman, who brought with him four thousand vines. He was followed seven years later by Louis Vignes, who came around the Horn from Bordeaux and planted French vines where the Los Angeles Union Station now stands.

These fascinating facts along with heaps of other lore one learns from Fred's book.

Probably more snobbery springs from wine than from any other subject, even including modern art and how best to make a martini, and bibber Fred goes a long way in his book to make the reader a wine authority. Tired of being confused when you approach the wine shelves in your liquor store? Cowed by those who speak so casually of pinot noir and semillon and who toss around such fancy words as varietal and generic? Know what the snob is talking about when he speaks of a wine's nose? Well, be the sage of the party and stun your guests with your erudition. Read *The Wine Book.*

Denisons of the Deep

I am not a professional whale-watcher. With me it's merely an avocation. However, I have devoted considerable time to the art and feel experienced enough to write of it with some authority.

The good whale-watcher, like the inveterate bird-watcher,

may or may not be schooled, but he or she must have a sharp eye, a romantic mind, a love of nature and a persevering patience.

The equipment for whale-watching is as follows: a good pair of Bushnell binoculars, at least 7x5 power, a copy of *Moby Dick* and a six-pack of beer. The art also requires a perch, a vantage point from which one may get an uninterrupted view of the briny deep. A house on an oceanfront cliff is best because it offers comfort and shelter in case of rain. If a house is not available the whale-watcher can fill a thermos and take it, a blanket (it's often chilly when whales pass Laguna on their way north or south to copulate and give birth) and a folding chair to one of the cliffs. Three Arch Bay used to have a fine place at the south end of the tract, but progress (meaning fences) has usurped it.

Once you get comfortable, with a can of beer at your side, take out the binoculars, wipe the lenses, pick up the copy of *Moby Dick* and begin reading. Pretty soon you may go to sleep, but from time to time, between sips raise your eyes and scan the surface of the vast Pacific. Flecks of white foam will appear on the blue expanse. Observe these closely with the binoculars. Determine if they are a moving body or merely the twitch of a nervous wavelet. Every now and then you will see the fin of a porpoise, a sword fish or the flipper of a seal. These the experienced whale-watcher ignores. At times one may observe a huge creature with purple eyes, pointed ears and a cat-like face with an undulating carcass. It could be, and probably is, a sea serpent. They are extremely rare. One twenty-nine feet long was found on the beach at Newport in 1904 and I espied one from our house in South Laguna in February, 1942 about four P.M. of a cloudless day. The visibility was excellent, the window was clean and the wind was about five knots from the northwest. An account of this appeared in the *Laguna Beach Post* and was picked up by the *New York Times*. The noted science writer, Willie Ley, wrote asking for details, which were supplied substantially as above.

From time to time a box or a crate will be seen floating

on the surface of the great sea and now and then a log or the body of an unfortunate Homo sapien. These too should be ignored. They are for the curious and the coroner. Quite often in spring and fall, your binoculars will find in their field the real thing—a spurt from an exhaling whale!

Zowie!

It will be followed by the huge body surfacing. Though weighing a ton, a male can use his flukes to lift himself out of the water. As it goes down again the last you will see of it is its tail.

Heaven has its beauties and diamonds have their glitter, but in all the world there is nothing so thrilling and awe-inspiring as this performance of the greatest mammal on our watery sphere.

Melville writes: "Other poets have warbled the praises of the soft eye of the antelope and the lovely plumage of the bird that never lights; less celestial, I celebrate the tail. Reckoning the largest sperm whale's tail to begin at that point of the trunk where it tapers to about the girth of a man, it comprises upon its upper surface alone an area of at least fifty square feet...at its utmost expansion in the full grown whale the tail will considerably exceed twenty feet across. Nor does its amazing strength tend to cripple the graceful fluctuation of its motion...."

Ever try a whale steak? They tell me it's delicious, that it has a beef-like texture and beats beef six days to Sunday. To hear whalers tell it, it even beats Sunday.

Whales are an order of mammals grouped under the Greek term Cetacea. Their ancestors were land animals. They are warm blooded, breathe through their lungs, have no scales on their skins and nourish their young with milk. There is some reason to believe they rarely sleep.

I once worked in a movie of *Moby Dick*. John Barrymore was the star. I was a stunt man. The script called for a whale to be harpooned and for Barrymore (me) to cling to the harpoon while the whale dived. I would have done this if we had gotten that close to a whale, but we didn't. We finally did the scene in a lake with a dummy whale. It turned out fine.

Another incident that contributed to my whale education took place off Santa Cruz Island about twenty miles west of Santa Barbara, and it likewise had to do with the making of a film, *Dante's Inferno.* While surfboading behind a speedboat I lost my balance and was dunked. While treading water, awaiting the boat's return, I was benumbed to see a few feet to my right a whale surface and exhale. As I frantically swam away from it another whale exhaled before me. Both were going northward. Using the Australian crawl, I barely touched the water headed the other way.

Rules for Successful Wives

How do you, as a wife, treat your husband? Do you tell him what to do or depend on him telling you? If you are the bossy type your tendency to guide and supervise comes from the ego: you won't be dominated.

The classic example of the domineering wife is the one who directs her husband while he is driving an automobile. She always does this when there are others in the car. When she cautions, "There is a stop sign!" or "Look out for that car," the other passengers get the impression the driver is either blind or an idiot.

I know a lady who falls into that category. In fact, I'm married to her. Whatever I am about to do, such as prune the roses, she will follow me and show me how it should be done. If I don't do it to her satisfaction she will wait until I am gone and do it her way. If I get the sniffles she will decide what medicine I should take and watch while I swallow it.

When we were first married I quietly resented this imperiousness. The first time I became aware of it I was about to drive a nail. It wasn't difficult. I had a hammer. She said, "Mind you don't hit your finger!"

Believe it or don't, I hit my finger. Once, when I was having difficulty screwing in a light bulb, she took it from me and did it easily.

In the beginning these actions of hers shriveled my id,

made me feel inadequate, wounded my pride. Sometimes my displeasure would bristle and once I shouted, "For God's sake, stop telling me what to do!" In time though I came to realize her bossy characteristic was an asset. She wasn't a shrew at all, but the kindest, smartest, noblest woman alive. It dawned on my muddled mind that she meant well, that I was awkward and inept, that she had my welfare at heart and was trying to protect me.

It took me years to realize she is smarter than I and knows more than I do how to live well and happily. Though she often treats me as if I were a child and she my mother, I find her knowledge and judgment superb. As a result I exercise regularly, eat properly and go to bed when I should. My weight doesn't change. I still have a fair head of hair and most of my teeth, sight and hearing. I'm seldom sick and when I am she pampers me. Because of her I am living the finest life in the best of all possible worlds. I don't believe I could have it any better if I were a four-wife Arab. She keeps our books, balances our budget, brings in from her professional activities (real estate) more lucre by far than I do from my scribbling. She manages our beautiful home, cooks our scrumptious meals, swims, plays backgammon with me and treats me as if I were a Grand Duke. I am not about to let my male ego offend her because she tells me what to do and how to do it.

Ancient Truisms for a Happy Marriage

When as a young girl you fell in love with a boy you were absolutely ga-ga about him. He was a hero, an idol, a paragon. He could do no wrong.

From the day you married, you and he set about to learn about each other, the good and bad, your strengths and weaknesses. You soon learned to your surprise that he has faults. However you don't stop loving him. You realize that, though he is far from perfect, he's better than widowhood.

Having found a weakness in him, take advantage of it. If he's lazy and shies from homework, find a few chores for him to do and prod him to do them, but don't nag. If he gains weight cut his calories, but don't forget the old adage that a man's affection comes not from his heart but from his stomach. If he is moody or cranky kid him out of it, but don't belittle him.

Don't criticize your husband when he does something wrong. Make light of it, even if he drops the pot roast on the dining room rug. Help him select the clothes he buys, but when he's at home permit him without criticism to wear whatever he likes, which usually will be much worn and probably may need cleaning.

If he's hooked on football and other sports, join him in attending them, even if you don't know much about what's going on. For your own sake you should learn the rules of the sports he likes so that you, too, can enjoy them.

When it comes to the marital bed, keep it from getting routine. Use imagination. Pretend it's sinful. Make it fun. Turn on some music.

If you'll do all of these things a happy marriage is guaranteed.

CHAPTER 26

My Friend, Jack Welch

I often read newspaper columns written by others, always comparing them with my own, of course, and generally finding them wanting. When I was writing one for the *Laguna Beach Post* I was known as "the Jack Smith of Laguna" and he was sometimes referred to as "the John Weld of Los Angeles." I'm pretty sure he wasn't flattered.

The other day in his column I read a report he quoted from a Santa Barbara man about Richard Haliburton, the adventure writer who became lost at sea in 1939 trying to sail a junk from China to California.

Haliburton was a Tennessean who, after graduating from Princeton, set out to stunt his way around the world and cash in on his exploits by writing books about them. He climbed mountains, swam the Hellespont and the Panama Canal and did other feats of derring-do which brought him fame and fortune. Indeed, when he died he was fast becoming a legend. His books sold well and he took some of the money he made from them and built a spectacular house on a hill in South Laguna, which is where I knew him. Before it was finished he took a few pals to China to serve as crew for the junk journey. For the navigator he hired my old pal Jack Welch.

Jack was an Australian who had worked his way to the U.S. as a seaman, had earned his ship-captain papers and had been master of a United Fruit Company banana ship. Eventually he became a technical advisor for films in which ships were featured. I met him while he was so employed and I was doing stunt work for the film *Peter Pan*. We became friends and shared an apartment. He was a flamboyant character who, when in his

"It's a sad little story. He stepped outside for a cigarette and never came back—and that was three weeks ago."

cups, had a proclivity for spouting poetry.

Besides being romantics, Jack Welch and I had another characteristic in common. We both wanted to become legends in our time. To this end we did what we considered unusual things so that people would notice, talk about and remember us.

Those days in Hollywood it was important to promote oneself, to become known as a personality. Greta Garbo became famous for eschewing publicity, by asking to be let alone. Jack and I tried it the other way, yelling "Hey! Look at us! Ain't we the lulus!"

Haliburton's idea of crossing the Pacific in a Chinese junk turned out to be his last adventure as it was for his pals and Jack. They went to Taiwan (that was before Chaing Kai-Shek took it over) where the boat was built. They spent weeks furnishing, outfitting and stocking the mahogany craft for the long voyage to San Francisco. The idea was to arrive for maximum publicity at the beginning of that city's "World Fair."

Because of the safety measures Jack insisted on, they were late getting started. But at last, loaded with oil, grub and whiskey, they set out across the prodigious Pacific, doubtless with Jack singing sea chanteys or quoting poets. One of his favorite quotations was from Arthur Simons: "Unto thee, dear disinherited, I leave a soul divine...." That would have been prognosticatively appropriate.

For the first few days, it must be assumed, everything went well. The automatic pilot was working, so were the compass and the engine. But then the worst thing that could have happened, happened. A typhoon came up and they got caught in its funnel. The whirling wind and the mountainous waves simply inundated the small, high-tailed craft.

Their wireless signal for help was picked up by the S.S *President Coolidge.* Assumedly it was the nearest help; it reported its position as about seven hundred miles distant.

"Advancing at full speed," the *Coolidge* message concluded.

Back came the last words from the junk: "Up to armpits

in water. Seven hundred miles too damned far. Having great time. Wish you were here instead of me. Welch."

Thus, when he was dying Jack uttered one of the great exit-this-life lines in history. It's about as dramatic, and a lot funnier, than Nathan Hale's "I only regret that I have but one life to lose for my country."

Architect William Alexander, who designed and built the all-cement Hangover House for the late Richard Haliburton, has built a house of his own on the same ridge in South Laguna. He invited me up last week to have a look. It's a very imaginative place, with two great views—fore and aft—up Aliso Canyon and out to the Pacific.

Bill told me this about the Haliburton house:

"It turned out that I was not only the designer, I became the builder. We had a contractor, but he thought we were crazy and tried to make us change the plan; so we let him go. We hired any labor we could get—very cheap in those days, fifty cents an hour.

"Though the house wasn't finished by the time Haliburton went to China to build his Chinese junk, he had spent $33,000 on it. It is built for the ages. Six-inch ceilings, walls and floors. Everything else on the hillside may crumble, but that house will be there as long as the hill holds up, presumably forever."

The half-built house sold for $9,000 in 1945. I wish I had bought it.

CHAPTER 27

Of Beards and Men

I'd like to wear a beard. It would save a lot of shaving bother and would enhance my looks by hiding certain facial deficiencies. But there's something about it—something that smacks of the pretentious and the pompous—that I don't like.

I think my attitude can be explained by a pair of trousers I bought recently. Katy had said to me, "I don't see why men don't wear brighter, gayer clothes. Seems to me that by being conservative they're going against nature. In the bird world it's the male which wears the bright plumage."

To make her happy, I bought a pair of checkered trousers, featured recently in *Life*. Idea was to give a lift to the old male carcass. God knows, mine can use some bewitchment.

Well, the first time I wore those pants in public I got so ridiculed by friends that I felt ashamed.

"Where'd you get the breeches, Buster?"

"What are you made up for—a costermonger?"

"Say, pal, your pajamas are showing!"

Wonder what it is in man that makes him poke fun at his fellows. Seems that whenever I put those pants on no one can withstand the temptation to tease me. Listen to the same remarks repeated over and over and you'll wish you'd stayed in bed.

Same thing happens when I wear my pink coat.

"Get a load of the jacket-ass!"

"Deer season's over, Mister."

I was in our convertible wearing a red beret and one of a group of teenagers hollered, "I saw him first!"

The remark cut me to the quick. I shouldn't be so sensi-

"Let's look at some houses. We have a couple of hours to kill."

tive. After all, wearing garments which are unusual in cut or color is a deliberate way of calling attention to oneself.

My psychiatrist probably would say I wear these garments because I haven't much self-confidence, that those who depend on clothes for attention are people who suffer from inferiority. And I'd guess he's right.

A man should not be ostentatious. As far as clothes are concerned he should wear the conservative patterns worn by other men. He shouldn't deviate from the accepted behavior: should speak quietly, think conservatively and make an effort at modesty.

The reason I don't wear a beard—because I'm afraid people will think I'm a beatnik, a hippie. As it is, my mustache makes me suspect. John McLaughlin, the noted sales engineer, tells me of a large corporation which will not hire a man who wears a mustache. They figure he'll be too flighty.

I've given my checkered pants to the Goodwill.

Doctors Rarely Make Housecalls

Homo sapiens go to physicians seeking physical relief; many go when Nature, given time, would correct their ailments. But doctors can be helpful. I remember the first time I went to one. I had whooping cough. My mother took me. The doctor didn't ask me a lot of questions but mixed a concoction which I forced down. I was taken home by streetcar. In twenty-four hours I felt fine. I think his fee, including the medicine, was three dollars. That was about 1909.

I don't need to tell you that things have changed. Last week my arthritic knees were hurting, so I went to see an orthopedist. An orthopedist, as you doubtless know, is a specialist who confines his "practice" to bones. (Practice is the proper word. Doctors practice on patients and learn from their errors.)

When I got to the doctor's office the receptionist gave me a physical history form to fill out. It got me to recalling how many times in my wayward, vigorous life I had needed the help of a doctor.

I was about three when I slid down a banister and broke a collar bone.

I was five when Mother thought I should lose my tonsils, so she took me to a doctor and he snipped them out, along with my adenoids.

I was seven when, playing "cavalry" (boys got on others' backs and tried to dismount one another), I broke a couple of bones in my right elbow. It was months before the bones reknitted and even today, fifty years later, the elbow is still crooked and the arm is slightly flaccid.

I had no idea what good this painful biography would do, but I put it all down. I wrote that at age eight, riding a bicycle down a steep hill, I hit a pothole, went tail over tea kettle, suffered a concussion and broke a leg. That wasn't the only bike accident I suffered. A few years ago I borrowed a ten-speed bicycle from a friend and was going down hill lickity-split; as I rounded a curve a ten-ton truck was headed directly at me. I hit the curb, went over the handlebars and broke my right shoulder, cracked my skull, four ribs and punctured a lung. It was forty-eight hours before I regained a glimmer of consciousness.

During the flu epidemic of 1918 I was in a hospital for ten days and almost died. I've had two operations for hemorrhoids, an appendectomy and a hernia operation. I almost had a foot cut off in a shipwreck off the coast of Japan. Going down with the ship my left leg was severely cut above the ankle and I almost bled to death before getting to the American Hospital in Yokohama. There my leg was improperly repaired. Again it was operated on, this time in St. John's Hospital in Santa Monica. There I got a streptococcus infection and had to be quarantined for ten days.

I wrote that while doing stunt work in a film starring Sidney Chaplin, brother of Charlie, I broke my left arm falling backward off the top of a hansom cab. I broke several ribs doubling for Tom Mix. By the time I got to telling about breaking my nose playing football at Auburn I had to have more paper.

I answered the questions on the form about my allergies,

what had caused my father to die (typhoid fever), and how many ounces of alcohol I consumed a day (usually three). By the time the good doctor got to me (about an hour later) he barely glanced at the form I had filled out. He had an assistant X-ray my knees and pointed out the arthritic nodules under my kneecaps. He suggested I build up the muscles of my thighs by bicycling. His bill turned out to be eighty-five dollars.

While I was in his office I did more work filling out the form than he did X-raying and tending my aching knees. As a professional writer, who sometimes gets as much as one dollar a word, I figured he owed me two hundred bucks. However, I didn't send him a bill.

The Medicine Cabinet

A newspaperman from San Francisco recently took his wife and children into the Sierra Nevada without food or fishhooks to see if they had the stamina and resourcefulness to live off the land. According to his articles they've been having a rough time.

Reading of their experiences got me to thinking about our opulence and how it is weakening the national character. We've come to depend on so many crutches that we have almost forgotten how to walk tall, the way our forefathers did. I began enumerating the little things we can do without.

First thing my eyes lit on was the big jar of bath salts. It sits on a shelf above the lavatory and looks right pretty—the way apothecary jars used to look in drug store windows before they went in for ceiling-to-floor greeting cards and alarm clocks. I figured that inasmuch as TLW and I use only the shower, the bath salts could go.

But it was when I looked in the medicine cabinet that I got the shock. Nowhere is our national insecurity and self-indulgence so mirrored as in medicine cabinets. Boy, do we pamper ourselves when we get a pain!

In ours there must be a dozen little bottles of pills. Most of them have my name on them (TLW almost never gets ill;

when she does she goes to bed) and all of them bear the typed instruction: "One every four hours."

It is a sad truth that when I am ill in any way—cold, earache, athlete's foot, ingrown toenail, nausea, biliousness, palpitations, hiccoughs or whatever—I either run to a doctor or pour out my symptoms to friends, all of whom, without exception, are quick to prescribe a remedy.

Inasmuch as the latter's fees are considerably less than a doctor's, I am prone to take their advice. Instead of paying for both the prescription and the medicine, I just pay for the pills.

I think our friends know more about pills than Mr. Upjohn. The ones they recommend usually come in red, green or white capsules.

Last week I complained of not feeling well and a friend was quick to offer a cure. I forget the name of it—something like euromorphathluminethane—but he said he often suffered from my identical symptoms, that it was undoubtedly galloping vertigo and prescribed this pill. "I take one every morning," he said, "whether I need it or not. Never felt better in my life."

I, the hopeful, romantic, insomniac, claustrophobic, neurotic hypochondriac that I am, carefully wrote down the name of the drug and hurried to the druggist with it. That white-coated gentleman counted a number of gaily colored capsules into a plastic container, said, "That'll be sixty dollars," and handed me the pills. Why is it that every time I buy any pills they cost sixty dollars? It's something the Interstate Commerce Commission should look into.

Well, I went home, took one, and after four hours, according to instruction, took another. Then I forgot them.

"What are these for?" I asked my wife several days later, and she said, "Don't you remember? They're for your vertigo."

I don't think the pills had any effect whatever. Time eventually took care of my ailment. Several weeks later I had the same symptoms, and another kind friend suggested another sure-fire remedy. Again I staggered off to the druggist to get sixty dollars' worth.

If I had any sense, of course, I'd postpone going to the

drug store for twenty-four hours, by which time I'd feel better and there might be no need for medication. Next time I get sick I think I'll just take an assortment of the pills in our medicine cabinet. Must be three hundred dollars worth there.

Two Talented People

Extraordinary people are rare but when two extraordinary people marry and live together happily it is rare indeed. Take our friends Ramona and Robert Sutton. She is one of the nation's outstanding organists and he is talented in many ways. They live in Laguna Niguel during the winter and on their yacht in the Mediterranean in the summer.

Right now they are "at home" and TLW and I visited them last Saturday. It was a farewell party. They are about to depart for Majorca to board their boat. They're going to bring it back across the Atlantic to Puerto Rico.

The boat's name is *Mona Mona* and what is remarkable about it is that Bob built it himself. Oh, he had one helper, but Bob did all the engineering and mechanical work, besides which he built a tiny automobile to serve as a gad-about-on-land tender.

Consider the improbability of this. Bob, a big man, six feet two, two hundred and twenty pounds, was practically born in a theatrical trunk, his mother and father having been vaudevillians, and he was brought up and educated on the stage. He grew up to write vaudeville acts and jokes. Drifting into radio, he became general manager of the CBS station in Minneapolis, which is where he met and married Mona. From there he was promoted to vice president and general manager of KNX in Hollywood.

Through the years there has been one yearning in Bob's mind. He wanted a boat in which he and Mona could roam the world at will. And when time came that he could retire from the Columbia Broadcasting System he set out at once to build it. The design he chose is nautically called "Grand Banks." It is fifty feet long, seventeen feet wide, has three sleeping cabins, two baths, a lounge-salon and a spacious galley. It took him more than a year to complete the job. Then one fine day, while dozens of his friends looked on, the *Mona Mona* was launched in Newport Beach. It floated perfectly, the engine performed beautifully and so did the rudder.

One would think that Bob, having completed that expensive job, would have been content to ply the local waters, cruise to Catalina, Dana Point and perhaps as far as San Diego. But no. He and Mona decided to take the boat through the Panama Canal, across the Atlantic and cruise the Mediterranean.

For seven summers thereafter they've been inviting friends, including at times, Katy and me, to join them, returning every fall to Laguna Niguel. They've plied the waters as far east as Turkey, pausing along the way to visit towns along the Spanish Gold Coast, the Balearic Islands, the French and Italian Rivieras, the Adriatic and the Greek Islands.

Having visited all of these fascinating places, this year they're bringing the boat back to the Caribbean and for the next few years intend to cruise the string of islands east of Cuba and the ports of South America.

Katy and I have had the great pleasure of spending weeks aboard the *Mona Mona*—along the Dalmatian coast from Dubrovnik to Venice, the Greek Islands, and Majorca and the islands around it. It has been marvelous, not only travel-wise but because every evening after a sumptuous dinner, Mona would give us a concert on her electric organ.

They have invited us to join them again, once they get to Puerto Rico. The waiting's going to be hard.

Real Estate Specialist

On our recent trip to the South Seas to photograph the coronation of the King of Tonga, Rod Yould, the cinematographer, and I were sitting on the terrace of the Mocambo Hotel overlooking the international airport at Nadi, Fiji, enjoying the soft night and glasses of New Zealand beer, when out of the shadows comes a tall, young, bald-headed man who spoke my name.

He turned out to be Robert Hunter, a real estate broker from Seattle. It was on his account that Rod and I were there. He had called to my attention the upcoming coronation, and while we had corresponded we had never met.

So far as I know Bob Hunter is the only real estate agent in the world who deals exclusively in islands. He seeks his merchandise the world over. An astute businessman, he claims he sells romance.

"People are patsies for isolation," he told us. "An island is a domain."

You want an island off Vancouver or in the Mediterranean, Hunter will find it for you. But right now he believes the most promising area for his unique business is Fiji. Unlike most of the islands scattered like emeralds across the South Pacific, where foreigners cannot purchase land, outsiders can own Fiji islands.

"Fiji is where Hawaii was one hundred years ago," Hunter said. "It is uncluttered by tourists, unspoiled by high-rise buildings and its natural beauty is enchanting. The people there are gentle and friendly. Whereas Hawaii land has become so expensive that it is beyond reach of any but the very rich, Fiji today is reasonably priced."

Bob told us he recently bought an 110-acre coconut plantation on a Fijian island for $29,000. "It has about a mile of white-sand beach and is as pretty a place as one can imagine," he told us. "The coconuts will bring in a profit of approximately three or four thousand dollars a year, and more, of course, when the place is well managed." He plans to build a thatched cottage on the property for a couple of hundred bucks.

From Los Angeles the flight to Fiji takes approximately eleven hours and costs about five hundred dollars. But with the coming of the super-jets in a couple of years, Bob figures both of these figures will be considerably reduced.

Hunter sells his islands by photograph. He has a thousand color slides of his listings. They bring out the romance in people and subsequently their checkbooks.

How much does an island cost?—They come in all sizes and prices. There's a nice little two-acre job in British Columbia for fifteen thousand dollars; you can buy a jewel in the Bahamas for one hundred and fifty thousand and you can pay millions for one off Vancouver. When you come to buy an island, don't ask Bob Hunter what the return on your investment will be. "What people are looking for is not an income," he said, "they're looking for romance."

Tonga is a cluster of approximately one hundred and fifty islands in the South Pacific—I say approximately because at times several of them are under water. The islands are closer to Fiji—about five hundred miles—than to any other landfall, and some seven hundred and fifty miles north of New Zealand. They lie almost exactly on the International Dateline and Tongans say Nuku'alofa, its capital and largest island, is where time begins. That is where Rod and I were headed.

The inhabitants of the Tongan islands are Polynesian and together they make up the last of the Polynesian countries that is ruled by a king. He is His Majesty, King Tupou the Fourth. He succeeded his mother, Queen Salote, who served her people well for almost fifty years before dying in 1965.

Much of the world might never have heard of this little Polynesian kingdom had it not been for Queen Salote's well-publicized appearance at the coronation of Queen Elizabeth the Second in 1953. The Tongan Queen won the affection and respect of mankind when she rode in the royal parade proudly erect in the pouring rain without benefit of canopy, hat or umbrella. She told Queen Elizabeth that Tongans do not cover themselves in the presence of their superiors.

Tonga is a member of the British Commonwealth and its history can be traced back through the Royal lineage as far as the Tenth Century. However archeologists have determined that there were people living on these islands as early as five hundred years before Christ. The present dynasty began in the middle of the Nineteenth Century when King Tupou's great-grandfather united the islands after a long civil war. He accepted Christianity as the State religion and religion plays a very important part in Tongan life today. The King is a Methodist. Others are Mormons, Presbyterians and Catholics.

Sunday is strictly observed as a day of rest throughout the Tongas. All businesses and endeavors of whatever kind cease. Even the radio closes down.

Tonga was discovered for the rest of the world by Captain James Cook during his famous voyage in 1764. Cook was impressed with the graciousness of the Tongan people. He referred to the archipelago as the Friendly Islands, and so they became known.

Long before Captain Cook arrived, the Tongans were well aware that they were not the only people on this earth. They not only knew about New Zealand and Fiji, they knew about Hawaii, more than two thousand miles to the north. It follows that some individuals must have made the long voyage to or from Hawaii in open canoes. Thus it may be said that Tongans knew celestial navigation long before Captain Cook called.

No one knows whence the Tongan people came to these islands nor when, but they must have come hundreds of years ago by canoe; and they must have been not only great navigators but ingenious in other ways as well. The journeys they made must have taken months and it is speculated that the coconut had been their main source of nourishment, along with the fish they caught. Coconuts not only supplied nourishment but water as well. Their outrigger canoes were as long as one hundred feet and they could carry lots of coconuts.

The Royal Palace, the most imposing building on any of the Tongan islands, is on Nuku'alofa. Like most of the permanent structures there it has a galvanized roof. Lesser houses are roofed with thatch. When the flag is flying over the Palace it signifies that the King is in residence.

The Tongan Royal family is treated with the same formality and respect by the Tongan people as the British Royal family is by the British. The King appears in public only for formal and ceremonial occasions and to go to church Sundays.

Because of their way of life and the abundance of food—coconuts, bananas, yams, breadfruit and taro, to say nothing of fish—Tongans do not work hard. While Tongan children generally speak their native Polynesian language, in the schools they are taught English. The King thinks it important that all of his subjects learn this important world language.

Methodist missionaries arrived in Tonga in 1822 and started the first school four years later. A Catholic school was started shortly thereafter. Today there are one hundred and fifty-seven Government and Mission schools on the islands with enrollment of more than sixteen thousand. King Tupou the Fourth is supposed to be descended from the mythical god Tangoroa, but Tongans no longer believe he can heal them of a disease merely by touching them with his bare foot.

Some of the Tongan islands are composed of coral; others were formed by volcanic action. Coconuts are the main sources of income on the Tongas. Every Tongan male, when he reaches maturity, is allotted two acres of land on which to raise food for his family.

On this plot he pays an annual tax of three or four dollars. No other taxes are charged. While the King takes little in taxes from his people, he owns all the land, operates practically everything and manages to make a profit.

One of the King's principal sources of revenue is postage stamps. Stamp collectors all over the world purchase this little monarchy's every stamp issue, and no inconsiderable amount of money comes to the King in this way.

Most Tongan houses are made of thatch from coconut fronds and have dirt floors. While few Tongan houses have any plumbing, water is available in every village; however it must be bucketed by hand, sometimes for long distances.

To supplement the food he raises on his land, the Tongan fishes, either at low tide or with a net from an outrigger. Even the Tongan pigs fish. When the tide goes out of reef or lagoon many fish will be left behind. Fittingly enough, Tongan pork tastes slightly fishy.

Tongan barbers charge ten cents for a hair cut, and if you don't have the cash you can bring the barber seven coconuts. Coconuts are used as a medium of exchange. Each is worth one and a half cents. They grow abundantly throughout the islands and are Tonga's principal export.

The capital city of Nuku'alofa has a population of about twenty thousand. A few of the streets are paved and there are electric lights. One can telephone, send a telegram and mail a letter. The motor scooter is the principal mode of transportation, but three-wheeled buses run to most of the villages. Otherwise people get around on foot, bicycles, horses or canoes. Nuku'alofa is about one hundred miles long and thirty miles wide. Whereas many people of the world have to struggle for a livelihood and are concerned therefore with the pursuit of wealth to give them security, Tongans take life relaxedly. They have plenty to eat, clothing is no problem because the climate is temperate, so instead of worrying about the future as people in many other countries do, they concentrate on the joy of living.

The film Rod and I made, *Coronation of a King,* was financed by Art Linkletter, with whom, at the time, I was associated. Rod and I were the only American team to photograph the highly newsworthy event. Other teams were from New Zealand, Australia, Japan, Sweden and England. For seven weeks Rod and I filmed the islands, the Tongans, the King and his family. We got lots of wonderful footage. After King Tupou bid us goodbye, we hurried home to edit the film and write the narration. Linkletter was to narrate. We expected to get $300,000 for the film's initial showing on TV prime time. Because Art was appearing at the Montreal World's Fair, we sent the film to a distributor in New York, where Art could fly down and record the narration. Unbeknownst to us, the distributor was in bankruptcy, and all of his assets, including our Tongan film, were seized by his creditors. To this day we have never been able to find it!

"Must be from South Laguna...."

CHAPTER 28

Nostalgic Journey, 1969

TLW and I are off on a nostalgic journey to Europe and by the time you read this we'll be gone. We're off to Switzerland, where as a young girl Katy went to school, and Paris, where during the 1920s and early '30s I worked as a reporter on the *New York Herald-Tribune*. We're going to visit old haunts and relive our salad days. We'll spend a month at Montreux on Lake Geneva, and perhaps two weeks in Paris. I say perhaps, meaning we'll stay until our money runs out.

At Montreux we'll hole up in a fancy hotel on the lake and from it we'll take boats, trains and buses to tiny Switzerland's fascinating and beautiful towns, returning each day to the hotel for sleeping. Thus we won't have to repack until we take off for Paris. If there is one thing I dislike about traveling it is packing and unpacking. That way traveling, more often than not, is hard work. And I don't like going on tours either. Up at some ungodly hour to catch a train, a plane or bus, you're often herded like cattle or sheep until, by day's end, you're exhausted. Even then you have to unpack for the night.

Katy went to the Ecole Superior des Jeunes Filles in Vevey, a public high school for girls. We'll visit the pension where she lived, the school she attended, if it's still where it was, and stroll the avenues she knew so well. The scenes will remind her of incidents and she'll tell me about them. For example, when she was there, aged fifteen, she fell in love with a nineteen-year-old Swiss soldier and she'll probably show me where he first kissed her.

In recent days, to prepare for our journey, we have been studying French. Not having spoken it conscientiously for years our tongues are rusty and so are our brains. Of course other languages are spoken there—German and Italian particularly—and English is quite common. The Swiss, I believe, are the most lingual people in Europe and the chances are that when we get there everyone will want to speak English to us and we won't be able to practice French. Ah me! 'Twas ever thus.

We'll go to Geneva, of course, one of the world's ancient cities. There we can get a tape in one of five languages for sightseeing. By following the map we'll walk through two thousand years, along streets where Rousseau, Voltaire, Byron and other illustrious people walked. With the Alps as background we'll cruise along the lake to Lausanne and the castle where Byron lived at Chillon. We'll take a funicular railway into sky country, train to Bern and bus to several towns, including Thun. We can also take the postman's bus. Switzerland allows anyone to ride with the postman wherever he goes.

When we get to Paris I'll be Katy's guide. We'll stay in an elegant but small hotel on the Ile de la Cité and sashay to many places: to the office of the *Herald,* to the place I used to live on the Rue Delambre, to the Ritz bar, to the Deux Magots, Lipp's, the Dôme. We'll go to Versailles and Saint Cloud, take a boat ride down the Seine, and attend the Folies-Bergère, the Lido and the Grand Guignol. We'll stroll the Champs Elysées and sit on cafe terraces sipping apéritifes while watching the eccentrics and weirdos go by.

For the present then, *au revoir.*

Travel Stress

If you're thinking of traveling to Europe, wipe it out of your mind. It's too far. We just arrived in Montreux, Switzerland, and getting here was so difficult it'll be a week at least before our bodies will adjust to the time schedule which is nine hours earlier than California's. Settle back and let me tell you what we went through to get here.

Up at 5 A.M. we left home for the airport at ten minutes to 6. Plane was due to depart at 7:25. We just managed to get aboard. The plane was due in New York at 5 P.M. and we were to board another for Geneva which was to depart at 7 P.M. Settled in our seats, we waited expectantly for take-off. We sat, seat-belted...and sat...and sat...for an hour and a half. Seems there was a fault in the hydraulic system. Mechanics finally fixed it and we got away at 9. The plane put down at St. Louis and we were there, still in our seats, for an hour. When we finally got away from the Mississippi River we were two and a half hours out of New York's John F. Kennedy airport. We landed at JFK at twenty minutes to seven. It was going to be a small miracle if we got on the Swiss airplane. TLW and I managed to be the first off the TWA plane and raced through the building and into the crowded street looking for a taxi to take us about four or five blocks to the Swiss Air check-in. The taxi we got was driven by a black boy from Puerto Rico who was not familiar with Swiss Air—or the English language. In fact, he had never heard of Swiss Air. We told him where its office was supposed to be and offered him five dollars to get us there in five minutes. He drove like a teenager, that is, fast. Too fast, as it turned out. He went right by it and when we finally got him to stop, we were more than a block away. We jumped out, me with my bad knees, and, carrying loaded bags, ran through traffic like those TV actors who have lost their traveler's checks.

It was two minutes to seven, fourteen hours since we had gotten out of bed. A Swiss Air attendant got us into the plane just before the door closed. There were only two empty seats, well apart from each other, and into these we were seated. Again, breathing hard, we buckled our seatbelts. The captain's voice came over the intercom and in English, French and German, welcomed us aboard. We would be arriving in Geneva at about 8 A.M., he said, and added "enjoy the flight."

We settled back exhausted, but pleased to have made the connection. Nothing happened. The plane didn't move. For some reason it was an hour before we took off. En route we were served cocktails and dinner. There was a movie I didn't watch. Being lonely, I asked the man sitting next to me if he would change seats with Katy, who was sitting at a window across from and behind us. He kindly consented to do so. It was then about 11 New York time. We were issued blankets. Three or four hours went by during which we napped fitfully.

As soon as daylight appeared the attendants came along with orange juice and warm, wet washcloths. We groggily gulped the juice and washed our numb faces. Then they brought breakfast and we munched drowsily.

It was 9 A.M. Swiss time when we landed in Geneva. It turned out that our luggage had not accompanied us. We reported its delay to the airline office, found a bus, were driven to a railway station, got on a train and rode an hour through the beautiful Swiss countryside to Montreux. A taxi took us to our hotel. When we got there it was eleven o'clock and all we wanted was to get into bed.

But there was one more hurdle. Checkout time at the hotel is twelve and we had to wait. At noon we were told we'd have to wait another half hour while the room was being "made up." We sat in the lobby, hardly able to keep our eyes open, and when finally we got to bed we collapsed. It had been twenty-four hours since we had left our bed at home.

As I write this, during our third day here, we are still suffering jet-lag and it will be several more days before we'll feel normal.

Montreux

This city on Lake Geneva is a tourist Mecca and August is its busiest month. The French and Germans come in hordes and so do the British and Americans. It is a hub from which spokes go to many other famous and historical places, such as Geneva, Lausanne, Vevey, St. Moritz, La Roche de Neige by train, bus or boat. Indeed, many other places too numerous to mention are nearby. Chateau de Chillon, the ancient fortress immortalized by Lord Byron in his poem "The Prisoner of Chillon," is on the lake within walking distance of our hotel. It is situated next to a boulder which rolled down a mountain in prehistoric times. The castle was built in the Ninth or Tenth Century and rebuilt in the Thirteenth. In its basement are dungeons cut into native rock. Many were imprisoned here, among them Francois de Bonivard, the hero of Byron's poem, who was incarcerated by the Duke of Savoy in 1530. For six years he was fettered to an iron ring because of his religious beliefs. According to the poem all of that time he had to stand up.

We have been by train to Chateau d'Oex where David Niven lived and just died, and to Gstaad, the famous skiing resort. We have been by boat to Evian, France, the famous watering place, and to Villeneuve on the Rhone River which flows into the lake from the towering Alps. We've been escorted to Vevey by Jim Shattuck, a relative of our friends Helen and Mark Shackelford. He took us to the farmer's market in the city square. The market functions only Saturdays and Tuesdays and people come from miles around to buy fruits and vegetables, meats and wines.

Wine is by far Switzerland's principal product. Mile after mile as you pass through the country you see terraced vineyards climbing to the sky. Almost every foot of land is cultivated. At the farmer's market we bought wine glasses ($1.50) and the vintners filled them time after time for free. That was the best bargain we found in this little but fascinating country.

There are many delights here. The weather is excellent, not exceedingly warm in the daytime and cool at night. The people are friendly. Tourism is Switzerland's principal industry and every Swiss is graciously helpful to foreigners. There is no tipping and none is expected. The scenery is spectacular. From the balcony of our room which hangs over the lake we can see the massive Alps. Even now, in late August, there is snow on the Dents du Midi.

We've been here more than a week and our jet lag fever has subsided. Whereas last week I told you not to come, I take it back. It's a marvelous place. But bring money.

Katy and I went to see our old friends Eleanor and Brian Ahearne who live in nearby Vevey. Brian, the famous actor, is eighty-one and in frail health, but Eleanor invited us for tea and we eagerly accepted. They live in a huge apartment on the third floor of an ancient chateau on the waterfront overlooking the town square and the dock for the side-wheel lake steamers. We had not seen them for many years, not since he was starring in *My Fair Lady.* They used to have a house on the beach in Santa Monica, a place at La Quinta and apartments in New York and London. "Too damn many houses," Brian said. Now they live mostly in Vevey but still have the apartment in New York where they go for the winter theatre season. In fact their apartment in New York is a duplex, one large, which they rent, one small which they occupy.

Brian has a blood-pressure problem and to get about he finds it necessary to use two canes. When he gets up from a sitting position he has to pause to permit blood to rise to his head; it has a long way to go because he is tall, about six feet three.

On the terrace overlooking the lake a maid served us sumptuous tea, a choice of iced or hot, and a tray of the most tempting petit fours and tarts—fresh raspberry and plum and thick-coated chocolate *gateaux*.

Our conversation was mostly reminiscence. Katy and I reminded Brian that we had first met him in 1939 when he came from Scotland to appear as Iago in Robert Edmund Jones' production of *Othello,* in which Walter Huston played the Moor. Brian told how he had gone to Scotland to appear in a play but when he got there the part was already being played by Lawrence Olivier. Because of the mix-up the producer was embarrassed and paid Brian five hundred pounds for the error. About that time Brian received a telephone call from Bobby Jones asking him to hie back to America and join the *Othello* company, then being tried out on the road.

Brian studied the part on the way across the Atlantic and joined the company in Philadelphia. He proved to be ready, letter-perfect in fact, and was absolutely stunning in the role—so much so that his performance over-shadowed Walter's. When the show opened in New York Brian was highly praised by the critics, but the production as a whole got a poor press and closed after two weeks.

"The trouble was," Brian said, "that Walter was too gentle and kind a man to play Othello. He was incapable of arousing the intense emotions the part demanded." Still speaking of Walter, Brian said, "There was as fine a man as ever lived. Whenever over the subsequent years I would see him he was always interested in my career and eager to help me. After exchanging personal news I would always ask him about his son. Usually he would report that John was not doing well. Once I was in the hospital and Walter came to see me. We got around to talking about John and he said, "Well, you won't believe this, but he has written a screenplay and Warner Brothers has accepted it. They think he's a genius."

"You're right," Brian said he replied. "I don't believe it."

"It's true," Walter said. "It's about Maximilian. And say, that gives me an idea! You should play that part. You'd be terrific! I suggest you get in touch with Warners and I'll tell John."

"Well," Brian said, "I did get to Warner Brothers and I got the part."

Brian went on to brief us on the history of Switzerland, probably the sanest country in the world. After Napoleon had occupied the area south of Lake Geneva (we could see it from where we were sitting) to ensure safe passage into Italy for his armies, France, Bavaria and Austria reorganized the need for a buffer between their mutual frontiers and agreed to create a federation to guarantee its neutrality. Thus was Switzerland formed and since then it has not been engaged in war.

That was the kind of entertainment Katy and I had during tea. Eleanor had been given a Yorkshire puppy which nestled in her lap while she told us about her first husband whose fabulously rich family owned nine miles of plantation along Chesapeake Bay. "If he was so rich why did you leave him?" I asked. And she said, "I didn't. He left me." He turned out to be an alcoholic and died at age forty-nine.

We chatted about how famous John Huston had become and Katy told about our visits to his hideaway south of Puerto

Vallarta. Eventually after much pleasure, tea and tarts the time came for Katy and me to leave. Brian autographed a copy of his book about George Sanders and Benita Hume, entitled *A Dreadful Man,* and we left with gay and appreciative goodbyes and with strong wishes that Brian would hastily recover.

Since then I have read *A Dreadful Man.* I could hardly put it down.

Longevity

The lives of Homo sapiens are being stretched ever longer in this century and it is reasonable to assume that they will grow older in the next. Not so long ago it used to be that people could expect three-score and ten years through this vale of tears, but today many are living to be ninety and myriad are passing the one hundred mark, some with their faculties and marbles in fair-to-middling working order.

The time may come—perhaps a thousand years from now—when people will live as long as Methuselah. (According to Genesis 5:27, he lived to be nine hundred and sixty-nine years.)

Because we are living longer there is a growing tendency to try and preserve the look of middle age. A vigorous man in his sixties or seventies may not feel as old as he looks. Indeed he might pass for forty-odd, he tells himself, were it not for his face which, sagged by the years, gives his age away. This is not true of women.

There is always a solution to any problem, of course, and the solution to mid-age women is having one's face "lifted." Face skin is heavier than body skin and as time goes on it is inclined to droop under the eyes and chin. Annoying wrinkles crease the cheeks and lips. Tucks here and there, at the temples and elsewhere, can take out the sag, and more and more women are resorting to this youthening expedient; so are people of the theatre who have to preserve their faces to keep the money coming in, and those who want to take another ride on the marriage merry-go-round.

The Blooming Buck

Money is in such short supply, the savings and loan associations are vying with one another for every single dollar. Instead of raising the interest rate to lure borrowers and investors, they have gone on a premium-giving tear to get them.

Pick up a newspaper and you'll find almost as much advertising space devoted to these loan company giveaways as to department store sales.

You want a set of steak knives, a coffee maker, some silverware? All you have to do is take your savings and deposit them in some savings and loan bank.

Katy and I had saved a few bucks and they were in a Bank of America branch. I went to the Laguna loan association and asked what I would get if I deposited them there. I was offered my choice of a pen and pencil set, a music box which plays "The boy stood on the burning deck, eating peanuts by the peck" or a recording of Verdi's *Othello.*

I deposited our money and took the pen and pencil set. The next day I withdrew it and took it to another loan company in Newport and got grocery coupons.

Used to be that savings institutions were the most conservative of businesses. Indeed, they were so august I used to get an inferiority complex whenever I went into one. I felt they were doing me a favor to accept my few shekels.

No more. Today they use a red carpet for the fellow with kash and bow from the waist. The way they're going I wouldn't be surprised to see savings and loan associations giving a free martini to everyone who deposits a dollar and a Mickey Finn to anyone who withdraws one.

If one deposits savings in one association on the first day of a month he can get a prize, take it out again on the second, deposit it in another, get another prize, and not lose any interest—on through the tenth.

If you're diligent and have a bicycle, you can get ten prizes every month. Dad-gondest thing. Beats saving green stamps all hollow.

"Another arts and crafts show!"

CHAPTER 29

The Rose of Jericho

If you are a horticulturist you probably know about the Rose of Jericho. It is, I think, nature's strangest, most mysterious, provocative plant. It is mentioned in the Bible and is considered a Syrian specialty, although it is to be found in the mountains here in the Southwest, always on the north slopes away from the sun. Its Latin name is *Anastatica hierochuntica*. Although that may not interest you, I include it to show my erudition.

In shape it is a small cluster of leaves not unlike a head of lettuce. Its mysterious character comes from the fact that it can lie dormant in a dry, mummified state for years, but when placed in water it will begin to "come alive." What happens is: its involucre (that's a collection of leaves which protect it) closes firmly over the flower head when dry.

Well, so much for the Latin. What makes the dried-up plant so fascinating is that as it "drinks" the water, the movement and rebirth can be seen with the unaided eye. In a short while, within twenty-four hours anyway, it becomes a beautiful green plant with fern-like leaves radiating from a central stem. Removed from water it will go back to sleep again—that is, it will dry up and to all intents and purposes die. Again placed in water it will flourish.

The reason I am telling you about the Rose of Jericho is that we recently were given one. It was a sad-looking thing, and had we not been told of its virtue we probably would have turned our noses up. Following instructions, we placed it in a bowl of water and were amazed at the result. We exclaimed and applauded. It was as if we had produced a miracle. It became a focal point in our house and when people called we would show it to them first thing.

Then one week we forgot to water it. It happened that Josefina, the Mexican girl who lives with us, and a delightful character if ever there was one, gave our house its weekly brush-up. The lady is very thorough; cleans everything and makes the house spic and span. When she encountered the precious plant she concluded it had had its day and threw it in the trash. Unfortunately TLW and I did not learn of this sacrilege until too late; the trash collector had come and gone.

You may have heard me screaming. Josefina wept. I particularly regretted losing the plant because it represented the only proof I had ever seen that life is eternal. Since I was a child I had held the belief that life and death are parts of a whole, as night is part of day. The Rose of Jericho lends substance to this concept.

When the Franciscan padres first came to California to convert the natives to Christianity, they used to demonstrate the miracle of the Resurrection of Christ by placing flies in water and "drowning" them. Removed from the water and dried in the sun, the flies would recover and fly away. The Indians were astounded by these performances, considering them miracles. And by using such tactics the padres inducted thousands of innocent and ignorant Californians into the Catholic Church.

Saga of Josefina

Before we left our beloved Laguna to start this long tour of the U.S.A. (I am on a lecture tour with travel film) we were very busy with myriad things—arranging our multiple affairs, helping Josefina get a driver's license and a car.

Getting her a driver's license was a spectacular achievement. Nothing I ever did in my misspent life was so fraught with hazards.

Before we broached the possibility to her, I'm sure she had never thought of driving, much less owning a car, which, I'm certain, was beyond her most extravagant dream. She had come to California to earn money to support her invalid mother in Guadalajara, but that was the extent of her ambition.

Josefina thought of cars as being exclusively for males, and when we suggested that she should learn to drive, she looked startled. "You think is possible?" she asked.

"This is an automobile world we're living in," I told her. "You'd better get with it. Learn to drive now, while you're young."

Dutifully she deposited fifty dollars a month in Laguna Federal Savings toward purchase of a car, and we arranged for her to take driving lessons. Her ignorance of a car was total. She had not the slightest—I mean not even the remotest—idea what gave an automobile mobility. The wheels she understood vaguely, and perhaps the doors and the seats; but as for the engine, it was as much a mystery to her as a man's brain.

When she wrote her brother about buying a car, he asked how many cylinders it had. He might as well have asked her the megathane rating of an isotope. She came to me to find out. When I told her six, she said, "Juanito, what is a cylinder?"

As for spark plugs, camshaft and transmission, she didn't even know the words. She probably thought a universal joint is a nightclub on the moon.

When she set out with the teacher for her first lesson, I held my breath. She did not know so much as how to turn on the lights or the windshield wipers. Fortunately, the teacher's car was equipped with dual driving controls or they would have come a cropper. As it was, as soon as she touched the accelerator she panicked and steered the car over the curb. Only stout braking by the teacher saved them both from a disaster.

But she waved to us gaily as, finally, they got under way.

She took one hundred and twenty dollars worth of lessons (at seven fifty an hour) before she felt confident enough to take the test for a license. I went to the license bureau with her. On our way there she had several close calls, and I pressed so hard against the floor boards that I got cramps in both legs. However, she knew the California Vehicle Code by heart and passed her written test with flying colors. But when she came to the driving test itself, she broke out in what fiction writers often refer to as a cold sweat.

It is against the rules for anyone other than an official to be in a car with an applicant for a driver's license, so I could not go with them. This suited me just fine, but the next ten minutes were an ordeal for all of us.

I felt that, when she was instructed to back into a parking position she would wreck something. But she did well. When they returned in one piece the official gave her a passing grade, but she was so unnerved by the experience that I had to drive her home.

The used car we found for her is a compact, powder blue and very nice. And her pride in it is almost indecent.

There she goes, free as a thunderbird.

More About Josefina

In trying to trace my idiotic penchant for penury I have come to the conclusion that it springs from the Civil War, or at least to the aftermath of that fratricidal conflict. I was born in the magnolia south and my mother and her parents had known what it was to be rich and poor. The Civil War devastated everything below the Mason-Dixon Line. Oftentimes mother and her family survived by ignominious scrounging. It must have been through the genes passed on to me that I inherited the tendency to conserve.

Then again, it may be the result of the Great Depression which began with the stock market crash in 1929. I was barely into manhood at the time—just entering the phase of life when I had to compete in the marketplace.

Somewhere along the path of life, when most of what we call luck is simply timing, I acquired a healthy frugality which makes me squeeze every dollar I let go. I truly detest this facet of my character. I would like to be extravagant, a big butter-and-egg free spender, but that built-in parsimoniousness won't let me.

Imagine the jolt I got at Christmas when Josefina, to

whom we pay a pittance for keeping our house clean (she also works as a nurse's aid at South Coast Community Hospital), presented me with a fourteen-carat gold pen and pencil set! I was flabbergasted.

Josefina's wages are modest and she sends fifty dollars a month to her improvident mother in Guadalajara. She has never had her share of this world's goods, but it would be difficult to imagine a more generous person.

She learned that here anything and everything can be bought on the installment plan or with a credit card. And she gets radiant pleasure from waltzing into a store and, with the flourish of her signature, coming out with things which have always been out of her financial reach. The pen and pencil set, for example, and the solid gold bracelet she gave Katy.

"You shouldn't have done it!" doesn't do any good. And it would spoil her pleasure if we insisted she take a gift back.

The Story of Julio

You may have heard of the navy captain who recently tipped a San Francisco taxi driver $5,000. Evidently the Samaritan was on the unbalanced side, and the cabby had to return the money.

The story reminded me of Julio Lara, a taxi driver Victor Andrews found for us in Mexico City this month. Julio, too, was the recipient of largess from an American. He was born to very poor parents in the backcountry. He never went to school. At the age of thirteen he was ambitious and made his way to Mexico City, where he found work as a laborer. He was tall for his age and strong, with a handsome face and a pleasant personality. And as he grew up his ambition was to own and drive a taxicab.

Now this may not seem much of a goal in the USA, but in Mexico those who own taxicabs are regarded as highly respectable businessmen. If one can accumulate enough money to buy a car, he must then purchase a license. And taxicab licences in Mexico are like liquor licenses in California—there are only so many of them, and they are expensive.

As a laborer Julio earned but fifty to eighty cents a day. But he had great trust in the Lord and faith in his destiny, and he reasoned that the first step he should take toward his ambition was to learn to drive. So he made friends with the owner of a taxicab, who taught him. Not only that, whenever the taxi driver was unable to drive his cab, Julio would substitute for him.

As he drove down the Reforma, an honest-to-heaven taxi driver, he felt he had come a long way in the world, as indeed he had. He had come so far, in fact, he went to a barber shop to have his hair cut.

The consequence was, he married the barber's daughter—for Julio another great step upward. Because his wife was very well educated she proceeded, as wives will, to smooth her husband's rough edges. By the time their third child was born he knew how to read and write. Furthermore, he had gained an appreciation for art and music.

One day he picked up an American at the Del Prado Hotel and drove him to Cuernavaca. They were together most of the day but had difficulty talking to each other. The American told Julio he should learn English and proceeded to teach him a few words.

Julio drove the American all during his stay in Mexico, and when the American left he told him he would be back in six months. "If you have learned to speak English by the time I get back, I'll do something nice for you," he promised.

Julio went to work on English in earnest. He did not really believe the American would come back, but he did, just when he said he would; and by the time he returned Julio was speaking English "very good."

The result was that the American loaned Julio $4,000 (American) with which to buy a second-hand car and a license. The license cost as much as the car, $2,000. Today Julio is one of the best and most sought-after guides and taxi drivers in Mexico. Furthermore, he is saving to send his son Julio, Jr., through law school. He fully expects young Julio to become president of Mexico. Indeed, in the father's mind there is not any doubt about it.

"I went to New York one time," he told me, "to drive a customer's car to Mexico. I saw the Empire State Building. When I got back I said to my son, 'When you get to be president of Mexico, I want you to build me a building taller than that.' He said he would."

Retiring?

People often ask me if I've retired and I usually answer: "From what? If you mean from a nine-to-five job, the answer is yes. I haven't had one of those for years. If you mean am I a man of leisure, the answer is no."

Retired is a much misused word. What is meant in relation to a man is that he has unlimited leisure, that he has run the labor race, has stacked up the kale and is free to pursue his hobbies and delights. While that is the way most people envision retirement, that's not the way it turns out. Even if you worked at a job for forty years and, at age sixty-five, are given a gold watch and pushed out to pasture with a pension you'll find your leisure is limited, perhaps more than it was when you were employed. You'll find that life still is to be lived and that its paths are full of fribbles, rocks and potholes.

You have "retired" but your wife hasn't. That lady still has to keep the house in order, do the marketing, the cooking and the cleaning, tend the garden, write to and entertain friends and relatives. This is a lot of work and she's generally at it from the time she gets up until she goes to bed. Nobody ever thinks to give her a gold watch, to pat her on the back and tell her to go out and have a good time. The way things are, she'll never "retire" until they box her and put her six feet under ground.

You learn that when you retire. You learn she has a harder and more difficult job than you had, and as you follow her about the house, getting used to your retirement, you'll be drawn into helping her. You'll find that you can't go off and play golf or fish or lie in a hammock with a tall drink reading while she toils away at the chores and duties of living; it wouldn't be fair.

So soon you'll be wiping dishes, helping make the bed, doing the vacuuming, washing the car, weeding the rose garden, writing checks to pay bills, answering the dad-gone telephone, making bank deposits, going for the mail, taking clothes to be cleaned and shoes to be repaired.

You'll have to replace light bulbs and washers, take whacks at repairing machines and appliances and do the correspondence.

It won't be long before you'll be arising in the morning before your darling and preparing breakfast, mainly because it takes her longer to get dressed, coiffured and "made up" than it does you, but also because you don't like to wait around until she gets to the kitchen. Gradually she'll wear you down and you'll make the mistake of asking: "What do you want me to do today?" That's fatal. She will always be able to think of a number of things and you'll find it's like being pecked to death by ducks.

After a while you'll be asking yourself: "How did all of these things get done when I was working eight hours a day at the office?"

As it is, there are not enough hours in the day to do them all. You'll feel you're up to your dew-lapped neck with drudgery.

Now that I've retired my days are cluttered with minutia. I can hardly find fifteen minutes a day to read or nap. Today the routine is quite different. My refuge from life's annoying details is bed and I begin looking forward to getting there as soon as Katy and I finish washing the dinner dishes, pots and pans. To build character, I sometimes wait until ten o'clock; beyond that it is difficult for me to stay awake. I'm a great yawner and anything that happens after ten o'clock, even if someone's giving away money, you can have and be my guest.

Once I start to bed it isn't as it was of yore. There are the duties of locking the fore and aft doors (man's distrust of man), that the grandfather clock's weights are lifted, that the furnace is turned off. And, oh yes, there is a window to be opened and teeth to be washed.

Ask me if I've retired and the answer is yes, but I long for the peace I had when I went to work.

Making a Will

The time has come when I think I should make a will. My lucre is modest and my possessions are not what you would call profuse, but when I am no longer able to control them I don't want the winds to scatter them. Many of them are keepsakes. One is a medal for swimming, which I won in Kansas City when I was seventeen, and one is a gavel, given last year while president of the Scripps Memorial Hospitals Foundation board. There are a trunkful of rejected manuscripts, the fez Katy bought me in Beirut and my bowling bowls.

I know these didos are not valuable. It might be well if I gave them to the Salvation Army. But they are mementos and I'd like to see one of them, the gavel for example, on display in a museum. Perhaps the UCLA Library, which has a collection of my published works and literary correspondence, might be interested in the rejected manuscripts. If not, there must be someone who collects such trivia.

Katy's and my problem, so far as wills are concerned, is we don't have any children. Thus there is no line of direct heirs waiting in the wings for us to pop off. The first things they would be interested in, of course, would be the kale and TLW's jewelry. After those, they would wrangle over our collection of art, not one piece of which is the work of a famous artist like Picasso.

I've never regretted not having a child, but now that I'm over the hill it would be nice to have a couple of offspring. They could come in, we could go over our goodies and I wouldn't have to find takers.

I remember how a late friend, Jane Antrobus, managed her estate in her will and I've decided to do the same. Jane was an absolutely darling lady who lived in Emerald Bay.

When her husband, John, died she was bereft, of course;

they had no progeny and, as they say, she was "getting along in years."

However, she had many friends, all of whom she loved and who loved her, so when it came to drawing up her will she made a list of the things she possessed and named those she thought would like them. Also in the will she asked that, at her demise, her estate provide the food, the music and the liquor for a wake.

She never told anyone, save her attorney, about the will, but, not knowing when or where she was going to die, she always carried a copy of it in her purse.

Katy and I were among those listed in the will and for us she specified a beautiful mahogany carving of a Zulu washer woman carrying a bundle of clothes on her head, a silver wine cooler, a set of thin, delicate martini glasses she knew we admired and a rare wooden bowl she and John had gotten in New Guinea.

As the days dwindled down she went hither and yon. The last place she went was Hawaii and she went there to see an ill friend, one of those mentioned in the will. While she was in the hospital with the friend she suddenly and abruptly died. She couldn't have found a more convenient place. Her remains were cremated, as specified in the will, and her ashes were scattered over the Pacific.

All of us mentioned in the will were notified by her attorney and we all gathered at Jane's house to help hasten her soul into Heaven. There were about thirty-five or forty of us and it was one of the best and gayest parties any of us ever attended. Each of us got his or her inheritance and as I write this I can see the figure of the washer woman. Every day Katy and I see the things Jane Antrobus left us and we thereby frequently are reminded of her, our good and imaginative friend.

Well, that's the kind of will I'm going to write. It will name all of my close friends and I'll carry it in my wallet.

Brooks Brothers

For some time TLW has been urging me to improve my attire. I have enough clothes in my closet to last me the rest of my life, but she complains that most of them are rags. "You are a man of quality," she told me, "and should dress accordingly. Just look at those shoes! They look as if they came from a missionary barrel."

One of the reasons she wants me to buy clothes is because she spends a bundle from time to time draping her beautiful body and feels guilty because I rarely spend a dime on my old frame.

I can endure only a modicum of nagging, so weakening last week I consented to be led into the market place. My dear wife is not a bargain hunter. She shops in deluxe stores and doesn't wait for sales. We headed directly for Brooks Brothers, whereas I, a person of penury, would have preferred Gemco or K-Mart.

Brooks Brothers in Fashion Island is housed in a very impressive stone edifice with its name carved in deep letters over the doorway. And as soon as we approached it I knew we were in for a shellacking. The brothers have to get a lot of money for their merchandise just to pay the rent. And as soon as we entered I smelled the haute couture. Moreover, the sales personnel were well groomed, all attired in Brooks Brothers best, their leather shoes shined and smiles on their faces.

There was none of the Gemco task of going and finding what we were looking for. A salesman guide took us in hand and led us like lambs to slaughter. The first place we went was for swimming trunks and Katy picked out a beautiful pair for me. After I had gone through the machinations and trouble of taking off all my clothes to try them on, we were led to the shirt section. She wanted me to buy some of Brooks famous button-down shirts. I talked my way out of them. I have almost fifty shirts of all styles and colors at home.

I also turned down a four hundred dollar cashmere sports coat that Katy liked. Although it was the price that staggered me, I said it was not my style. Fortunately the salesman didn't ask me what my style was, because I don't have any.

Then we got to the shoes. Summer is just around the corner and Katy thought I should have a new pair of white shoes. Having been adamant about the sports coat I did not dare refuse to consider shoes. She liked a pair with moccasin toes, but they did not please me. I picked out a pair of seamless buckskins, plain, simple, classic with red rubber soles and agreed to try them on.

I didn't ask the price. That, I thought, in such a well-mannered, gentlemanly place, would be gauche. When I had seated myself the salesman presented the right shoe and was surprised when I removed my left one. I did this because I suddenly remembered that my right sock had a hole in the toe. Horrors! A client of Brooks Brothers with a hole in his sock! Perish the thought.

The salesman brought the left shoe, we got it on finally, though not without effort, and I stood up to ascertain its comfort and fit. Katy asked, "How is it?" and after taking a few steps I said, "Fair to middlin'." She said, "Try on the right one. Your feet aren't the same size." She then explained to the salesman that my left foot had been injured in a shipwreck. He wanted us to tell him all about it, and Katy would have done so, but I said we didn't have time.

Reluctantly I removed my right shoe and there, shining like a beacon was my big toe. I blushed and said, "I've got a hole in my sock," about as stupid a remark as I could have made, it being evident.

The salesman said, "Oh, that's nothing," to mitigate my shame, and added, "It's a sport sock. You won't want to use it with this dress shoe."

"Of course not," I said.

The shoes fit well. "How much?" I asked.

Katy picked up the box and said, "Only seventy-five dollars."

I didn't have the courage to protest. We bought them. Then, passing the silk neckties Katy picked out three beauties and asked if I didn't need some trousers. I said no, and we managed to get out of the place for a little more than three hundred dollars.

Greetings, Salutations and Best Wishes

Much as I yearn to write about Kasavubu, Mobutu and Lumumba, the latter-day Shadrach, Meshach and Abednego who have conjured up their own version of the "fiery furnace," I can't do so because this is the last chance to wish faithful and dissident readers of this space a Happy New Year.

To the blessed and the sinful, the virtuous and the worthy, the weak and the strong, the sick and the well, the whole and the crippled—best wishes.

A warm salute to all our friends, from (A) the Brian Ahearnes to (Z) the Nello Zavas.

To Winston Churchill, "the greatest man of our time," who was an inspiration to everyone, except Hitler and the Russians. Despite his addiction to brandy and cigars, there is a good prospect he will live forever.

To Dwight David Eisenhower, probably not the greatest president this country ever had, but a good man nonetheless. May he now play golf to his heart's content without incurring the ridicule of the righteous.

To Dag Hammarskjold, poor fellow, who, like Lucky Adolph, always finds himself in the middle. May he avoid claustrophobia. To Eleanor Roosevelt, top candidate for "the greatest woman of our time," a salute. And to the readers of this compilation my thanks for your fidelity and endurance.

The Greeter

Eiler Larsen was the Dane who became nationally famous standing for years at the corner of Forest Avenue and Pacific Coast Highway, waving at passing motorists. Children called him "Mr. Laguna." He was a bachelor and a gardener by trade, and lived in a rent-free room over a client's garage. His income was sparse. For his endeavors he received one dollar an hour but he could always get a free meal at Dad Benton's restaurant on the beach or at Trotter's Bakery on Forest Avenue. Everyone liked him.

Considering him a great advertising ploy, the day I opened the Ford agency I hired him to wear a tailor-made pair of white overalls on which, fore and aft and in large blue letters, were the words JOHN WELD FORD.

I paid him fifteen dollars a day for a week. It was the first time he had ever been paid to perform and it pleased him. He had no automobile and had never driven one. Wherever he wanted to go he walked. When we were living in Dana Point I became ill. He came to see how I was faring and to wish me well. It was six miles from Laguna. He walked both ways and brought me a letter he had just received.

> To Laguna's Famous Greeter
> Dear Sir:
>
> I have been through Laguna many times and each time I have seen you. I must say it is a pleasure to see anyone so happy. I hope I'm not asking too much, but I would like to know something. I have heard you are very old and I have heard you are young. Just how old are you?
>
> [Editor's note: Eiler was 66.]
>
> There are a dozen different stories about you. One is that you were in the last war.
>
> [Editor's note: Eiler was a member of the 4th Division, U.S. Army, in World War I.]
>
> I have a son sixteen months old and he loves to see you. If you have a picture of yourself would you please autograph it and send it to me for my son?
>
> I hope you keep on enjoying life as much as you seem to. There are very few of us left.
>
> Mrs. Isa E. Parsons, San Diego, Calif.

During an unusully cold winter Eiler decided to go live in

Palm Springs. To get there he went the short but mountainous way—about a hundred miles—over the Ortega Highway which climbs the Sierra Nevada before descending into Coachella Valley. He found a room to rent and chose a busy corner on the main drag where he began greeting motorists. At once he was considered an anomaly, a crackpot, a *weirdo.* People complained to City Hall, saying he was disturbing the peace, and two policemen were dispatched to tell him he was unwanted. They escorted him to the edge of the town limits and told him not to come back.

Eiler sashayed back to Laguna as a prodigal son. All of us Lagunatics were pleased to have him back.

We considered him a treasure.

His younger brother was the Mayor of Arhus, Denmark's second-largest city. He once came to Laguna and Eiler invited me to have lunch with them. It was a delightful time. Danes are famous for their humor and the brothers were droll, whimsical and witty telling their family's history. It seems that Eiler had been a derelict, a wanderer. He had come to America and never returned home.

Unfortunately I did not record all of what was said.

Eiler died in Veterans' Hospital in Long Beach. He was about seventy-five years old. His image is still in Laguna. Roy Childs had a life-size sculpture made of him. It stands on Pacific Coast Highway in front of what used to be Roy's Pottery Shack. Every time I drive past it I tip my imaginary hat and say hello.

Crusade

Eugene Douglas, artist, writer and author of *The Romance of Flowers,* a newspaper feature which is carried in thirty papers around the country, has written me a passionate letter asking that I use this space to "force the city to buy the main beach and beautify it."

His letter is compelling, and I am in such agreement with him that I cannot deny his request.

•

> Laguna's downtown beachfront, south from the famous Victor Hugo restaurant, is one of the reasons we live in this quaint town. Close up, however, it is a community disgrace: shacks, sheds, and an ancient, inadequate boardwalk and a jerry-built and antiquated lifeguard tower. The beach is beautiful, but it is framed so badly its effect is spoiled.
>
> Think of the money the rich have spent for pieces of canvas, the money Getty, Hearst and Huntington have lavished on works of art and given them to museums.
>
> Isn't cleaning it up worth the price of one or two pictures or sculptures?
>
> Henry Kaiser is spending millions for his dream place in Hawaii. The Rockefellers took oil money gathered from all over the United States and rebuilt wonderful Williamsburg, for which we are thankful. Civic-minded people in New Orleans woke up just in time to save the famous French Quarter from being inundated.
>
> Think of what millionaire Harold McCormick could have done for Laguna when he was here thirty years ago.

The second richest man in the world has a house here.

I am in accord with Eugene Dupont, who says the Chamber of Commerce, the Lion's Club and the Real Estate Board should rise up and make our beachfront the walk of the coast.

A number of uninformed people have an idea that the majority of the residents of Laguna, who had a chance to pass on this great civic improvement, voted it down. Nothing is farther from the truth. Only forty-five percent of those registered voted for the bond issue to make our front yard our own.

Those who stayed away from the polls that day should be ashamed. Are we a democracy?

It is well past midnight that charity should begin at home.

Ah, if only the Coffee Club, the Optimists, the Rotarians,

the Elks, the Ebells, the Garden Club, the Zontas, etc., etc., etc., would stand together, we could swing this thing. Come on, everyone. Let's try again.

P.S. The next time we tried, we won. Shacks were removed, a boardwalk was built, the lifeguard station was renovated, grass and shrubs were planted and the entire beach area is a work of landscape art. People come from all over to frequent and enjoy it.